D0359602

ENTRENCHMENT

ENTRENCHMENT

Wealth, Power, and the Constitution of
Democratic Societies

PAUL STARR

Yale

UNIVERSITY PRESS

New Haven and London

Yale University Press books may be purchased in quantity for
educational, business, or promotional use. For information, please
e-mail sales.press@yale.edu (U.S. office) or sales@yaleup.co.uk
(U.K. office).

Set in Janson type by IDS Infotech Ltd.
Printed in the United States of America.

Library of Congress Control Number: 2018965635
ISBN 978-0-300-23847-1 (hardcover : alk. paper)

A catalogue record for this book is available from the British Library.

This paper meets the requirements of ANSI/NISO Z39.48-1992
(Permanence of Paper).

10 9 8 7 6 5 4 3 2 1

To my colleagues and friends M.D., P.D., and V.Z.,
and to the next generation

Contents

Preface and Acknowledgments

READERS WHO GLANCE AT a book about "entrenchment" may expect it only to be about the perpetuation of unjust power. One acquaintance, on first hearing this book's title, said what a discouraging subject this must be. But in the following pages I use "entrenchment" in a general sense, applying to foundational rules of all kinds, and am concerned not only with unjust regimes but also with the entrenchment of rights and democracy and institutions promoting equality. Anyone hoping to defend those values when they are threatened, as they are now, should be interested in the means of entrenching them. Instead of being discouraging, the subject of entrenchment ought to awaken us to what is at stake when foundational rules and systems of power, just or unjust, hang in the balance.

I began working on this project and giving talks about it in 2013, so I did not cook up the ideas especially for today's political situation, though the political turns of our time have influenced how the book developed. I originally began writing about entrenchment in regard to race and other social categories for a 1992 volume, *How Classification Works*, edited by the anthropologist Mary Douglas and philosopher David Hull. It was only after using the concept in several different contexts that I decided to give it more systematic attention. I am much indebted to Stanford's Center for Advanced Study in the Behavioral Sciences and to Princeton University for affording me the 2014–15 academic year to begin that work.

I also owe a debt to colleagues and students at several universities, including my own, for criticism of an early paper ("Three Degrees of Entrenchment"), which was thankfully never published but nonetheless continues to float around the internet. When the manuscript for this book was complete, I had the benefit of criticism from Stephen Holmes, Robert Keohane, Andreas Wimmer, and Sean Wilentz. I am also grateful to two Princeton students: Jeremy Cohen, for his close reading of Chapter 5, and Julu Katticaran, who did excellent research on the legacies of slavery and colonialism for a chapter that I decided in the end not to pursue.

Lucky is the writer who can count on a partner for love and support through the years of working on a book. I am among the lucky ones, and I thank my wife, Ann, for that.

Introduction

The Stakes of Entrenchment

TRYING TO CEMENT CHANGE—to entrench it—can be a dangerous game. The deeper and more lasting the change we seek, the higher we raise the stakes and the more fraught we make the contest. There is nothing so much to be feared in politics as the other side permanently getting its way, and no temptation greater than the opportunity to get one's own way decisively and for good.

Yet it is impossible to keep everything open to choice, so even without anyone's intending it, many things become relatively fixed. As social and political institutions develop, their constitutive features—the basic elements that make them what they are—often become increasingly difficult or seemingly impossible to change. The process may be sudden or slow, the result of deliberate decisions or an unintended byproduct of actions taken for other reasons. As people come to regard the fundamentals as settled and perhaps as natural facts of life, they are likely to give low odds to changing them, if they think about those opportunities at all.

We can describe the same process in a more positive way, however, from the standpoint of innovation. Unlike passing fads, the most significant innovations in both institutions and technologies are generally long-lasting. Innovators have an interest not only in having their ideas adopted but also in making them stick. They may want to ensure that once their innovations go into effect, those who opposed the ideas beforehand do not have the opportunity to undo them. They are interested, in short, in entrenchment—durable innovation, they might call it.

Entrenchment per se is not a bad thing. We could hardly organize our lives, make plans, or have any confidence about the future if not for some more or less fixed aspects of law and society. This confidence is partly what political constitutions are intended to provide, and constitutional entrenchment—adopting a legal rule in a form that makes it hard to change—is one of the principal forms entrenchment takes. As the example of political constitutions indicates, entrenchment may be a means of protecting values of high importance, such as freedom, rule of law, and democracy. Constancy in fundamentals may be the condition for innovation in other dimensions.

As the constitutional example also indicates, entrenchment may be a carefully thought-out choice, the result of a publicly deliberated decision to make an arrangement difficult to undo. In such cases, entrenchment is often traceable to specific historical moments and known historical figures whose reasoning we may be able to reconstruct. In the many contrasting cases where entrenchment emerges without any conscious plan, it often results from the unanticipated effects of chains of decisions, or from the choices of countless anonymous people accumulating slowly over long periods.

We usually notice entrenched institutions, interests, and beliefs only when they obstruct change. But we also need to see entrenchment from its beginnings, not only as a condition but as a process—as a type of change structured, intentionally or not, so as to be difficult to reverse. Entrenchment is not the opposite of change. It is the making of changes that then become hard to undo and that increase the resistance to stress at the foundations of society.

These considerations make the phenomenon of entrenchment more complicated than it may seem. A society's entrenched features—the foundational features that are hardest to change—shape what kind of society it is. They establish its moral and political character and influence its economic performance. They have often arisen through great struggles and may again become the subject of high-stakes conflict. Whether we want to preserve or reform those entrenched realities, or to entrench new ones, we need to understand entrenchment itself. That is the general motivation of this book. But there is a more particular one as well: to understand the foundations of power in the troubled democracies of our time.

Much of our politics today is a struggle over entrenchment—over efforts to bring about change in a form that the other side will find hard to undo. The three decades after World War II were a period of liberal democratic entrenchment in the West: all the relevant parties accepted the terms of democratic institutions. The arrangements adopted as part of that settlement initially kept the power of concentrated wealth in check and created the basis for a widely shared prosperity. That order, while not entirely undone, has been shaken. The last quarter of the twentieth century saw a surge in economic inequality, and after an era when democratic forms of government were expanding worldwide, liberal democracy itself has come under attack. Even the nations with the longest and deepest democratic traditions are haunted by the twin specters of oligarchy and populist nationalism. The conflicts today are testing just how well-entrenched—or how fragile—the institutions are that underlie constitutionalism, democracy, and the economics of shared prosperity.

Democracies have two kinds of politics. In ordinary politics, the conflicting parties take entrenched rules and institutions as given and fight over what they understand to be temporary power positions and reversible policies. Other times, they fight over the rules themselves and power positions and policies that they anticipate, or realize only too late, will be hard to reverse. This is the politics of entrenchment. Democratic politics usually lies in the realm of the ordinary: battles over budgets, tax rates, and alterable legislation subject to swings in the partisan balance of power, fluctuations in the economy, public opinion, and other variable influences. Losing a battle does not mean losing the war. But in the politics of entrenchment, the consequences may stretch far into the future.

The deeper struggles are often over rules that govern power itself. Democracy abhors entrenched power—at least in principle. The democratic idea presumes that power is temporary, conditional on continued public favor, and reversible at elections. But a democratic government cannot exist without foundational rules that determine how its institutions work, and those rules are never immaculately conceived. The risk of entrenched rules is that they lock in a bias in favor of whatever interests were in control at the time they were adopted. The benefit of entrenched rules is that they reduce the ability of subsequent power-holders to manipulate the rules for their own advantage. If rules are entrenched, they are enforced even against the desires of the powerful. If power is entrenched, those who possess it are able to keep it, use it, and enlarge it despite public preferences and rules to the contrary. Constitutionalism is a gamble that although the rules incorporated into a constitution may be imperfect, it is better to entrench them than to let those in power make them up as they go along.

The politics of entrenchment is not just about the powers of government. It is also about the structure of power in civil society and the private economy. The stakes here are at least as fundamental: the rules of property and inheritance; family structure and the position of women; capital and labor; the forms of independent organization and association; and other relations that determine where power lies before the curtain opens on the everyday political drama. However the formal institutions of government are framed, the meaning of democracy depends on those power relations in society. If society itself is to be compatible with democracy, it cannot be constituted on the basis of personal or class domination.

It is not a new discovery, nor should it be a controversial point, that democracy is untenable when private wealth and power are overwhelmingly concentrated in a few hands. Eighteenth-century revolutionaries in America and Europe knew that systems of patrimonial inheritance concentrating landed wealth in an aristocracy kept political power concentrated too, and that changing the rules of inheritance was vital to the consolidation of a republic. Nineteenth-century opponents of slavery saw the ownership of other human beings as a form of domination and a basis of oligarchic political power that was inimical to democracy. Later opponents of industrial monopolies and trusts confronted aggregations of power that threatened not only the livelihoods of farmers, small businessmen, and workers but also the possibilities of popular self-government.

Today the problem of monopoly power has been reduced to questions of economic efficiency, but earlier generations knew better. Limiting the political power of wealth is an old concern of republican and liberal political thought, often framed as a concern about corruption. The classical constitutional problem was how to organize politics not simply to stop bribery, or what is now called quid pro quo corruption, but also to secure leadership that would place the greater public good before its own private interests and those of its friends. Like all forms of government, democracy faces the danger, wrote John Stuart Mill, "of class legislation, of government intended for (whether really effecting it or not) the immediate benefit of the dominant class, to the lasting detriment of the whole."[1] Yet as damaging as it is to the efficacy and legitimacy of a democratic government, corruption for purposes of enrichment is not the greatest threat. Corruption for purposes of entrenchment— the use of power to perpetuate concentrated power in both its private and public forms—is even more dangerous.

The political interest in entrenchment arises especially at historical moments of uncertainty and fragility. Some of this interest reflects a reasonable concern for stability, including an interest in consolidating what might otherwise be short-lived victories for democracy and equal rights. But as we shall see in the following pages, there is another pattern at times of uncertainty. When those who have enjoyed privilege and power face threats of political decline, they have repeatedly sought means of entrenchment. In a representative system, they have often turned to two strategies: electoral engineering to prevent the opposition from gaining power, and control of counter-majoritarian institutions like constitutional courts to provide additional backup protection. The same pattern is at work today, when oligarchy and populism have been fused and threaten to entrench illiberal and undemocratic values.

Serious and consequential matters are at stake in everyday politics. Even reversible policies may have irreversible effects. But the stakes in the politics of entrenchment are especially high.

My approach to these questions is historical and analytical, and although the developments I cover are necessarily selective, they tell a story about the struggle over democracy amid an evolving capitalist economy and the changing forms of wealth and oligarchic power. But before we get to that history—to the entrenchment of landed wealth and racial slavery and their overthrow; the varying forms of entrenchment in both domestic and international political institutions; the entrenchment of progressive change in systems of social protection and taxation; and the politics of entrenchment today—I begin with a more general question: How does entrenchment work? What mechanisms produce hard-to-reverse change at a society's foundations?

CHAPTER ONE

Understanding Entrenchment

L IKE MATERIAL OBJECTS, SOCIAL institutions and organizations vary in how they respond to stress. One political regime will be unyielding in the face of popular protests, while another crumbles. A centuries-old church that counts its followers in the hundreds of millions will survive a scandal that would destroy a more fragile organization. A corporation with deep reserves of capital will endure economic reverses and continue to dominate a market, or even become more dominant, while other enterprises flounder and never recover.

But unlike material objects that persist without human effort, the structures of society depend on people's continuing choices, practices, relations, and beliefs. Social facts are facts only insofar as people regularly reproduce them. Laws do not regulate social life just because they were once recorded in statutes. Wealth and power do not exert their influence only as a result of having once been accumulated. They must all be constantly renewed to have any force. Yet some foundational features of the social world are more tenaciously reproduced than others. They resist stress, they defy pressure, they overcome opposition. The process by which those features of society become stress-resistant is what I mean by entrenchment.

Entrenchment, like the closely related terms "lock-in" and "consolidation," can refer to any process whereby an institution, a technology, a group, or a cultural form—any kind of social formation—becomes resistant to pressures for change. The focus of this book, however, is specifically on *hard-to-reverse change in constitutive aspects of society and politics.* I use the term "constitutive" in line with a distinction that John Searle, borrowing from Kant, makes about two kinds of rules. All rules regulate behavior (or are meant to do so), but some rules, like the rules of chess, are also constitutive: Take away the rules, and there is no game of chess. Other rules, such as highway speed limits, regulate activity that exists independently: Take speed limits away, and the road and traffic remain.[1] Constitutive choices are choices about the social and material basis of things, without which they would not exist in the same state, or at all. In the development of institutions and societies, a constitutive moment is a time when such high-stakes choices are made. But the full constitutive process, from the initial stages to their entrenchment, may be slow and incremental, and the significance of entrenching developments may be lost at the time they take place.

The historical cases that form the body of this book illustrate what I mean by "constitutive." In England and other European societies from the late feudal through the early modern era, the rules for the inheritance of rank and property, notably primogeniture and entail, were constitutive of the aristocratic, patriarchal, and monarchical order. The rules of racial slavery that emerged in colonial America were constitutive of the social system that became entrenched in the American South. Both of these were cases of oligarchic entrenchment, with political implications ranging from the local domain of aristocrats and slaveholding planters to their national governments. The rules of constitutional democracies— rules about rights and powers, elections, courts, and so on—have also been constitutive of both their governments and societies. Constitutional entrenchment is central to our story, but the terms "constitutional" and "constitutive" do not exactly coincide. The fundamental rules of property rights, family and kinship, labor, and social protection, while generally not encoded in political constitutions, have constitutive significance for those institutions and for society more generally.

Entrenchment places two kinds of constraints on change. The first is a constraint on reversibility. At a minimum, entrenchment makes it difficult to undo a development or a decision. Second, it constrains further change, channeling it in particular directions. It may perpetuate features of a society that would otherwise have been expected to evolve. But entrenchment is not synonymous with complete stasis or inertia; it requires active reinforcement, renewal, and resilience. When the character in Lampedusa's *The Leopard* says that for "things to stay as they are, things have to change," he is talking about entrenchment, specifically the new steps needed to entrench privilege against the threat of a republic.[2] Inflexibility is never a good formula for survival.

Entrenchment is also not the same as institutionalization. The political power of concentrated wealth may be entrenched without being directly institutionalized. Power may be entrenched by brute force or through an overwhelming preponderance of resources. Conversely, institutionalization may not be sufficient for entrenchment; many things are institutionalized without becoming entrenched. A government may be set up one day and soon collapse; a principle may be encoded in law, but the law may trigger opposition and be repealed the next year or never be enforced. Institutions are systems of rules and practices, dependent on widely (though not necessarily universally) shared understandings. Unlike more voluntary aspects of culture, institutions have socially recognized and often formally organized means of identifying, enforcing, and changing rules. They therefore necessarily involve power and authority.[3] They give a stable form to fluid and variable relations and more predictability to social action—at least, they do to the extent they are effective. Whether they can withstand pressure for change at their foundations is a separate matter.

Entrenchment, in this view, refers not only to a condition but to a process, and it is always a matter of degree. The more all parties, even the powerful, are constrained by rules and see no possibility of reversing a constitutive development, the more thoroughly entrenched it will be. Determining where an institution, technology, or cultural form falls on that continuum is a formidable challenge. But if we think of entrenchment as a capacity to withstand pressure for change, one kind of evidence comes from what are, in effect, *stress tests*. A political regime's survival of stress—economic depressions, popular protests, changes in top leadership, military defeats—is evidence of its entrenchment. Elections are stress tests for emerging democracies (and sometimes for established ones). A commonly used measure of the entrenchment of a democracy (democratic consolidation) is the peaceful transfer of power, even possibly a double turnover, that is, power transferred back and forth between parties. A test for the entrenchment of a law or policy is whether it survives a changeover from one administration or government to another. A test for the entrenchment ("lock-in") of a technology is whether it continues to dominate a market despite the availability of a more efficient design or substitute. A test for the entrenchment of a belief system is whether it continues to prevail despite contradictory evidence, dissonant experience, and social pressure for revision.

None of these tests is perfect, in part because entrenchment is greatest when an institution or belief system is subject to no challenge or stress whatsoever and people are not conscious of alternatives. We can conceive of any individual's actions, Jon Elster points out, as being subject to two "filtering processes." The first limits actions to a "feasible set"; the second influences choices within that set.[4] Entrenchment arises from the first type of filtering: A constitutive aspect of society is entrenched from an individual's standpoint if undoing it is not an option in the feasible set. That set of alternatives, however, depends not only on technical feasibility and the objective realities of power but also on individuals' knowledge and understanding. Social realities are entrenched if instead of being regarded as products of human will, they come to be treated as part of the order of the universe, aspects of a world where people as well as things have their natural and rightful place. Taken as given, some features of society may not even register in consciousness: they may be entrenched through invisibility. When people become aware of alternatives, that in itself may be a sign that the institution or condition is less entrenched than it once was.

My central concern here is with mechanisms that impede or constrain change in constitutive elements of society. We need not attribute entrenchment to the inherent nature or immutable cultural dispositions of a society. In Molière's *The Imaginary Invalid*, a physician explains that opium puts people to sleep because of its *virtus dormitiva*—its sleep-inducing nature. Some social explanations are of the same type. Why do some societies adhere to traditions? Because they are "traditionalist." Why do others accept and even promote change? Because they are "modern" and "progressive." If this were a good way to account for entrenchment, we could stop right here.

A more satisfactory way to proceed is to identify the recurring mechanisms in the production of social regularities. People act under given historical conditions, and they remake those conditions. But despite the unending variety of history, there are patterns in how people respond to structural realities and then maintain or change them.[5] In offering the following framework for understanding the mechanisms of entrenchment, I begin with a straightforward distinction. Entrenchment is sometimes intended, sometimes unplanned and emergent, and most often a mixture of both. A concern for the intentionality of entrenchment focuses our attention on those who have the power to make hard-to-reverse changes in society's constitutive rules, and on the conditions that motivate and enable them to do so.

STRATEGIC ENTRENCHMENT

When entrenchment is deliberate and purposeful, I call it "strategic." In such cases, individuals and groups try not only to achieve an objective but also to ensure that the achievement sticks. They do that in part by anticipating their opponents' countermoves in an effort to make a subsequent reversal difficult or impossible. The choices they make may be unilateral and one-sided, or they may result from a settlement among conflicting parties. Strategic entrenchment is the pursuit of irreversibility: the conscious effort to make a change in a way that prevents it from being undone and sets the direction for the future.

Creating Facts on the Ground

Strategically created facts on the ground are the most elementary basis of entrenchment. Whether through military power, population movements, or economic forces, states and societies may entrench themselves de facto in a territory or a market. Although usually a prologue to claims of legitimacy and sometimes to negotiations with an adversary, realities established on the ground serve as means of entrenchment when they are objectively hard to reverse, or even just believed to be hard to reverse, and therefore taken as faits accomplis.

In its original military sense, entrenchment means digging in to resist assault, as when an army digs a line of trenches to defend the ground it holds. An entrenched position can result from any marshalling of power and presence that deters or defeats potential challenges. Like armies, social groups may entrench themselves by occupying an area without any recognized legal right, as invading tribes and empires did for millennia, often killing, expelling, or subjugating and enslaving indigenous populations. Colonization throughout the world and continental expansion in the United States involved establishing facts on the ground with settlers and arms. Today, as in Israel, groups and nations continue to use settlements as a means of creating facts on the ground and entrenching a position with an armed population.

In the economy as well, predatory groups and firms have also entrenched themselves de facto. Bandits, brokers, and cartels have occupied strategic economic positions or created a "constellation of forces" to bar potential rivals. Firms sometimes introduce products or promote practices of dubious legality, anticipating that if they become widely used, governments will have no choice but to accept them. It is not just possession, but practice, that is "nine-tenths of the law."

Power rarely leaves itself naked for long; it soon puts on the clothing of justice and the armor of institutions. But even where governments and dominant groups and firms make claims of legitimacy, the ultimate basis of entrenchment may lie in the facts they have created on the ground. The obedience of subjects may be a sign not of reverence but of resignation, as James Scott argues, quoting an Ethiopian proverb, "When the great lord passes, the wise peasant bows deeply and silently farts."[6]

Rules of Change

Although the significance of raw power should never be underestimated, the choice of rules in the design of institutions is the principal means of strategic entrenchment in modern societies. No rules are more important for entrenchment than rules that confer power, especially those governing change.

A rule of change is a secondary or meta-rule determining how changes are made. Raising the procedural requirements for change is a means of entrenchment. For example, compared with the ordinary rules for enacting legislation, constitutional provisions are entrenched in the United States because the Constitution's rules of change—that is, the procedures for amendments—are especially onerous. The rules for changing regulations, laws, and constitutions may be arranged in a hierarchy of entrenchment according to the number of veto players (institutions or parties that can block change) and the thresholds of support required to overcome each potential veto. The higher the *threshold of adoption* for a change, the greater is the level of entrenchment.

Even without more demanding procedures, rules of change may entrench decisions by producing winners who have both the incentive and the power to keep the rules that have enabled them to win. For centuries, primogeniture produced winners with the power to maintain the rules of inheritance and succession that gave them control of landed wealth and power. A system of "first-past-the-post" electoral rules typically yields two major parties with the power and motivation to keep those rules in place, to the disadvantage of third parties that would benefit from a shift to proportional representation.

Economists and political scientists usually refer to basic rules as "rules of the game." Rules of change are rules of the game that determine how easy it is to change the game's other rules, so the term is more specifically relevant to entrenchment. The concept of a "rule of change" comes from H. L. A. Hart's theory of law. In Hart's analysis, law encompasses two sets of rules: primary rules, such as those of criminal law, which impose duties, and secondary rules, such as those of constitutional law, which confer powers. Besides rules of change, the secondary level includes rules of recognition, which identify sources of law, and rules of adjudication, which govern the application of law to cases. These secondary, power-conferring rules, Hart writes, "specify the ways in which the primary rules may be conclusively ascertained, introduced, eliminated, varied and the fact of their violation conclusively determined."[7] Rules of change confer powers on governmental bodies to modify laws, and they empower individuals and private organizations to adapt the law to different circumstances and create legally binding relationships—for example, through contracts, wills, and corporations. Through these legal facilities, people create private legislation and even private legal universes, with their own rules of change. Rules of change may be a means of entrenchment for a policy or institution by creating and empowering groups or constituencies likely to support it. While rules of change allow for flexibility, more exigent rules make change difficult. In other words, they represent an institutional procedure for strategic entrenchment.

The standard meaning of entrenchment in law is the establishment of a binding constraint on governance that cannot be overcome through ordinary politics culminating in a simple majority vote of a legislature. "Constitutional entrenchment" refers to two levels of constraint. In the most common usage, it means writing a rule into a constitution, which can then be changed only by a constitutional amendment. In addition, the constitutions of many countries entrench some clauses in an even stronger way by designating them as unamendable. For example, Article V of the U.S. Constitution bars any amendment depriving a state of its "equal suffrage" in the Senate; an effort to give more populous states greater representation would arguably have to replace the Constitution entirely through a new constitutional convention or a revolution. Germany's Basic Law includes an "eternity clause" prohibiting any change in certain fundamental provisions, such as those guaranteeing the inviolability of human dignity and human rights and the federal structure of the German state. Eternity clauses are the highest degree of entrenchment that law can attempt to provide. They are as close as modern government comes to aspirations of divinity.

Governments may also entrench power and policy through other kinds of rules of change. Legislatures may try to entrench a statute or procedural rule by attaching a stipulation that it can be modified or repealed only by a supermajority vote. The tendency of ordinary legislation to become entrenched may also reflect the number of veto players in a government. Compared with a parliamentary system with a dominant lower house and no division between the legislature and executive, the federal government in the

United States may have stronger tendencies toward status quo bias, making it hard to enact a major institutional change and perhaps even harder to repeal it.[8] In the most familiar kind of political entrenchment, incumbents may try to keep themselves in power by modifying the rules of change that determine who can vote, who can run for office, how votes are translated into representation, and other aspects of elections. In addition, laws and policies may be entrenched through the establishment of semi-autonomous governing institutions, such as supreme courts or central banks, or through adoption of an international treaty or entry into an international organization from which a state may not readily extricate itself. In all these cases, entrenchment means shielding from the pressures of ordinary (domestic) politics certain policies and means of governance, as well as the values and interests embodied in them.

The motivations for strategic entrenchment may seem so overwhelming as to make it ubiquitous. But there are risks in the use of entrenched rules to entrench power, even for decision-makers who may see immediate benefits from a particular change. The long-run effects of hard-to-reverse changes are hard to anticipate. A "veil of ignorance" may not just be a hypothetical constraint on decision-making about foundational rules; it may accurately describe how little decision-makers know at critical moments of institutional design. Even when the stakes seem to be clear, complications emerge. The prospect of entrenchment often arouses intense opposition. The opponent who would willingly concede the first round of a conflict may use every available resource to win that first round if it will be the only one and the outcome will be irreversible. The entrenchment of laws, policies, and institutional structures entails a loss of flexibility. Those who initially get what they want may be stuck with arrangements that do not work as they expected. Strategic entrenchment therefore carries a significant risk of regret. Conservatives may support a constitutional court with strong powers of judicial review as a safeguard of property rights, only to discover it gives priority to other rights. Socialists and liberals may be disappointed for the opposite reason. The history of institutional design is strewn with examples of miscalculation.

Faced with such risks, decision-makers may not always try to entrench rules or institutional arrangements. Their choices will often depend on their expectations about changes in power and what the opposition would do if it gained control. If incumbents are confident about the future, unworried about the opposition, and anxious to preserve flexibility, they may not see sufficient reason to pursue the entrenchment even of highly partial rules and structures, with all the opposition that move will arouse and the inflexibility it may bring. But if they think that their power is at a peak and their successors cannot be trusted, they may decide that now is the time to try to entrench rules and arrangements they prefer. Entrenchment may serve as a kind of insurance policy against political change.

These considerations apply to such measures as the adoption of constitutions or constitutional amendments and restrictions on immigration. A party or group in society that thinks it is endangered by ongoing political or social trends may try to entrench itself with constitutive rules that limit what its successors can do, or even who succeeding generations are. Some of the same considerations apply to organizations of all kinds, even to private relationships. Both public bureaucracies and private organizations (for example, the media) may become a basis of entrenched power for whatever partisan, ideological, religious, or ethnic groups are able to colonize them and secure the adoption of rules and procedures that help perpetuate their own interests. "Managerial entrenchment" refers to the use of "lockup" devices such as "poison pills" and different classes of stock to make it difficult for outside investors to wrest control of a corporation from insiders.[9] In a more balanced way, entrenchment may make an agreement between two private parties hard to alter after the fact. In many private negotiations, the parties try to entrench agreed-upon rules by assigning dispute resolution to an independent party. Mandatory arbitration is an entrenchment device (in this case based on a rule of adjudication rather than a rule of change), though in practice it is often a means of entrenching one party's power at the expense of another.

Rules of change may also be encoded in devices and software, denying users the ability to modify a program or a device. Like institutions, technologies are systems of rules that include rules of change. Entrenching a feature in a technology, like a constitution, may be a way of trying to make a system tamper-proof. Legal code may back up the technical code, as when the law bans efforts to "circumvent" digital rights management. But even without law's involvement, some features of a product may effectively be entrenched in a technology if as a practical matter the vast majority of users are unable to change them. The more people have come to inhabit digital environments such as social media, the more the corporations that control those platforms set constitutive rules with wide implications for social life and politics. Platform monopolies can thereby become sites for strategic entrenchment, though the platforms themselves may develop into monopolies from the tendencies toward lock-in that I turn to next.

LOCK-IN AND THE COSTS OF CHANGE

People may be unable or unwilling to undo a decision not because the rules make it difficult to switch, but because the costs of switching are too high. The costs may be too high because of increasing benefits from sticking with an earlier choice, even though that choice may not, in retrospect, have been the best. Increasing returns help explain how technologies, industrial locations, and institutions that had a head start or other early advantages continue to dominate alternatives that, if adopted, could have yielded equal or better results. Increasing returns, however, have less application to contexts where the outcome depends less on net social costs and efficiency than on the power of parties with conflicting interests. Costs may deter change because of the resisting power of those who would bear the losses and the weakness and disorganization of the potential beneficiaries. In concrete historical cases, the opportunities for constitutive change are not constant but depend on continually shifting configurations of forces. After decision-makers have seized a moment ripe for change, the costs of undoing their choices may become prohibitive when the window of opportunity closes.

In all these cases, the outcomes are path dependent—that is, they depend on the nature and timing of contingent events that might have sent developments down one of several paths. Path dependence per se does not necessarily lead to lock-in; some path-dependent processes have fragile outcomes that are easily disrupted. Some outcomes may also be circumvented or converted to other ends without being directly confronted and formally overturned. Lock-in depends on the difficulty (that is, the cost in the broadest sense of that term) of getting off one path and onto another.

Following the usage in economics, I use the term "lock-in" for entrenchment that results from high costs of change that emerge over time, whether through increasing returns or from other effects. Lock-in is a potential outcome of any self-reinforcing process, such as cumulative advantage ("the rich get richer"). Any institution is likely to have "feedback" effects that positively or negatively affect its stability; positive feedback (self-reinforcing) effects lock in a choice only when they are significant enough to shut off alternatives. The term "lock-in," however, lends itself to two misunderstandings. First, it suggests that once selected, a particular technological or institutional form does not evolve. What gets locked in, though, is usually not a static institution or technology but one element of its design or structure, while the institution or technological system continues to develop, perhaps reaching other branching points. While reversing those earlier choices is difficult, lock-in doesn't usually bring development to a full stop. Second, the term "lock-in" highlights whatever emerges as dominant, but the same processes also produce exclusion, marginalization, and subordination. The flip side of cumulative advantage is cumulative disadvantage.[10] Lock-in implies lock-out.

Path Dependence with and without Lock-In

Big effects, we often assume, must have equally big causes. But in a path-dependent process the outcome may hinge on minor, random events or on the sequence in which events occur. By definition, path-dependent development begins with more than one potential outcome. It is the path taken—the intermediate events, rather than the initial conditions—that determines where the process comes to rest. Multiple equilibria are possible, and path dependence explains which of those equilibria emerges. Under diminishing or constant returns and perfect competition, the market would "forget" chance events or their order of occurrence—their effects would average out. But when the effects of those events are magnified by increasing returns, the market "remembers" (the technical term for this is "hysteresis") and may lock in the result.

Lock-in thus contradicts standard expectations about markets: a technology, institutional form, or industrial location may continue to dominate despite the availability of more efficient alternatives that market forces would ordinarily lead producers and consumers to adopt. Under standard conditions, increasing production leads to diminishing or at best constant returns; for example, as farmers plant more acres of a crop, they may bring less-fertile land into production, and the yield per acre falls. But the opposite happens in many situations where returns per unit increase as production increases or as others adopt the same technologies and institutions.

Increasing returns result from several well-established mechanisms.[11] *First*, if production involves high fixed or setup costs, returns will increase as those costs are spread over a larger volume. High fixed costs are typical in large industrial plants and communication and transportation networks as well as knowledge-intensive goods for which the bulk of the cost goes into creating the prototype or first copy. *Second*, both producers and consumers may "learn by doing and using," improving their mastery of techniques as they gain experience. Such learning economies may be especially important during early stages of adoption, as in the most famous (albeit trivial) case of technological lock-in, the QWERTY keyboard, which became standard for typewriters in the late nineteenth century.[12] *Third*, and also relevant to the QWERTY case, the value of a particular option may increase if many people make the same choice (these are called coordination effects or network externalities). In a communications network, for example, the value of owning a device to connect with others increases as more people join the network. The location of an industry may become locked in as new firms develop near the industry's pioneering companies, the region's labor pool with relevant skills expands, and workers move from one firm to another. *Fourth*, if people expect an option to emerge as dominant, that expectation may be self-fulfilling. Such "adaptive expectations" come into play, for example, if buyers anticipate that one format for a new electronic device will win out over rivals.

The development of nuclear-reactor technology, as described in the work of Robin Cowan, is a good example of how institutions become locked in through increasing returns. Nearly all of the elements in increasing-returns path dependence figure in the history: rival technological designs, early events leading to the adoption of an alternative that many experts doubt was the best, and increasing returns as a result of high fixed costs, learning economies, network externalities, and adaptive expectations. In the early 1950s, several competing designs for nuclear power—light-water, heavy-water, and gas-graphite reactors—were under consideration in the United States and Europe. One of those technologies, however, had a head start because the U.S. Navy had chosen a light-water design for its nuclear-powered submarines, the first of which, the *Nautilus,* was launched in 1954. Worried at that time about Soviet nuclear advances, the U.S. government made civilian nuclear power an urgent priority, sought to have a nuclear power plant built quickly, and chose the light-water design, the only one with which it had experience. This early sequence—military use first, civilian second—proved crucial: "The effects which followed from the military's definition of 'best' have been felt ever since," Cowan writes. The light-water design benefited from government subsidies of early research and development costs as well as from substantial learning economies during early commercialization; the result was a "bandwagon market" for light-water nuclear plants. In 1958, when a group of six European countries decided to cooperate with the United States in developing nuclear power, Britain and France gave up on the gas-graphite design in favor of light water. Network externalities in information influenced adoption decisions; according to a report on nuclear power by the International Atomic Energy Agency, "The best countermeasure against technical problems is to have a production system which is common all over the world." By the time the "other, potentially superior, technologies were developed to the point of being marketable," Cowan concludes, "it was too late. Light water was entrenched."[13]

Other examples of institutions intertwined with technologies subject to increasing returns come from the development of network industries, such as electrical-power transmission and transportation systems.[14] Once commitments to a network design have been made, it often becomes extremely costly to switch, especially to an alternative that would destroy the value of sunk investments.

As a result, choices among technological alternatives may get locked in at an early stage before the full implications of the choices are known. That does not mean the choices are a dead end: the technologies and policies may co-evolve. The term "lock-in" still applies, as long as the switching costs block the development of other technologies that might have had greater potential.

But lock-in does not necessarily follow from path dependence, as another example of path dependence—information cascades—illustrates. Information cascades arise when people make choices sequentially, knowing only the prior actions of other people, not the information they had. Suppose as a stranger in a town, with no local knowledge or access to reviews, you are looking for a place to eat and come upon two restaurants. If one of them is crowded and the other is deserted, you will likely infer that the first is the better choice. When a choice is sequential, those who make decisions later may base their choices on inferences from what others have done, even setting aside their own information. As a result, the individuals who act first may set in motion an information cascade, whether or not their choices are the best.[15]

Two demonstrations of path dependence illustrate the difference between increasing returns and information cascades. The classic example of increasing returns, from the work of the mathematician Gyorgy Polya, involves an urn of infinite capacity, which starts out with one red marble and one white marble. Without looking inside, an individual chooses one marble in each round, returns it to the urn, and adds another marble of the same color as the one picked at random. After each round, the probability of the next marble being red exactly equals the proportion of red in the urn. Depending on early random choices, the makeup of the urn will become locked in as marbles of one color or the other come to dominate.[16]

In a second demonstration—this time of an information cascade—an urn containing three marbles may be either majority-black (two black, one red) or majority-red (two red, one black). Unable to observe the contents, subjects draw one marble from the urn, put it back, and announce their guess to onlookers as to whether the urn is majority-black or majority-red. The onlookers cannot see which color marble has been drawn. If the first subject draws a black marble and makes her best guess, she will announce that the urn is majority-black. If the second subject also draws a black marble, his best guess will be the same. But if the third subject then draws a red marble, she may put aside her own information because her best guess, based on the two earlier picks, will still be that the urn is majority-black. In fact, the urn may be majority red, but by that point, chance events—the first two subjects each drawing a black marble—will have started an information cascade.[17]

This kind of path-dependent process unfolds in many situations of sequential choice, as people who act later base their choices on what they know about earlier choices, not simply out of mindless imitation but because they infer that the earlier choices reflect more or better information. For example, in an online experiment testing social influence, visitors to a music website were invited to download free songs by little-known bands and then randomly assigned to eight different "worlds." In worlds where visitors could see the cumulative downloads of previous visitors, songs that got an early lead rose to the top—but in other worlds, different songs rose and remained at the top. The stronger the social influence, the more unequal and unpredictable were the outcomes. "Quality" mattered less than luck and cumulative advantage.[18]

Although increasing returns and information cascades both exhibit path dependence, the mechanisms and outcomes are different. While direct benefits drive the increasing-returns process, information effects—inferences from other people's previous choices—drive the cascade. And since the inferences reflect limited information, the outcome of the cascade is vulnerable to additional information, which may not be costly. For example, if the subjects in the second urn experiment were to announce the color of the marbles they each draw instead of their guess about the makeup of the urn, the cascade would end, and the group would quickly arrive at the right answer. So while increasing returns often lead to lock-in, the outcomes of cascades are highly changeable. Cascades primarily explain short-term phenomena such as fads and fashions, though they may have lasting effects if they trigger an institutional or political change that becomes entrenched through other means.[19]

Chance, Choice, and Political Lock-In

The idea of increasing-returns path dependence has had wide influence in the analysis of social and political institutions.[20] The model has been so influential, in fact, that it has been stretched to apply to cases of path dependence that are fundamentally different. Like some technologies, institutions and societies have key branching points in their history when contingent events or minor influences may tilt development in one direction or another, leading to an outcome that becomes increasingly costly to undo. Those costs may result partly from the mechanisms responsible for increasing economic returns. Like industrial plants and complex technological systems, political institutions have large setup costs.[21] Just as firms achieve learning economies from experience in production, so party leaders and high-level bureaucrats may acquire mastery in organization. And just as there are coordination effects in the economy, there are bandwagon effects in politics. Adaptive expectations have their direct counterpart in Carl Friedrich's "rule of anticipated reactions": Those in power often do not need to exercise it because others change their behavior in anticipation of what the powerful would do.[22]

But especially in the political cases of path dependence, there may be no increased utility or efficiency from sticking with an earlier choice. If choices about institutions become locked in, it may be because of self-reinforcing effects on power and beliefs and on the distribution of the gains and losses between winning and losing parties. The early choices may have initiated a chain of decisions that is difficult to unravel because of the elaborate web of arrangements that has grown as a result, entangling the interests of diverse groups. Wittingly or not, decision-makers may have set in motion self-reinforcing processes that, for better or worse, are hard to reverse. The economic model of lock-in is an amendment to the theory of perfect competition; the social and political cases of lock-in have no such reference point. What gets locked in is not necessarily any more or less efficient or functional than what would have happened otherwise.

Historically minded studies of path dependence often see the inflection point of change as a *critical juncture*, the outcome of which leaves *legacies* that shape future development. Such studies tend to conceptualize social change as an alternation between relatively short bursts of change and long periods of stability, a pattern sometimes called "punctuated equilibrium," after the concept from evolutionary biology.[23] The focus on critical junctures, however, is not a necessary aspect of the theory; it works for some cases and not for others. It has served primarily as a way of reintroducing chance and choice—contingency and agency—into social explanations that are otherwise structural and deterministic.[24] In the increasing-returns model, chance events give an edge to one of several alternatives, and increasing returns to that choice drive the system from openness to closure. In political models of path dependence, choice matters because contingent historical events expand the feasible set of alternatives for whoever has power at the time choices open up. Critical junctures, Giovanni Capoccia and Daniel Keleman write, are moments when structural constraints are "significantly relaxed for a relatively short period, with two main consequences: the range of plausible choices open to powerful political actors expands substantially and the consequences of their decisions for the outcome of interest are potentially much more momentous."[25]

Still, even after such "momentous" choices are made, there may be opportunities for a variety of counterstrategies to limit or redirect institutions that are otherwise entrenched. When barriers to outright reversal are high, the opponents of a policy or institution may succeed in blocking adaptations in response to new practical realities, producing a condition Jacob Hacker calls "drift." For example, as work has evolved in the past half century away from standard, full-time employment, the opponents of broad protections for workers have limited their extension to people with part-time or other contingent jobs. Short of formal revision, the opponents of an institution or policy may also try to convert it to different purposes.[26] Adopted to protect the rights of African Americans after the Civil War, the Fourteenth Amendment became a basis for upholding the rights of corporations.

The development of institutions is politically path dependent and results in lock-in when two conditions are fulfilled: Historical contingencies motivate and enable political actors to change institutions and choose among alternative rules and structures, and the long-run institutional outcome "remembers" those choices because of self-reinforcing effects that constrain further change. The historical contingencies may arise because of chance events, the sequence in which events occur, or the intersection between changes in different spheres (for example, between international conflict and domestic politics, as when a war enables leaders to raise taxes and make other changes they could not make in peacetime). A large class of events, originating both internally and externally, can break down entrenched structures and create opportunities for alternative constitutive choices. Examples include international and civil conflicts, economic crises, and natural disasters. Not all such moments are brought about by adversity; growth spurts in population and wealth may also become critical junctures by simultaneously creating new pressures and opportunities for change. Foundings of various kinds—the creation of new states, colonies, and communities; the establishment of new forms of political and social organization, new taxes, and public programs; and the advent of new technologies—are among the prime occasions for the formulation of new constitutive rules and forms of organization.

In some cases, critical junctures may just be switch points between "alternative tracks" that have already been laid out in other societies or other domains of the same society. But to see critical junctures exclusively in these terms is to underestimate the potential for social and political creativity. New paths may emerge. Critical junctures may be constitutive moments when alternatives are invented and designed and the history of ideas intersects the history of power. When old institutions and practices no longer work—or at least when people come to power who hold that belief—the window may be open for those in power to search for new ideas, and for new ideas to find their way to power.[27] People in search of solutions are not necessarily limited to ideas developed within the domain of the immediate problem at hand. They often have multiple roles and relationships, live in societies with competing institutions and ideas, obtain information from a distance as well as locally, and have the capacity to recognize failure and reflect critically on a range of experience. While "learning by doing" does generate increasing returns, people learn different lessons from other people's doing as well as their own, which they sometimes remix and apply across domains.

These recombined and transposed ideas may then become the basis for the emergence of new institutions, technologies, and cultural forms.[28] These are moments not of path dependence but of path departure, or at least of paths bent in new directions. Yet while ideas are crucial to such transformations, they are also subject to their own tendencies toward entrenchment.

SOCIAL STRUCTURE AND CULTURAL ENTRENCHMENT

Changing our beliefs might seem easy to do. After all, believing something different requires no physical effort, no expenditure of resources, and no originality of thought; merely accepting someone else's beliefs will do. Yet beliefs are often tenacious because we cannot separate what we believe from who we are, and we generally do not hold beliefs by ourselves alone. Many of our core beliefs we hold in concert, together with other people, often under the sway of institutions that have inculcated those beliefs from an early age. When we share beliefs with others, we often share rituals and holidays, moments of grief and celebration, and rules for living. Those shared beliefs and experiences may be constitutive of our sense of self and community—they define who we are in one another's eyes. Giving up a belief may set off a chain of consequences that threatens our faith and identity, closest relationships, and public standing—possibilities that may be so painful as to be literally unthinkable.

From a logical standpoint, a belief system is entrenched when people do not change their beliefs, or make only superficial adjustments, in the face of contradictory evidence. If we are unsympathetic, we may describe their responses as "dogmatic" or "ideological." Even the most perfectly rational individual, however, would not necessarily give up an entire belief system on the appearance of a single piece of contrary evidence. Rationally, the response should also depend on other evidence in favor not only of that belief but of other beliefs that are logically interconnected. In general, one belief is more epistemically entrenched than another in a belief system when an individual rationally holds on to that belief despite conflicts between the two, perhaps because the first is more useful in explaining a wider range of phenomena.[29]

From a sociological viewpoint, beliefs are entrenched when they persist despite the stress of contradictory evidence, dissonant experience, and social pressures for revision. Cultural entrenchment arises from a combined epistemic and social process: the binding together of beliefs and practices with social ties and institutions, entangling them in bundled systems that emerge historically and resist pressure for change. Those bundled systems may also include technologies and other material features of the built world. At the individual level, beliefs are embedded in social relations and social structure and, at an institutional level, incorporated into dominant institutions and propagated by them. The mechanisms of entrenchment at these two levels are different, and they do not necessarily produce the same result.

Embedded Beliefs

On many matters of opinion and taste, people may hold a belief one day and change it the next without worrying about being consistent or occasioning any distress for themselves or others. They may drift from one opinion to another on public issues depending on their recent experiences or what they have heard on the news, particularly from figures they respect. But beliefs that sit at the core of individual and group identity, or that serve as well-recognized symbols of membership and shared worldviews, are not so easily given up. The threshold of adoption for new constitutive beliefs and related symbols of identity and social practices is likely to be high. Reaching that threshold may require reinforcement and affirmation from others, perhaps even a severing of old ties and the formation of new ones.

The concept of a "threshold of adoption" for a change in beliefs is analogous to the impediments created by onerous rules of change and high costs of change.[30] None of these guarantees permanence; they create hurdles for constitutive change, whether in institutions, technologies, or cultural forms. By the same token, they may enable a change, once adopted, to become entrenched in turn. So just as we have asked what mechanisms lead to exigent rules of change and to high costs of change, we can inquire into the mechanisms that raise the threshold of adoption for new beliefs.

Individual and group identities arise, in the first instance, from the bonds people form, usually at an early age, from their immediate social relations. These attachments, Clifford Geertz writes, stem from the "assumed givens" of kinship and locality, of being born into a religious community, speaking a particular language or dialect, and following particular social practices—"congruities of blood, speech, custom, and so on [that] are seen to have an ineffable, and at times overpowering, coerciveness in and of themselves."[31] When I noted earlier that some aspects of social reality are taken to be natural and objective aspects of the world, I was referring to the same phenomenon of "assumed givens." It is from those givens that people derive many of the beliefs that they *think with* (for example, social categories), as opposed to the beliefs they *think about*. The taken-for-granted categories include distinctions between "us" and "them," which define who belongs and can be trusted and who is an outsider and perhaps an enemy.

Stepping outside those givens is inherently difficult for anyone who inhabits them. To be sure, many people now remake their identities during their lives, especially when they live in diverse communities or are able to move to one. But the social networks and hierarchies of more homogenous communities may considerably raise the costs of breaking away. Accepting a new belief may risk a loss of social connections and reprisals from the group, especially from people with greater power. Beliefs are more strongly entrenched when an individual's social ties are more embedded. In a social network, an embedded tie is a tie between individuals whose neighbors (in a social, not necessarily a geographical sense) also have ties with one another, as in a close-knit community where neighbors all know one another. People with dense, embedded ties are likely to have less exposure to new beliefs, and if they are exposed to alternatives, a high threshold for adopting them. The result may be the "closure" of a network and the local entrenchment of beliefs—resistance to change introduced from outside. The threshold of adoption will be greater still if the locally powerful are determined to keep out disruptive external influences.

Different thresholds of adoption affect how beliefs spread. When a new belief or new piece of information fits readily into existing frameworks and confirms preexisting biases, the threshold of adoption is generally low. Like highly contagious viruses, such beliefs can spread through a single contact—old-fashioned word-of-mouth sped up today by social media. People may learn more from casual acquaintances who have new information than from kin and close friends, whose knowledge is likely to be redundant with their own. This is the "strength of weak ties," the interpersonal basis on which new information and memes can jump from one group to another.[32]

But when new information and beliefs conflict with existing frameworks, and accepting them entails substantial personal cost, a single contact with a weak tie is unlikely to be enough to get people to change. Before they will revise beliefs that affect their identity, faith, and social position, they may require multiple sources of activation and reinforcement—for example, from early converts who lend legitimacy to new beliefs and provide alternative sources of solidarity and emotional energy.[33] Consequently, the diffusion of such identity-changing and socially disruptive beliefs usually takes a different form, involving intensive, locally focused communication and personal relationships. Religious and political movements that have sought to change people's identities and commitments have necessarily proceeded on that basis. Here we come full circle, back to questions about strategic entrenchment, now in connection with the cultural constitution of power.

Institutional Deepening

The dominant institutions in a society do not necessarily reach deep into most people's lives. They may reach only the metropolitan centers, not the countryside; just the higher social strata, not those below them; only what people say publicly, not what they say in private, much less what they think. In Czarist Russia, according to Florian Znaniecki, "the vast majority of peasants were utterly unconscious that they were supposed to belong to a Russian society united by a common culture."[34] The French Revolution may have "invented" the modern nation-state, but France's national culture, according to Eugen Weber, penetrated rural areas slowly. So persistent were local languages and dialects that French was a foreign language for nearly half the children reaching adulthood in the late 1800s.[35] Mass conscription into national armies, national educational systems, and national media in the twentieth century all contributed to the deeper cultural penetration of the nation-state into local communities, individual lives, language, and popular consciousness.

Institutional deepening, as I will call this process, is not limited to the state's penetration of society. The term "democratic deepening" refers to the integration of democratic ideas into popular thought and political practice.[36] Technological systems may become so pervasive that the assumptions embodied in them become a cultural subconscious. The market can also vary in how deeply it permeates social relations and everyday thinking, even thinking about the self (or, as a marketing consultant might put it, your personal brand). Political, religious, and economic institutions often become entrenched in a society's metropolitan core and among its elite before extending to its periphery and down to subordinate groups. This was the pattern in Europe from the late medieval to the modern era in the spread of manners governing interpersonal relations, basic bodily functions, and eating (the classic case is the spread of the fork from court society to the middle classes).[37] Institutional deepening is not synonymous with hegemonic imposition and social control; the sources of institutional deepening come from below as well as above. Adopting the ways of dominant classes and institutions is for many people the means of escape from poverty or stifling parochialism and entry into more varied and complex cultural experiences.

As institutions develop, they often demand more of people even as they create wider opportunities for them. As I noted earlier, those who control wealth and power cannot just sit on their accumulations; they have to renew them lest they become vulnerable to challengers. Eliciting moral commitments from others, in part by elevating institutions to a sacred trust and a higher cause, is part of the continuing process of replenishing institutional power.[38] Institutional deepening also typically involves systematizing beliefs and practices, turning them into the more structured form of an ideology. Ideologies are weaponized ideas, critical to the identity-shaping ambitions of proselytizing religions, revolutionary parties, and nationalist movements.

Since states have to categorize people for administrative and statistical purposes, they are necessarily in the business of shaping individual and group identities. Both the distinctions they make and the inferences they draw from those distinctions are important political choices. Religion or race, for example, may be either highlighted or banned as a relevant category for decisions about employment, educational admissions, and other purposes. The social categories states adopt, or allow private decision-makers to use, affect how people organize themselves in relation to government. If politics is partly about who gets what, the choice of official categories affects who the who is in the first place. Asked to fill out official forms from an early age, people learn who they are partly from the options presented to them. The choice of categories used in censuses and other official data also affects what becomes known and measurable in a society, which has its own consequences. The more extensive the scope of state intervention in social and economic life, the more its categories are likely to frame both personal identity and the understanding of how society as a whole is constituted.[39]

The two social processes I have been describing for the formation of individual and group identities are not cleanly separated. The attachments Geertz wrote about, which he called "primordial," typically descend not from time immemorial but from long-forgotten political struggles that shaped the structures of kin and community. Social categories and identities that start out at the level of social relations may move up to the dominant institutions; those that start out in the dominant institutions may move down to everyday relations. At the individual level, Andreas Wimmer points out, an ethnic boundary consists both of categories that divide the social world into "us" and "them" and of social scripts that indicate how to relate to members of different groups.[40] At any given time, though, the officially drawn social boundaries may not match the boundaries the people in those groups draw for themselves. The official and local "maps" may not agree on who belongs where, much less on how they ought to act toward one another. This potential dissonance applies more generally. Beliefs entrenched locally do not necessarily match beliefs entrenched in the state or other dominant institutions. The results of different processes of entrenchment may be in tension with each other—or outright contradiction—and rather than being incidental misalignments, those conflicts may be of central significance to a society.

ENABLING CONSTRAINTS, TRAPS, AND CONTRADICTIONS

Institutions last, according to some theories, because they fulfill the needs of society or satisfy demands for efficiency. As should be clear from the preceding discussion, I do not adopt either of those views, but it is a pity they are not correct. If an unfailing social or economic logic predictably weeded out dysfunctional and inefficient institutions, all societies would be more harmonious and efficient, and progress would be universal. History has not been so kind. Dysfunctional and inefficient institutions have often been highly agreeable to people with sufficient power to maintain them. Nor have societies had the unity and coherence that these and other theories suggest. If a single imperative force, like a great magnet, pulled all the elements of a society into alignment, social explanation would certainly be easier. We would only need to understand the magnet, whether it was individual rationality, class interest, or a hegemonic culture.

Instead, competing forces push institutions in different directions, often with contrary effects that have been historically overlaid on one another. Many aspects of a society are like the meandering streets of old cities: the entrenched results of paths of activity laid down long ago for reasons no one remembers, persisting because people have grown attached to their own ways and byways, and the costs of tearing them up and carrying out a master plan would be too great.

While not necessarily advancing interests in efficiency, functionality, or unity, the mechanisms of entrenchment I have set out do enable constitutive rules and other foundational elements in a society to withstand pressure for change. Strategically creating facts on the ground may make the outcome of conflict a fait accompli and consequently deter challenges; the deliberate adoption of onerous rules of change may make foundational decisions hard to undo. Early choices about technologies and institutions may get locked in because of increasing returns. Other choices may get locked in politically because of who happens to hold power or to acquire it at a moment of constitutive choice, before the window of opportunity closes and a do-over becomes impossible. Embedded social ties raise the local threshold of adoption for new beliefs about core questions of identity, while dominant institutions propagate social categories and cultural forms, impressing them more deeply in social structure and popular consciousness.

These mechanisms of entrenchment fall into a pattern (see table, "Summary of Conceptual Framework"). Under each of the general forms (strategic entrenchment, lock-in, and cultural entrenchment), there are paired types, varying in the extent to which they rely on institutionalized systems of authority and claims of legitimacy. The use of brute facts on the ground for strategic entrenchment relies on raw power and a preponderance of resources. Increasing returns lock in path-dependent outcomes through material advantage. Embedded social ties entrench beliefs through local and direct interpersonal pressure. The second set of mechanisms—rules of change, political lock-in, and institutional deepening—all

Summary of Conceptual Framework

	Strategic entrenchment	Lock-in	Cultural entrenchment*
Force/material advantage/pressure	Created facts on the ground; faits accomplis	High costs of change from increasing returns, cumulative advantage/ disadvantage	High threshold of adoption for new beliefs and identities from embedded social ties
Institutionalized system of legitimate authority	Exigent rules of change; deliberately institutionalized supporting interests	Political lock-in; high emergent costs of change from choices at critical junctures	High threshold of adoption for new beliefs and identities from institutional deepening

Note: The terms listed in each box are illustrative, not exhaustive.
* Cultural entrenchment may develop through strategic action (as in religious or ideological proselytizing) or through cumulative and emergent effects.

call for more complex formal institutions. These are all ways in which foundational rules and relations become resistant to pressure for change.

To acknowledge that institutions, technologies, and cultural forms become entrenched is not tantamount to endorsing any form of historical or structural determinism. None of these mechanisms spells the end of history. They create tenacious structures, not eternal ones. As the following chapters illustrate, entrenched structures may ultimately fall victim to external shocks like wars and depressions; to cumulative changes in economic and social conditions that prevent rules and arrangements from working as they had in the past; to their own internally destabilizing effects; and to transformations in moral beliefs and political regimes to which the institutions are closely linked. Entrenched regimes may have vulnerabilities that no adversary has yet figured out how to exploit. "Entrenchment," Steven Teles points out, "is the joint product of the structure of the incumbent regime and the failures of rival agents"—if, that is, there are rivals of any consequence.[41]

Understood in this way, entrenched institutions have a range of possible consequences that can be divided, from a moral and political standpoint, into three general types, according to whether they enable or constrict freedom and human welfare, or are internally contradictory.

Ideally, entrenchment is a basis of enablement—enabling not the powerful alone but society as a whole, and especially those with less wealth and power, to secure opportunities for greater flourishing. This is the vision of constitutionalism as a set of enabling constraints, ultimately empowering to those who would otherwise have no power at all. Entrenchment, as I suggested earlier, implies constraints on the reversibility of past decisions and on paths of future development, and those constraints may suggest that entrenchment only shrinks the set of feasible options for individuals and societies. But especially when entrenched constraints reflect mutual agreement or a public deliberative process, they may also create new alternatives that would otherwise be infeasible, and they may improve the quality of decisions from the standpoint of democratic values.

The concept of an enabling constraint is fundamental to the ideal of the rule of law, and indeed to any system of binding rules.

People are able to act together more effectively when they have greater clarity about the behavior of others and means of holding them to expectations. By constraining changes in rules, entrenchment may take this institutional solution to collective-action problems to a higher level. An entrenched constraint is enabling if it filters out options for later changes that the affected individuals or groups, knowing their own limitations, would rationally prefer to have closed off.

It may seem counterintuitive that people would willingly choose to deny themselves alternatives, but there are well-recognized reasons for making precommitments.[42] In the paradigmatic case of a self-imposed constraint, Ulysses has his crew bind him to the mast and tells them to ignore his cries when their boat comes within earshot of the Sirens. A more prosaic example is setting your alarm clock for an early hour and putting it too far away for you to reach from bed. In both cases, the precommitment reflects an anticipated weakness of will.

Mutually imposed constraints sometimes reflect the same logic. People enter into marriages and other binding relationships in part because they anticipate their own limitations as well as the other party's and expect to enjoy reciprocal benefits in return for credible commitments that they themselves will find hard to break. Constitutionalism ideally follows similar principles. In constraining its own powers, a liberal government announces that it is tying its own hands, anticipating weakness of will in the future, when, for example, circumstances might tempt its leaders to abrogate individual rights.

The actual motivations for entrenchment, however, often do not meet this high standard. In practice, entrenchment is liable to capture, with more malign consequences in some cases than others. Rather than tying their own hands, the parties interested in entrenching rules frequently want to tie someone else's hands, generally those of rivals and potential successors they distrust. Choices about institutional design are no different from other political decisions in being subject to capture by interests that hold power when the decisions come up. Concessions to preexisting power are the price that many democracies have had to pay to resolve conflicts at the moment of their founding. Constitutional provisions often consequently protect wealth and privilege acquired in a pre-democratic period. The rules that constitutions entrench for that purpose—including rules for electoral and counter-majoritarian institutions, cases I take up later—may not turn out in the long run to serve the interests that sought them. But like the capture of regulatory agencies by the industries they are supposed to regulate, constitutional capture has at times succeeded, and it is an ever-present risk to democracies—as it is today.

Entrenchment fails in a particularly disastrous way when it results in institutional traps, arrangements that not only foreclose collective gains to society but also provide no means of self-correction. A repressive regime may condemn its subjects and itself to a low level of economic development if ruling elites seek to entrench themselves by blocking productive innovation out of fear that it will reduce their power.[43] "Opportunity hoarding" and other forms of elite social closure may deny excluded groups skills and other capacities that would redound to the advantage of society as a whole.[44] Increasing returns may perpetuate technological and institutional infrastructures that threaten a society's long-term prosperity and even its survival.

This is exactly the problem with the dirty-energy trap today. Sunk investments in the existing carbon infrastructure provide a massive base for increasing returns, simultaneously creating incentives to keep investing not just in fossil fuels but in fossil-fuel innovation (fracking, for example) and generating the political power to stymie alternative policies at the level that would be needed to overcome the fossil-fuel economy's self-reinforcing tendencies.[45] Health-care policy in the United States has some of the same features.[46] Escaping an institutional trap requires political power, but the very reason the institutions in these cases block an escape is that they are politically self-reinforcing—unless there are vulnerabilities in the incumbent regime that opponents can be mobilized to exploit.

In an institutional trap, a society is caught in a loop and cannot readily get out of it, but entrenchment can go wrong in another way as well, when institutions develop on the basis of principles that are in outright contradiction to each other. A social contradiction is not just a matter of moral hypocrisy (professing one thing and doing another) or logical inconsistency (professing two things that cannot both be true). In a social contradiction, opposed principles and forms of organization clash with each other, lead to overt conflict, and make change unavoidable. Opposed elements on both sides may be entrenched, as was true in the struggle over slavery in the United States, in which case the resolution requires transformative change at the deepest constitutive level.

Like democratic governments, democratic societies require a "constitution," not a single formal document but a body of entrenched principles, rules, and arrangements that counteract tendencies toward personal and class domination and the monopolization of wealth and power. The struggles over the constitution of society would deserve our attention for their historical interest alone, but they are all the more important because of their continued bearing on freedom and human welfare. In the next two chapters, I take up two cases of oligarchic entrenchment that stood in the way of democracy as we have come to understand it—Europe's landed aristocracies and the slaveocracy of the American South. I then turn in the following two chapters to the entrenchment of core features of constitutional democracy and the welfare state—to democracy's many compromises with wealth, and wealth's many compromises with democracy in the liberal order that developed in the nineteenth and twentieth centuries. Whether that order will survive or a substantially different one will emerge in its place is the subject of a final chapter on oligarchy and populism, constitutional capture, and the politics of entrenchment today.

CHAPTER TWO

Aristocracy and Inherited Wealth

P ROPERTY IS ALWAYS AN eminently political matter, not just an economic one. How wealth, particularly great wealth, is acquired and passed on to the next generation is closely related to the foundations of political power. The rules for inheriting wealth, as opposed to accumulating it through work, are especially important for power if two conditions are met. When economic growth is relatively slow, the inheritance of existing wealth tends to be correspondingly more important because opportunities for new accumulations are limited. And where the ownership of wealth is highly concentrated, political power is likely to be concentrated as well. These two conditions generally occurred together before the industrial revolution, often making inherited wealth and power so closely aligned as to be all but indistinguishable.

In early modern Europe and its colonies, no one would have doubted the supreme political significance of property and the rules governing its inheritance. The supporters of monarchy, even constitutional monarchy in Britain, argued that a stable social order required a concentration of landed wealth in an aristocracy. In contrast, Thomas Jefferson and others in late eighteenth-century America were convinced that a republic demanded not just the overthrow of monarchical power but a wide distribution of property among independent yeoman farmers. These rival theories of political entrenchment shared the same premise: Strategic choices about rules determining the ownership of land—the most important form of wealth at the time—could solidify a regime and make it difficult to overturn.

Two rules of inheritance, primogeniture and entail, were widely acknowledged as crucial to the monarchical social and political order. Primogeniture is the right of the firstborn, usually the firstborn male, to succession or inheritance. An entail is a private, legally enforceable restriction on inheritance, typically requiring the family estate to remain forever undivided and to descend in "tail male" (through the eldest son or surviving male relative). These rules, or variants of them, underpin systems of patrimonial inheritance such as the one that long prevailed in Britain. A patrimonial inheritance system channels property and status through a line of male heirs, and it seeks to maintain intact the patrimony, the estate, as the foundation of the family's durable status and identity. In English law, the head of a landed family was merely the "life tenant" of an estate—or as Roy Porter puts it in a colorful analogy, "the ancestral baton-carrier in the relay race of family destiny."[1] The rules and practices of patrimonial inheritance sought to prevent the current life tenant from exhausting or squandering the patrimony and limited whom an heir could marry and often whether a younger son could marry at all.

What these rules entrenched was not so much individual possession as the family line. They promoted not only dynastic rule in the state but also family dynasties throughout the top echelons of society. Patrimonial inheritance thus served as a means of oligarchic entrenchment, perpetuating a dominant class of wealth holders.

This relationship between inheritance rules and entrenched power was precisely why Jefferson and other revolutionaries of his time opposed primogeniture and entail. Alexis de Tocqueville was so convinced of the centrality of inheritance as the ultimate determinant of state and society that he wrote, "When the legislator has once regulated the law of inheritance, he may rest from his labor. The machine once put in motion will go on for ages." According to Tocqueville, where the law "unites, draws together, and vests property and power in a few hands," it yields an aristocracy, and where the law "divides, distributes, and disperses both property and power," it leads to democracy.[2]

Tocqueville's confidence in the durable political effects of inheritance laws now seems naïve. Partible inheritance did not turn out to guarantee that property and power would be divided and dispersed. Jefferson, Tocqueville, and others who developed their ideas about property and power before the growth of industrial capitalism and the modern corporation failed to anticipate the emergence of forms of wealth that would dwarf land and its owners. Jefferson also failed to anticipate the consequences of his generation's failure to end slavery. Entrenching democracy against the threat of domination by concentrated wealth would become an evolving political project, requiring new means to keep wealth's power within bounds.

But patrimonial inheritance and the system of power it undergirded lasted a long time. In England, primogeniture arrived with the Norman Conquest in 1066 and was finally extinguished as a legal rule through the Administration of Estates Act in 1925—nearly a millennium after its establishment, surely enough to qualify it as an example of an entrenched institution. Today, novels and historical dramas are the main sources of popular knowledge about the workings of patrimonial institutions and their effects on inheritance and marriage. So alien are these arrangements to a modern sensibility that it must seem puzzling how they ever began, much less survived so long. That is the puzzle this chapter addresses. But because it is only part of the larger problem of entrenched power, I turn first to some general analytical considerations about the relationship between wealth and power and the role of rules of inheritance.

WEALTH, POWER, AND RULES OF INHERITANCE

Wealth is a source of power in social relationships of all kinds, even within families and between generations. It may translate into political power in at least four different ways.

First, ownership of property conveys *control over a specific domain*, and it conveys more complete control to the owner the more limited the rights and powers of other parties in that domain. The seigneurial privileges and military power of a feudal lord exemplify entrenched power based on domain control. Modern business enterprises are also governments of private domains, exercising power and influence over their employees, local communities, and even their customers (think of Facebook), sometimes setting standards and norms with wide ramifications. For both the feudal lord and the modern corporation, the extent of domain control depends on the rights and powers enjoyed through law or custom by parties such as tenants and workers, as well as those groups' opportunities for "exit" and their capacities for "voice," including their capacity for collective action, disruption, and violence.

Second, wealth holders become more powerful as a class through the *concentration of ownership* and other forms of combination and monopoly. Greater unity of control magnifies the power of wealth in its local environment and helps overcome problems of collective action in coordinating at higher levels. Monopolization affords political power, not just opportunities for profit.

Third, wealth has been a basis of *privileged political and legal representation and access*. In the early stages of representative government, aristocratic upper chambers of legislatures and other classes' restricted access to the franchise fortified wealth's power. Even after such formal privileges were abandoned, those who controlled great wealth, whether as individual owners or through corporations, continued to enjoy privileged influence through informal channels to political leaders. They could also use financial assets at their disposal to secure elite legal representation and to make political investments—for example, in political organization and campaigns to support preferred leaders (including themselves) and in lobbying, media, and advocacy to win favorable treatment and promote congenial ideas.

Fourth, wealth conveys political power because of its *structural indispensability*—that is, its role as capital for investment, the basis of economic growth and therefore the growth of government revenue. Insofar as capital is mobile, those who control it can punish governments that adopt policies hostile to their interests by withholding investment and transferring capital across local or national boundaries—at least, if the government allows them to do that.

The power of landed wealth in a preindustrial society depends primarily on the first three sources of wealth's power—domain control, concentration of ownership, and privileged political representation. The owners of land, oil fields, mines, and other immobile forms of capital cannot move their assets elsewhere when they face a state that is less than friendly. Consequently, they may be especially implacable opponents of democracy, which they may see as threatening to deprive them of their property through outright expropriation or confiscatory taxation. The taxation of inheritances and other reforms of inheritance laws may be particularly abhorrent to great landowners and other owners of immobile capital because such changes jeopardize their dynastic ambitions.

Rules of inheritance and succession are examples of the "rules of change" I described in the previous chapter. The changes that these rules govern involve the transmission of status, property, and power from one generation to the next. In societies where legal status is heritable, the rules may determine who is free or slave, aristocrat or commoner, citizen or alien. It is no exaggeration to say that rules of inheritance are often constitutive of the dominant class and political elite and that the choice of rules may therefore be a way of strategically entrenching a social and political order. As Lawrence Friedman writes, the rules of inheritance and succession "act as a kind of pattern or template through which the society reproduces itself each generation ... guarantee[ing] that the next generation will, more or less, have the same structure as the one that preceded it."[3]

The extent to which the rules for inheriting property actually do reproduce social structure depends on the rate of economic growth. People acquire wealth in two ways: through accumulations from work during their own lifetimes, and through inheritance, either directly or by marriage. Rapid economic growth expands the opportunities for new accumulations and therefore tends to diminish the ratio of inherited wealth to total wealth and consequently the importance of inheritance rules. But when economic growth is slow—as it was before the industrial revolution—inherited wealth generally dominates the distribution of wealth in society. If, as some forecasts indicate, future economic growth rates will be relatively low, inheritance will again become an increasingly important source of wealth, with possibly profound implications for social structure and politics.[4]

The significance of inheritance rules has also depended critically on changes in birth and mortality rates and family structure. High birth rates among propertied families reduce the concentration of wealth under systems of partible inheritance, yet they have also led families and governments to institute rules such as primogeniture to resist the diminution of family fortunes. While low birth rates and high mortality reduce that pressure, they leave many dynasts without a preferred heir, creating crises of succession and opportunities for social mobility. Inheritance rules are closely related to kinship systems and gender relations. In societies where a woman's property becomes her husband's upon marriage, inheritance is unilaterally from the father (as opposed to a bilateral system where children inherit from both parents). Rules restricting marriage for daughters and younger sons may also concentrate property in a single line of male descent. The choices that people make, however, do not always reflect a society's laws or even its informal norms. People are not always rule-followers. Like other rules, rules of inheritance create a context for individual and family strategies.[5] These strategic adaptations may then lead to changes in law and institutions, as arrangements get incrementally renegotiated.

Systems of inheritance and succession are also spelled out in law to different degrees. Legal rules may define who among potential heirs is to succeed to a particular status or title or to inherit specific assets, while other rules are social norms, that is, widely shared expectations about the practices of inheritance that may be regarded as customary and proper. Custom may become law, as it did, at least in theory, in the development of the English common law. Whether defined informally or formally, inheritance rules range across a spectrum from restrictive to permissive. The more restrictive may dictate, for example, the exact shares of an estate that go to a spouse, sons, and daughters. The more permissive afford greater discretion to the individual testator, as when the law provides a facility such as a will. The more discretion afforded, the greater is the *testamentary freedom*, at least for the individual who initially leaves property. If the law allows it, a testator may be able to bind heirs for more than a generation, even in perpetuity, as in an entail. Consequently, restrictive rules governing inheritance may originate not only in law or custom but in the private decisions of earlier testators.

The very concept of a will rests on a series of assumptions about social institutions: that individuals own heritable property; that law and custom provide owners a degree of freedom in determining who will own that property after they die; that individuals can create a binding testament to transmit those choices; and that society will honor those choices and institute procedures to carry them out. The historical development of these practices of testamentary succession was a subject of central interest when the discipline of legal history first arose in the nineteenth century; the early legal historians debated whether Western institutions owed more to ancient Roman or Germanic law.[6] But on one point, historians have been in agreement: Neither Roman nor Germanic law included a rule of primogeniture for the inheritance of property. That absence makes the origin and entrenchment of primogeniture all the more interesting.

THE POLITICAL ORIGINS OF PRIMOGENITURE

Primogeniture has served historically as a rule for both the succession of political power and the inheritance of property, usually in the form of a right of the eldest son. Primogeniture is not the only form of unigeniture, that is, inheritance by a single heir. The rule in some societies has favored the youngest child (ultimogeniture) or called upon a ruler or testator to designate one successor or heir.

Primogeniture may result from law, custom, or private choice. All three were involved in Britain's system of patrimonial inheritance, the remnants of which lasted into the early twentieth century. Inheritance law in Britain was divided into two domains: real property (land, buildings, and other improvements) and movables or personalty (all other possessions, including liquid investments), a division that roughly corresponds to the distinction between immobile and mobile capital. As a legal rule, primogeniture applied only to real property, and it served as a default—that is, it was the rule when there was no will (intestacy) or wherever a will was ambiguous about realty. In cases of intestacy, the law called for the eldest son to receive all the real property and for the movables to be split equally among all the decedent's children.[7]

But since those with great wealth usually did not die without a will, the more important British legal institutions for inheritance were entails and family settlements. Once land was entailed, a later will could not reverse it; entailment was a strong entrenchment device. Family settlements were agreements, usually drawn up at the marriage of the eldest son, accomplishing the purposes of entail while also setting aside resources for a surviving spouse and younger siblings. Although these arrangements overwhelmingly favored male heirs, they did not always prevent a daughter from inheriting. Where real property passed to a daughter, however, control typically resided with her husband. As "femmes covert," married women had no independent property rights. Indeed, if they died first, their husbands inherited their property, whereas if their husbands died first, they generally received use of only a third of the property for their lifetime or until they remarried (at which time the property went to one or more of their children or a collateral heir). Patriarchal values underlay the entire English system of real property ownership.[8]

It is not accurate to call primogeniture a "traditional" institution, as if it was generally practiced in the pre-modern world. Inheritance rules vary in pre-industrial societies. Primogeniture was not the prevailing law or practice in Anglo-Saxon England or in continental Europe before the twelfth century. It had specifically feudal origins. In France and much of Europe, primogeniture dominated inheritance practices among the aristocracy from the twelfth century until the French Revolution (and was revived or maintained in varying degrees under different regimes in the nineteenth century). But just as it is incorrect to think of the practice as "traditional," so it would be a mistake to attribute its persistence merely to inertia. Primogeniture remained entrenched for so long only because those who controlled the rules of inheritance repeatedly counteracted the forces threatening the institutional foundations of their power.

Primogeniture originated as a response of feudal elites to conditions between the eleventh and thirteenth centuries. The overriding realities of feudal society were the weakness of states and of centrally imposed public order and the high levels of violence. Although kings sat atop the social hierarchy, power largely devolved to local lords, each with his own knights and other retainers. A king or lord could reward his vassals—those who swore homage to him—in two ways. He could house and equip them, or he could give them estates ("fiefs") from whose income they could provide for themselves. "By fief," Marc Bloch explains, "was meant a property granted not against an obligation to pay something . . . but against an obligation to do something."[9] The most important of these obligations were military; a king's or a lord's military tenants were the foundation of his army and his power. Lands under military tenure were granted in return for a knight's service.

The development of primogeniture involved the establishment, first, of the heritability of fiefs and, second, of the rule that the entire estate went to the eldest son. In the early feudal period, vassalage began with a rite of personal homage and ended with the death of either the lord or the vassal; a fief might only involve a life tenancy, without any right to pass the land on to heirs. By the late 800s in France, according to Bloch, there developed a strong sense of "family reversion—the feeling that the services rendered by the father created a right for his descendants." In Lombardy (northern Italy) in 1035, a war broke out between the great nobles and their vassals, who claimed their fiefs as family property. The vassals defeated the nobles' army.[10]

The move toward primogeniture took place in different ways in England and on much of the continent. The Norman invasion of England in 1066 led to what was effectively a military occupation and the creation of a new aristocracy. Rewarding his vassals with seized estates, William the Conqueror stipulated that they be passed on undivided to the eldest male. Primogeniture thus originally applied only to knight-service estates but spread to others by the late 1100s. The usual explanation for William's action is regime consolidation: Large undivided estates would provide the Norman barons and their heirs a surplus capable of supporting a strong enough military force to subdue popular resistance. Once established as a norm for the greatest nobles, primogeniture spread throughout the aristocracy and became a legal requirement for civil as well as knight-service land. A statute adopted in 1285 is usually cited as the source of entails lasting in perpetuity.[11]

On the continent, there was no single, top-down imposition of primogeniture, but the strategic interests were similar. Demographic pressure from a rising population may have been a factor.

Princes and lords adopted primogeniture and entail as a way to prevent the division of estates and the disintegration of the power they had accumulated. By the end of the twelfth century, the aristocracy had generally embraced the new rules of succession. According to Georges Duby, the adoption of primogeniture reflected the consolidation of the knightly aristocracy in the twelfth century and a sharpened division between the aristocracy and commoners. Although some peasants had managed to accumulate land and tenants, their estates eroded from one generation to the next as a result of "pious gifts" and partible inheritance. At death, one part of a wealthy peasant's estate would go to the church, while the rest was split among sons and daughters. Nobles, meanwhile, obtained compensatory grants of ecclesiastical property when making gifts to the church, and they adopted new kinship and inheritance rules. "In the upper levels of society," Duby writes, "family ties were being arranged with a rigid framework calculated to safeguard the unity of the inheritance—in a word, lineage. For each family there would be one line of male descent." Not only would the patrimony pass to the eldest son; the family would allow only the eldest or at most two sons to marry, while directing other sons into the clergy or monasteries. (This pattern leads some historians to suggest that the church, with its rules of celibacy, operated as an adjunct of primogeniture.) When daughters were married off, they received a dowry in movable goods but were denied any claim to the land.[12]

What drove the adoption of primogeniture in feudal Europe? The primary forces fall under two headings. The first involve military and political imperatives in an age of weak legal order. No one has better described the military imperative than Adam Smith, in his account of the origins of primogeniture in *The Wealth of Nations*:

> When land was considered as the means, not of subsistence merely, but of power and protection, it was thought better that it should descend undivided to one. In those disorderly times, every great landlord was a sort of petty prince. His tenants were his subjects. He was their judge, and in some respects their legislator in peace and their leader in war. He made war according to his own discretion, frequently

against his neighbours, and sometimes against his sovereign. The security of a landed estate, therefore, the protection which its owner could afford to those who dwelt on it, depended upon its greatness. To divide it was to ruin it, and to expose every part of it to be oppressed and swallowed up by the incursions of its neighbours.[13]

The forces driving primogeniture in the succession of both states and estates, Smith argues, were therefore the same. To avoid being weakened by division or conflict, the patrimony had to descend according to "some plain and evident difference which can admit of no dispute." The answer to this need, Smith says, lay in the unambiguous characteristics of sex and age and the "universal" preferences for males and firstborns.[14] In fact, as the historical and anthropological evidence shows, those preferences are not universally inscribed in human nature. But we need not assume that they are: it matters only that feudal monarchs and aristocrats adopted male primogeniture in the belief that it served their military and political ends. Then, like many other norms that spread from high elites to those below them, primogeniture diffused downward and across societies through the familiar processes that generate similarity in institutional structure. Power breeds imitation, even when it does not demand it.[15]

Besides this military and political logic, a second set of interests in the adoption of primogeniture involved class consolidation. The basis of membership in the aristocracy underwent a transformation in the late feudal era. By the mid-thirteenth century, according to Bloch, nobility had become a hereditary status, though a noble's son could forfeit his position by marrying beneath him or engaging in manual labor. "The nobility," Bloch writes, "had ceased to be defined by the exercise of a function—that of the armed retainer. . . . It remained, however, a class distinguished by its mode of life."[16] Like rules about marriage, primogeniture and entail served to protect this mode of life by concentrating wealth. In Max Weber's account, the distinctive characteristic of the feudal aristocracy was its claim to military honor, which served as a basis of legitimacy for monopolizing high status. The process exemplified the closure of a status group—the attempt to draw sharp boundaries separating that group from others and to reinforce its claims to privilege.[17]

Even when the military logic of male primogeniture disappeared, these interests in class consolidation and closure remained.

PATRIMONIAL INHERITANCE AND OLIGARCHIC ENTRENCHMENT

The decline of feudalism brought developments that threatened to weaken the hold of primogeniture. Between the fourteenth and sixteenth centuries, property relations in the rural economies of western Europe underwent a transformation. Under feudal tenures, tenants owed their lords labor service, and the lords exercised seigneurial powers over the inhabitants of their land. Modern conceptions of ownership did not apply; different parties, from king to lord to tenant and local villagers, had legal and customary rights in the same land. Although the timing of change varied from one region to the next, the general tendency was to reduce the burdens of tenants' customary service, to convert their labor obligations to cash rent, and to reframe the relationship between landlords and tenants as a periodically renegotiated lease. Property relations were increasingly simplified.[18] The evolution of inheritance law showed some of the same tendencies toward the stripping away of old feudal restraints, as the heads of land-owning families gained increased legal power to devise their property.

In England, the Statute of Wills in 1540 ended the legal requirement that real property descend entirely to the eldest male; testators could now leave two-thirds of knight-service land and all freehold land to heirs of their choice. A century later, knight-service tenures were abolished entirely, making all land devisable (other changes increased testamentary freedom in disposing of personalty). But instead of dividing their estates among their children, the great landowners at first entailed their land, preventing their heirs from breaking it up and trying to ensure that the family estate remained within the patrilineage. In short, they used their testamentary freedom to curb the freedom of their successors. Devices similar to entail emerged in France (*substitutions*), Castile (*majorats*), and Germany (*Fideikommisse*).[19]

Entails, however, often became straitjackets that heirs sought to overturn or modify so as to apportion their estates differently among their children, or to sell land to meet immediate financial needs. Lawyers in England created a maneuver known as "common recovery" that made it possible to "bar" an entail, but that weakening of entail led to a reaction. Among the nobility and gentry, status and identity continued to depend on lineage. Aristocrats remained committed to perpetuating the ascendancy of their families, and primogeniture was the time-honored way to do that, even if the law no longer required it. Moreover, when negotiating the marriage of their eldest son, landowners had to contend with the demands of the bride's family, who wanted guarantees that the estate would be unimpaired and descend to the "heirs of her body." The solution to these competing pressures was called "strict settlement," an irrevocable agreement usually drawn up at the time of the eldest son's marriage or upon his majority. Strict settlement typically transmitted the family's landed estate to the eldest son while setting aside portions of the inheritance, usually from ancillary property, for daughters and younger sons, as well as resources for a surviving spouse. The eldest son did not gain unlimited possession of the estate; he received a life interest in it and bound himself to pass it on to his "contingent remainders," that is, his unborn children, according to a prescribed line of descent, in line with the norm of primogeniture.[20] These efforts to perpetuate the direct male lineage did not always succeed in a genetic sense; a male heir might be childless, or his marriage might produce only daughters, in which case the estate might pass to a male relative on his father's side or, if a daughter inherited, to her husband, who would take the family name. According to calculations by Peter Laslett, three-quarters of direct male lines were broken by the fifth succession.[21]

But in a fundamental social and political sense, the entrenchment of aristocratic dynasties was extraordinarily successful; property and power in England and the British Isles as a whole remained highly concentrated. A study of great landowners in three English counties from 1540 to 1880 shows an "extremely tenacious core" of older families, with surprisingly few new owners buying their way into the landed elite.[22] Data for 1688, 1759, 1803, and 1873 show about the same high level of concentrated land ownership.[23]

Not all of Europe embraced primogeniture and entail as fully as Britain. Even within England, there were local exceptions. For idiosyncratic reasons, some localities followed ultimogeniture, known as "borough English," while Kent maintained the pre-Norman system of gavelkind, which called for equal partition of estates among sons in cases of intestacy. In continental Europe, the German nobility stood out for its resistance to primogeniture. There, too, the equal partition of estates among sons—"equality of brothers"—was held to be a guiding principle. In 1158, Frederick Barbarossa, emperor of the Holy Roman Empire, declared that all honorary fiefs (that is, with titles) would be indivisible and hereditary, a principle that was reaffirmed by Frederick II in 1232. But the empire had only limited control, and from the thirteenth to the sixteenth centuries, German territorial princes divided their lands when they had more than one son. They shifted to primogeniture after 1650, but too late to prevent the multiplication of German principalities. The princes' adoption of primogeniture is generally ascribed to their new status as sovereigns in the wake of the Treaty of Westphalia (1648) and the political advantages of maintaining the unity of their territories. Even then, German nobles did not formally or consistently adopt primogeniture in the inheritance of property. According to one study, they tailored their inheritance practices to economic conditions, favoring the eldest son when the patrimony could support only one descendant in a noble style, but subdividing the estate among sons and establishing collateral family lines when economic conditions allowed.[24]

The British colonies in North America also presented a mixed picture. Although land was more easily available to sons striking out on their own, the colonists brought with them the basic structure of the English inheritance system and the cultural ideals it expressed. As Gordon Wood writes, "Gentry families in many of the colonies, in emulation of the English nobility, created the legal devices of primogeniture and entail, built 'seats' for themselves in the country, and strenuously sought to amass estates they could pass on to their heirs."[25] The partial exception to this pattern was New England, whose founding settlers rejected strict primogeniture in cases of intestacy and divided inheritances among all children, except that the eldest son often received a double portion. Under

New York law, the eldest son received all the realty and a double share of the movables—a more unequal arrangement than in Britain itself. In 1705, Virginia passed a law requiring a special act of the legislature to bar an entail, making entails more strictly enforced than they were in Britain. On the whole, however, as of the early eighteenth century, inheritance laws in the colonies followed those of the mother country. "The English," Carole Shammas writes, "had a narrow unilateral [male descent] system with great individual freedom for family heads and, basically, that was what the colonists had as well."[26]

Reading later history back into the colonial period, some historians see America as having been destined to diverge from Britain in its rules of inheritance as in other aspects of law and society. But as wealth in the colonies increased, plantation owners and others with property were better able to realize the cultural ideals they took from Britain. Today we may believe that things had to turn out differently only because we know that they did—after America had a revolution.

ENTRENCHING A REPUBLIC: THE EIGHTEENTH-CENTURY SOLUTION AND ITS LIMITS

The politics of inheritance changed in the eighteenth century. Between 1500 and 1700, European writers on primogeniture overwhelmingly praised it on the grounds that the stability of a state required deeply rooted, wealthy families with imposing authority.[27] Dividing landed estates would only weaken the aristocracy as a bulwark of order. A few dissident voices expressed sympathy for younger sons, but even during the English Revolution and Interregnum (1641 to 1660), Parliament made no changes in the law, and primogeniture and entail continued.

In the eighteenth century, however, the patrimonial inheritance system came under sharp intellectual criticism and political attack in the developments that culminated in the American and French revolutions. The general trends toward economic growth and modernization do not explain this shift; primogeniture and entail were repudiated and replaced for political reasons and only because of broader political change. The revolutionaries identified the rules of patrimonial inheritance with the regimes they were seeking to overturn, and they changed those rules in an effort to entrench the new social and political order they were hoping to build. Where there was no revolution against aristocratic power, as in Germany and Britain, primogeniture and entail survived into the early twentieth century, despite economic growth and other changes associated with modernization.

Three distinct lines of criticism of primogeniture contributed to the transformation of inheritance. I will refer to these as belonging to the civic republican, liberal, and radical democratic traditions, though I do not mean to suggest that their arguments are mutually exclusive. Jefferson's views about inheritance, for example, show the influence of all three traditions.

The civic republican or neo-Roman tradition in political thought saw widespread ownership of land as the foundation of a free citizenry. As originally developed by Niccolò Machiavelli in the early 1500s and James Harrington in the following century, republicanism emphasized the relationship of real property to freedom and military effectiveness; the independence afforded by owning land promoted the virtue and toughness men needed to defend a republic. Soldiers who had no other means of support, Machiavelli wrote, were a threat to public order in peacetime; the ideal soldiers would rally to their country's defense in war and return to tend their fields in peace.[28]

Harrington's major work, *Oceana*—written in 1656, while England was at least nominally a republic under Oliver Cromwell—was also concerned with the implications of landed property for power. The "balance of property," Harrington thought, determined who had power. Men, he wrote, are "hung" upon riches, not of choice but of necessity because "he who wanteth bread" is the "servant" of whoever feeds him. "Where there is inequality of estates there must be inequality of power; and where there is inequality of power there can be no commonwealth."[29] Yet Harrington was not interested in property from the standpoint of economic relations; as J. G. A. Pocock points out, he was thinking of the power that feudal lords drew from their military tenants, who were bound to fight on their behalf.[30] The history of property since the second century AD, according to Harrington, had seen a shift from feudal to freehold tenure, and it was only as freeholders that men could be genuinely independent citizens and patriots. Although not opposed to an aristocracy, he favored limits on the size of estates and was no fan of primogeniture; he marveled "how it comes to pass that we should use our children as we do our puppies—take one, lay it in the lap, feed it with every good bit, and drown five!"³¹

Harrington's republicanism echoed in the thinking of America's revolutionary generation, as in this letter that John Adams wrote in May 1776:

> The balance of power in a society accompanies the balance of property in land. The only possible way, then, of preserving the balance of power on the side of equal liberty and public virtue, is to make the acquisition of land easy to every member of society; to make a division of the land into small quantities, so that the multitude may be possessed of landed estates. If the multitude is possessed of the balance of real estate, the multitude will have the balance of power, and in that case the multitude will take care of the liberty, virtue, and interest of the multitude, in all acts of government.³²

It is exactly on the basis of this kind of republican argument that eighteenth-century revolutionaries believed that ending primogeniture and dividing up the ownership of land would help entrench a republic.

Smith's *Wealth of Nations*, also from 1776, best exemplifies the liberal argument against patrimonial inheritance. In Smith's eyes, primogeniture and entail were obsolete, unjust, and inefficient. Primogeniture persists, he suggested, because it supports "the pride of family distinctions," even though "nothing can be more contrary to the real interest of a numerous family than a right which, in order to enrich one, beggars all the rest of the children." Entails, he wrote, "are founded upon the most absurd of all suppositions ... that the property of the present generation should be restrained and regulated according to the fancy of those who died perhaps five hundred years ago." Yet entails survived because they were believed necessary to maintain the "exclusive privilege of the nobility to the great offices and honours of their country; and that order having usurped one unjust advantage over the rest of their fellow-citizens, lest their poverty should render it ridiculous, it is thought reasonable that they should have another." According to Smith, concentrated ownership reduced land's productivity: "To improve land with profit, like all other commercial projects, requires an exact attention to small savings and small gains, of which a man born to a great fortune, even though naturally frugal, is very seldom capable." Smith noted that some great estates in the United Kingdom had remained in the hands of the same family since feudal times: "Compare the present condition of those estates with the possessions of the small proprietors in their neighbourhood, and you will require no other argument to convince you how unfavourable such extensive property is to improvement."[33]

These views about the inefficiency of great landed estates were not peculiar to Smith. Other writers of the era also maintained that land was more productive in the hands of owner-occupiers. According to Bas Van Bavel and Richard Hoyle, two economic historians, the belief in "a free peasantry with full property rights in land was as much an intellectual and economic fashion in [the eighteenth century] as collectivization, nationalization and privatization were in the twentieth century."[34] The comparison to twentieth-century theories of privatization and property rights is particularly apt, although the advocates of privatization are more tender-hearted toward large corporations than Adam Smith was to the large land-owners of his time.

Neither the republican nor the liberal positions in the eighteenth century necessarily implied a commitment to popular self-government. Republicanism was consistent with property qualifications for voting and popular deference to rule by men of great wealth; Smith's economic liberalism was associated with constitutional limitation, but not necessarily popular control of the government.

In the radical democratic tradition, however, primogeniture was abhorrent because it perpetuated aristocratic domination. Primogeniture, Thomas Paine wrote in The Rights of Man, "is the law against every other law of nature, and Nature herself calls for its destruction. Establish family justice, and aristocracy falls." The very experience of "trampling on all their younger brothers and sisters," he suggested, rendered an aristocratic beneficiary of primogeniture unfit for government: "With what ideas of justice or honour can that man enter a house of legislation, who absorbs in his own person the inheritance of a whole family of children, or doles out to them some pitiful portion with the insolence of a gift?"[35] *The Rights of Man* was Paine's response to Edmund Burke's *Reflections on the Revolution in France*. Burke, answering Paine in turn, defended primogeniture, claiming it had a "happy tendency" to "preserve a character of consequence, weight, and prevalent influence over others in the whole body of the landed interest." Seizing on Paine's claim that "aristocracy falls" without primogeniture, Burke wrote that primogeniture's opponents "call loudly for its destruction ... for political reasons that are very manifest."[36] On that point, the two agreed. The rules of inheritance were ultimately about who would rule.

The political purposes behind the abolition of primogeniture and entail show up clearly in Jefferson's account of his role in Virginia's reforms at the time of the Revolution. In 1776, as a state legislator, Jefferson made the abolition of entail his first priority. Here is the explanation he gave in his autobiography:

> In the early times of the colony when lands were to be obtained for little or nothing, some provident individuals procured large grants, and, desirous of founding great families for themselves, settled them on their descendants in fee tail [in other words, they entailed their estates]. The transmission of this property from generation to generation in the same estate raised up a distinct set of families who, being privileged by law in the perpetuation of their wealth were thus formed into a Patrician order, distinguished by the splendor and luxury of their establishments. From this order too the king habitually selected his Counsellors of State, the hope of which distinction devoted the whole corps to the interests & will of the crown. To annul this privilege, and instead of an aristocracy of wealth ... to make an opening for the aristocracy of virtue and talent, which nature has wisely provided for the direction of the

interests of society, & scattered with equal hand through all it's conditions, was deemed essential to a well-ordered republic.[37]

As Jefferson proposed, Virginia abolished entail in 1776; a separate bill to end primogeniture was enacted in 1785. As he saw it, these two measures along with two others—a bill abolishing tax support for the established church, which he called "the religion of the rich," and a bill for public support of primary education—all had one underlying purpose. They formed "a system by which every fibre would be eradicated of antient or future aristocracy, and a foundation laid for a government truly republican."[38]

Other colonies changed their inheritance laws in similar ways. In 1776, South Carolina and Delaware ended entail; Pennsylvania and Georgia put the abolition or limitation of entail into their Revolutionary-era constitutions. By 1800, nearly all the states had done away with both entail and primogeniture. Some legislative statements of purpose express the political intentions behind these measures; in 1794, when Delaware repealed an inheritance law giving eldest sons a double share, the statute's preamble declared it the "duty and policy of every republican government to preserve equality amongst its citizens, by maintaining the balance of property as far as it is consistent with the rights of individuals."[39]

According to some historians and political scientists, these changes were insignificant because, as Bernard Bailyn put it in 1962, "primogeniture and entail had never taken deep roots in America, not even in tidewater Virginia."[40] The latter claim largely reflected an unpublished 1926 analysis of Virginia wills, which Holly Brewer showed in 1997 to have suffered from elementary mistakes in calculating the prevalence of entail. By the time of the Revolution, according to Brewer's reestimates, "entail controlled three-fourths of the land in tidewater Virginia," and the evidence suggested similarly high levels in the piedmont and even on the frontier.[41]

Inheritance law was central to a more general debate about the social consequences of the American Revolution. Mid-twentieth-century historians tended to portray the Revolution as socially conservative, a political revolt rather than a social revolution. The subsequent reevaluation of the changes in inheritance went along with a renewed acknowledgment of the radical social changes brought about in the Revolutionary era.

Moreover, the relevant question about primogeniture and entail is not their general prevalence in the colonies. Jefferson objected to the "distinct" class of ruling families that dominated colonial Virginia and feared the emergence of future aristocracies of wealth. Many previous revolutions had ended with restorations. The abolition of primogeniture and entail should be understood as part of an effort to prevent an aristocratic reversal. Together with the writing of constitutions, changing the laws of inheritance was a critical part of the eighteenth-century republican solution to the problem of political entrenchment.

The relevance of inheritance law to political entrenchment becomes clear if we turn back to Europe and to the development of inheritance rules in France, Germany, and Britain. In France, as in the United States, revolutionary leaders saw primogeniture and entail as undergirding the system of power they wanted to change. In 1789 the National Assembly abolished primogeniture; in November 1792, the assembly's successor, the National Convention, abolished entails. But unlike the United States, France soon returned to its earlier institutions of inheritance, first under Napoleon and then during the Restoration. Although Napoleon had opposed the old system of entail, he changed direction after being crowned emperor. To strengthen his hold on power, he created a new system of entail and primogeniture under the Spanish term *majorats*, for a new class of hereditary nobility loyal to his regime. After he fell, the restored monarchy reestablished a Chamber of Peers with a hereditary landed elite, and in 1826 the government passed legislation to restore the old regime's system of entailed property to prevent the division of estates. But with two more revolutions, in 1830 and 1848, France finally broke with the old regime. In 1830, the government abolished hereditary peerages, and in 1835 it barred the creation of new *majorats*; after the Revolution of 1848, most existing *majorats* were converted into ordinary property.[42]

In one respect, the French changes in inheritance law went further than American reforms. Rather than leave the decision to the testator, France in the 1790s required equal division of property among all children, daughters as well as sons. Although this requirement was later modified to allow greater testamentary freedom, French inheritance law continues to reflect the eighteenth-century shift toward equality among siblings.[43]

Inheritance rules also figured centrally in conflicts over the system of power in Germany. *Fideikommisse*, estates held in fee tail, gave the nobility special legal protection—for example, creditors were barred from seizing a noble's land for unpaid debts—as well as privileged political representation. Property had to be passed on undivided and undiminished to the eldest son, though he had obligations to his siblings. During the nineteenth and early twentieth centuries, the nobility sought to expand *Fideikommisse*, while liberal and commercial interests tried to abolish or limit them. But unlike the United States or France, Germany did not undergo a revolutionary upheaval on behalf of republican or democratic values, nor were *Fideikommisse* weakened by economic growth. According to Jens Beckert, they spread in the second half of the nineteenth century; the nobility clung to *Fideikommisse* and supported their expansion in a defensive effort to protect their position against industrial and commercial forces. "The stronger the pressure on large aristocratic landownership," Beckert writes, "the more it looks for a *political* guarantee for its property structure."[44] It took Germany's defeat in World War I to initiate change. The Weimar Constitution in 1919 abolished entails, but it was not until after 1945 that the process was fully carried out. For Germany, the loss of the two world wars served as the functional equivalent of liberal revolutions in France and the United States in bringing about linked social and political changes.

Britain did not have to lose a war to end primogeniture and entail, but both institutions survived into the twentieth century. The economic and political power of landed wealth in Britain declined in the late 1800s as agricultural rents and the value of agricultural land fell, while commercial and industrial wealth increased and reform laws expanded the franchise. In the 1880s, as the British landed elite lost what David Cannadine calls its "unifying sense of territorial identity," legislation eliminated the old restrictions on the sale and mortgaging of entailed property; the Administration of Estates Act in 1925 was the final coup de grâce to primogeniture and entail (with the now-modified exception of the royal family).[45]

But the institutions of patrimonial inheritance had had an extraordinary impact on the "balance of property," to use the old republican phrase. Thanks to surveys going back to the Norman Conquest, more is known about the ownership of land in England over a longer time than anywhere else in the world. From the eleventh to the nineteenth centuries, land ownership remained highly concentrated. In 1086, when the Domesday Book was compiled, the crown held one-quarter of England's land, the church another quarter, and the aristocracy most of the rest. The crown's and the church's shares had diminished sharply by the seventeenth century, but the aristocracy's had not.[46] As late as 1873, just 710 aristocrats owned one-fourth of the land of England; 5,000 landowners held three-quarters of all the land in the British Isles, and six of every seven households owned no real property.[47]

The American and French revolutions may not seem especially egalitarian today; indeed, they may seem contradictory and hypocritical because they failed to accord equality to women and non-whites. But for all their limitations, it is a mistake to say they were concerned only with political rights and not with social or economic equality. Land was the most important form of wealth at the time, and the revolutions sought to make its distribution more equal. Social rank at birth determined forms of personal as well as political domination, and the revolutions sought to abolish the hereditary principle. As Pierre Rosanvallon argues, the eighteenth-century vision of republican equality was "relational": it posited a basic "similarity" of human beings, elevated the concept of citizenship, and sought to make (white) men independent in the sense of not being subordinated.[48]

Moreover, considerable evidence suggests that the eighteenth-century republican theory of political entrenchment was correct. In agrarian societies, high levels of landholding inequality are inhospitable to stable democracy. As Alexander Gerschenkron, Barrington Moore, and others have shown, a dominant landlord class obstructs democratization.[49] "The absence of landlordism," Carles Boix argues, "constitutes a necessary precondition for the triumph of democracy." In an analysis of a data set on political regimes from 1850 to 1980, Boix finds that although a higher percentage of family farms does not increase the probability of a transition to democracy, it does reduce the probability of a democratic breakdown.[50] Other research supports the view that concentrated landholding is inimical to successful democratization.[51]

Although eighteenth-century revolutionaries were right about the crucial political importance of widely distributed landholding, they were naïve to think that if they removed legal privileges such as primogeniture, titles of nobility, and politically granted monopolies and other favors, equality would inevitably follow. Condorcet, for example, wrote that without civil laws perpetuating inequality, fortunes would "tend naturally toward equality."[52] The optimism of John Adams—if "possessed of the balance of real estate, the multitude would have the balance of power" and "take care of the liberty, virtue, and interest of the multitude, in all acts of government"— was characteristic of his age, even though Adams himself became far less sanguine later in life. As great as their achievements were, the revolutionary generation failed to anticipate how social and economic changes might overtake their vision—or how racial slavery could distort and destroy it.

CHAPTER THREE

Racial Slavery as an Entrenched Contradiction

ALTHOUGH AMERICANS LIKE TO think of their country as never having had a ruling class, the slaveholding planters of the antebellum South surely qualify as one. Their power stretched from the estates they ruled as masters and patriarchs to the nation's highest lawmaking and judicial authority. Like European aristocracies at their peak, the planters drew their power from fundamental rules concerning property and political representation. The distinctive property of slave-owners, however, consisted of human beings, and their distinctive political advantage lay in provisions entrenched in the Constitution that enabled them to protect that property and extend its reach. Two property-rights regimes emerged in the United States before the Civil War: one in the South that recognized a right to own other people and coerce labor from them, and one in the North that didn't. Slaveholding affected the entire structure of the South's economy and society and the nation's politics, and like the overthrow of patrimonial systems of inheritance and aristocratic privilege, the overthrow of slavery had far-ranging democratic political implications.

Contrary to an old mythology, the South's planters on the eve of the Civil War were not a declining class engaged in a hopeless defense of an outdated, precapitalist institution. Slave plantations were highly profitable enterprises enmeshed in the global capitalist economy.[1] As of 1860, the South's cotton, nearly all of it slave-produced, accounted for 61 percent of U.S. exports; three-fifths of America's wealthiest men were southern slaveholders.[2] Legal and political institutions supported their economic position. The law gave slaveholders more absolute power over their slaves than European landlords had over their tenants, and rather than shrinking, slavery had expanded into America's western territories since the nation's founding. But despite their legal privileges and political influence, slaveholders had reason to fear that their property and power were vulnerable—vulnerable to slave revolts; vulnerable to whites who questioned the legitimacy of slavery and opposed its extension; vulnerable because their section of the country was growing more slowly than the free states; and vulnerable not least because they had joined a nation that announced itself to the world with the words "All men are created equal."

Slavery is not inherently unstable. After its emergence during the Neolithic Revolution around 8000 BC, slaveholding persisted for millennia. But slavery in the modern West created a distinctive situation. As of 1500, northwestern Europe was the one region in the world where chattel slavery had virtually disappeared. Yet during the next three centuries—through the Renaissance, Reformation, and Enlightenment, eras often identified with the growth of individualism and freedom—the northeast European states created a system of chattel slavery of unprecedented global scale, transporting some ten million Africans to the Americas (another million and a half died in transit). During this time, the English, French, and Dutch operated under two sets of rules. While enslaving non-Europeans abroad, they generally did not import slaves into their own societies or reestablish slavery at home. This distinction between the "outside" and "inside" social worlds—much like the difference in rules for war with outsiders and civil peace internally—helped the imperial powers, at least for a time, manage the tensions between slave and free labor.[3]

Slavery presented a different political problem in the United States because the "outside" was "inside" the same nation. The American republic was born in ambivalence and division over slavery.

Unlike any other society with large-scale slavery, it wrote contrary principles into its founding declaration, federal constitution, and state laws, and then developed half slave, half free. When the nation was established, some of the slave-owning founders who acknowledged slavery was wrong consoled themselves with the thought that their successors would end it. Instead, as the early republic developed, slavery became more extensive, and more brutal.

The growth of slavery in the United States has been described as a paradox. In a paradox, however, the opposed elements only appear to be contradictory; a deeper understanding of their relationship reveals them to be consistent. In a contradiction, the opposed elements negate each other; a contradiction can be resolved only by change.[4] To be sure, societies can often live with logically contradictory beliefs and morally inconsistent institutions. A social contradiction exists only where the relationships are unstable, and institutional change in one direction or another becomes unavoidable. The relationship between slavery and freedom in the United States was not merely a paradox, a logical contradiction, or an example of moral hypocrisy—it was a contradiction in a true sociological sense, at the most fundamental, constitutive level. Opposed principles were entrenched in the structure of both state and society. Rather than one of them receding, the two varieties of capitalism in the North and South both had strong expansionary drives. Neither freedom nor slavery alone but the contradictory relation between them defined what America became.

It is easy to assume that this contradiction was destined to be resolved through the disappearance of slavery. That outcome conforms to the standard American narrative that treats freedom as the dominant story and slavery as a deviation from it. But the early history of the United States did not follow that story line. And if the later history did, it was only because of economic forces, demographic change, and political movements and leadership that no one could have predicted. The adoption of the Constitution's Thirteenth Amendment, which abolished slavery, was a highly contingent event, impossible to separate from the Civil War that preceded it.

The slaveocracy of the American South, however, was not the only propertied class in history ever to face rising threats to its wealth and political power, nor the only one to resort to war to defend its privileges. A "peculiar institution" in some ways, American racial slavery was also representative of a larger phenomenon, entrenched domination unstably combined with representative political institutions. Both sides of this process—how racial slavery became entrenched in the American republic, and how it came undone—require our attention.

THE COLONIAL DIVERGENCE

Since the English in the seventeenth century did not practice slavery at home, it was not a foregone conclusion that they would adopt it in their colonies. Villeinage, the primary form of servitude in feudal England, had meant subjection to a lord's power, but not to being bought and sold or deprived of rights of marriage and kinship. By the era of colonization, villeinage had practically disappeared and did not provide any direct influence, much less a legal foundation, for chattel slavery in the Americas.[5] Earlier forms of servitude and slavery in Britain, going back to the Roman Empire, had also not been based on race. The New World allowed colonists not only more freedom from monarchical rule but also the opportunity to create a system of hereditary racial slavery that was unknown at home. Not all the colonies, however, followed the same path. Only some became full-fledged slave societies, with black populations so large and so frightening to whites that emancipation came to seem impossibly dangerous and costly.

Racial slavery arrived in the New World originally via the Portuguese and Spanish, who had never entirely done away with slavery internally. Even as it died out in northwestern Europe after the Middle Ages, slavery had survived in the Mediterranean. Italian slave traders hauled away captives from the Balkans and the coast of the Black Sea, and it was the Latin term for these peoples (*slavus*, that is, Slavs) that gives us the English word *slave* and its cognates in other western European languages. Ottoman advances leading to the capture of Constantinople in 1453 cut this supply line. By then, however, the Portuguese were making their way down the West African coast and buying African slaves who had previously reached Mediterranean markets through a trans-Saharan circuit.

The Portuguese also led the way in exploiting African slaves as plantation labor in colonies they established in the eastern Atlantic, beginning with Madeira in 1419 and continuing in the Azores and Cape Verde Islands and down the African coast through the fifteenth century.[6]

Settler colonialism of this kind was one model for exploiting new territories. In the New World, the Spanish employed another model for forced labor, conquering native peoples and exacting tribute from them. But the massive die-off of indigenous populations from disease in the post-Columbian period limited the profits from tribute and prevented the Spanish from relying wholly on Amerindian workers. In Spanish as in other European colonies in the New World, African slaves became a solution to the labor shortage.

Although the English arrived in the Americas later and generally disdained Iberian institutions as inconsistent with their free traditions, they confronted the same fundamental problem, a shortage of labor, and ended up following the same course in importing slaves from Africa. Economic interest, combined with beliefs about the inferiority of darker peoples, inclined the English to accept racial slavery and drove some of their colonies toward an overwhelming reliance on it.

In the quest for labor the English had three options: free whites, temporarily bound white labor, and slaves. There were never enough whites who crossed the Atlantic free and unencumbered. From the early 1600s to the American Revolution, three out of every four people who arrived in the colonies were bound to temporary or lifetime service. The temporarily bound—indentured servants, apprentices, debtors, convicts, and others—typically came under arrangements that were more onerous than the annual master-servant contract in English agriculture. Instead of one year, their obligations ran from four years to seven. Servants received such food, clothing, and shelter as their masters provided, but no wages since their transport to America had already been paid for. If they survived long enough, they would be free and could work for wages or strike out on their own. Slavery—perpetual, hereditary subjection—was reserved for blacks and, to a lesser extent, native people deemed to be enemies.[7]

At first there were ambiguities in the distinction between servitude and slavery and in the definitions and boundaries of racial groups (especially in cases of mixed ancestry). White servitude in the colonies entailed a more severe deprivation of freedom than in England: servants were unable to marry or travel without their master's permission, and subject to harsh discipline for any displeasure they caused. They could be sold, seized for their masters' debts, and bequeathed to heirs—in short, like slaves, servants were property. Consequently, servitude and slavery in colonial America differed only in degree. Virginia in the first half of the seventeenth century also accorded slaves rights that it later denied them; the law of slavery had yet to define how completely slaves had lost all rights of their own. These customary practices and legal ambiguities may have slowed the pace of slavery's adoption.[8]

Slavery did not begin in the English colonies with an edict, legislation, or public debate; it emerged as a social practice that was haphazardly acknowledged in law and then clarified and modified through it. The first colonial settlements, in the early 1600s, supplemented free immigrants primarily with indentured servants, but all the colonies recognized slavery. In the second half of the seventeenth century, however, the colonies took different paths in solving the labor problem that confronted any settlement where land was readily available, but labor was not. In an agrarian society with abundant land, why should any freeman hire himself out for less than he could make on his own? In the hypothetical case where land was free, unless landowners had some way of tying down labor, the rent left over for them—that is, the surplus over wages—would have been zero.[9] To solve their labor problems, agricultural colonies could basically go in one of two directions: toward plantations with forced labor or family farms with (mostly) free labor. Virginia and Massachusetts illustrate those two responses. Virginia shifted from servants to slaves on a large scale in the late 1600s (as British settlers in Barbados had already done), while Massachusetts, despite its early embrace of the institution, never made a transition to large-scale slavery.

Conceived as a commercial enterprise and dominated by an elite of gentlemen fortune hunters, the Virginia colony struggled economically from the first settlement in Jamestown in 1607 until the colonists hit on tobacco as a crop, the source of a boom in the 1620s.[10] From that point on, the key constraint on profits was the supply of labor, since planters had plenty of land for growing tobacco. Africans had first arrived on a Dutch ship for sale in Virginia in 1619, but their numbers grew slowly, as planters continued until the 1680s to rely chiefly on white servants. Several factors may account for the roughly sixty-year delay in the large-scale importation of slaves after the advent of tobacco farming. During its early decades, Virginia suffered from a staggering mortality rate, a consideration that probably influenced planters' choices whether to buy indentured servants or slaves. Servants were cheaper, making them a rational choice for planters interested in a quick return on a smaller initial outlay, whereas slaves were a larger and longer-term investment. Declining death rates through the seventeenth century tended to favor the purchase of slaves. By the 1680s, as economic conditions improved in England, the flow of servants to Virginia also declined.

But perhaps the key factors in the substitution of slaves for servants were political. In the second half of the seventeenth century, the planter-controlled colonial government followed two strategies to satisfy the demand for labor, one involving servants and the other involving slaves. From the masters' standpoint, the limited term of servants was a problem. Once they finished their service, instead of working for wages or as tenants, ex-servants could produce tobacco on their own, increasing competition and reducing prices. Between 1656 and 1666, the state adopted new laws lengthening terms of servitude; ex-servants also found it harder to obtain land as a result of a land grab by wealthy planters. But the various steps the planters took to keep ex-servants working for them excited discontent, contributing to an uprising in 1676 known as Bacon's Rebellion. In the same period, the colonial assembly also passed a series of laws clarifying slaveholders' property rights and power over slaves. A 1669 law, for example, said that masters would not be guilty of any crime if slaves died in the course of being disciplined because no master would intentionally destroy his own property. The guarantee of unrestrained power over slaves enabled masters to drive them harder than white servants.[11]

Other laws in this period also began clarifying the racial basis of slavery. In the 1660s and 1670s, the assembly established that non-Christian servants brought "by shipping" (in contrast to Indians brought by land) were to be slaves forever and that conversion to Christianity did not affect a slave's status. A 1680 law called for thirty lashes "if any negroe or other slave shall presume to lift up his hand in opposition against any christian." By the late seventeenth century, the early distinction between Christians and heathens began to give way to racial language as the term "white" came into increasing use. But instead of recognizing intermediate mixtures among blacks, whites, and indigenous peoples (as the Spanish, Portuguese, and French did), Virginia's laws had a binary structure. They began treating blacks, Indians, and those of mixed ancestry together and imposed punishments for racial mixing between whites and all others. The law also began limiting one power of masters—the power of manumission. A 1691 law said masters could not free slaves unless they paid to transport them out of Virginia (the assembly would later prohibit private manumission unless the governor and council agreed to it). Other southern colonies also adopted restrictions on manumission, an enormously consequential step for race relations because it blocked the emergence of a large population of free blacks and mulattos such as developed in the Spanish, Portuguese, and French colonies in the Americas. In the American South, the binary system of racial classification became almost perfectly aligned with the categories of slave and free; blackness in any degree became congruent with enslavement. By 1705, when Virginia consolidated its previous statutes in a systematic slave code that denied virtually all rights to slaves, the colony had become overwhelmingly reliant on slave labor and unambiguously committed to a racial caste system. This was the critical phase for the cultural entrenchment of the racial order of the slave South.[12]

As a religious colony, indeed a theocracy at its inception, Massachusetts had different origins from Virginia, though Puritanism was no barrier to slavery or racism. The Puritans held both Indian and black slaves, and they sold captives from Indian wars into slavery in the West Indies. The Body of Liberties adopted in Massachusetts in 1642 said "there shall never be any bond-slavery, villenage or captivitie amongst us, unless it be lawfull captives, taken in just warrs, and such strangers as willingly sell themselves,

or are solde to us"—the last exception, in particular, wide enough
to eliminate any limits on keeping slaves provided someone else
did the enslaving. Family connections and trade linked the Puritans to the Caribbean slave plantations. In 1630, some of the same
people who founded the Massachusetts Bay Colony that year were
also involved in founding Providence Island, a Caribbean settlement based on slave labor that experienced one of the first slave revolts before it fell to the Spanish in 1641. Massachusetts merchants
were active in the West Indies trade, including traffic in slaves, and
it was through those connections that the Winthrops, Hutchin-
sons, and other prominent families became slave-owners themselves. But the numbers of slaves in Massachusetts remained
relatively small, about 2 percent of the population, and they were
widely dispersed in households rather than concentrated on large
plantations.[13]

A distinction originally developed in studies of the ancient
world helps to illuminate the different paths of slavery's evolution
in Britain's North American colonies. In a *society with slaves*, slavery
is one of several forms of labor, whereas in a *slave society*, slavery is
integral to the productive system and social structure. The difference is not only in the prevalence of slavery. In a slave society, Ira
Berlin argues, the master-slave relationship provides a model or exemplar for other social relations—between men and women, parents and children, employer and employee. Slavery affects the
public world as well as intimate life, since slaveholders form a ruling class whose power extends beyond their own estates into civil
society and government. In short, slavery is constitutive of social
and political relations in a slave society in a way that it is not in a
society with slaves.[14]

The transition to a slave society in the Americas typically
began with the development of a commodity for export. The profits from that trade enabled the dominant producers to monopolize
resources, import slaves, and marginalize other forms of labor. The
establishment of a slave society required political power to back it
up—to define property rights in human beings and to maintain the
system against insurrection from within and meddlesome reformers in the metropole. In the Atlantic slave trade, slaves were taken
to regions of the Americas where their use in producing profitable

exports justified the buyers' investment. Virginia developed such an export crop, whereas Massachusetts did not. But Virginia was also a far more unequal society even before its planters adopted large-scale slavery. Their shift from servants to slaves was only a continuation, not a reversal, of earlier trends. From the time it discovered how profitable tobacco could be, Virginia had been "drifting" toward slavery.[15] The advent of large-scale slavery was the culmination of a process that reflected high levels of political inequality from the start as well as the ratio of land to labor and the economic opportunities created by tobacco. If sugar or rice could be grown in Massachusetts, the entire process of settlement would have been different, and slavery might have grown there too. But having begun differently, Massachusetts evolved differently. Settled by families of Protestant dissenters rather than royalist fortune-hunters, it had a more equal distribution of land among freemen who enjoyed rights of political participation. Ill adapted to slavery in its formative period, Massachusetts later became positively resistant to it.

Beginning in the 1720s, some northern colonies did see a significant increase in slavery. The importation of slaves often came as a result of interruptions in the flow of indentured servants and primarily affected the Middle Colonies as well as Rhode Island. From 1732 to 1754, more than a third of new arrivals in New York were slaves, whose share of the population there ranged from 11 percent to 15 percent. From about five hundred in 1720, the number of slaves in Rhode Island increased to more than three thousand in 1750, 10 percent of the colony. Much northern slavery was urban and concentrated in elite households, although it also filtered down into artisans' workshops and spread into pockets of the rural economy. But northern agriculture was not reorganized into large plantations using the gang system, and slavery did not become central to the northern economy.[16] On the whole, slavery's spread in North America followed a geographic gradient; the further south a colony, the more it relied on slaves for labor. In 1770, slaves made up only 4 percent of the population from New Hampshire to Pennsylvania but 37 percent of the population in the Upper South (Delaware to North Carolina) and 58 percent in the Lower South (South Carolina, Georgia, and East Florida).[17]

Whether a colony relied on slave or free labor had pervasive implications for the structure of government. Slavery did not foster democracy or a broad definition of government's responsibilities.[18] But in the crisis that followed the American Revolution, many southern leaders agreed with those in the mid-Atlantic states and New England about the need for a stronger national government rooted in ideas of popular sovereignty—as long as that government did not imperil the slave system that was the foundation of their own wealth and power.

CONSTITUTIONAL ENTRENCHMENT AND THE COSTS OF CHANGE

Even after slavery had taken root in the colonies, Americans might have abolished it when they achieved independence and framed a new political system ostensibly on the principles of liberty and equality. The Revolution did lead, over several decades, to the emancipation of slaves in the states north of Delaware, but the Constitution entrenched the power of southern slaveholders in the national government and, by so doing, entrenched slave societies in the southern states.

The use of the Constitution to protect slavery exemplifies strategic entrenchment—the deliberate effort, in this case, to make an institutionalized system of property and social relations difficult to change. Slavery also became entrenched because of the growing costs of change—the relevant costs, in this case, being the costs of emancipation to groups with political power, as they imagined the alternatives, given their commitments to property rights and expectations about black-white relations in the absence of slavery.

The prospective costs of emancipation were of three kinds: *labor costs* (the additional cost of alternative forms of labor), *compensation costs* (compensation to slaveholders for loss of their property), and *social costs* of the freed black population. While all three types of costs were barriers to emancipation, reigning assumptions made the second and third especially formidable. Property owners, Americans generally believed, were due compensation for property taken from them, but if that principle were applied in this instance, who would bear the cost of compensating slaveholders for the value of their freed slaves? The social costs associated with emancipating blacks posed at least as difficult a problem, given the racist worldview of the time. Even many whites who disapproved of slavery could not imagine living together with blacks on equal terms—or indeed any terms at all other than slavery. They therefore entertained plans for sending former slaves to colonies in Africa or resettling them in the West. In 1820, Jefferson wrote that the cessation of slavery would not cost him "a second thought" if "a general emancipation and *expatriation* could be effected," but as it was, "we have a wolf by the ears" and "can neither hold him, nor safely let him go. Justice is in one scale, self-preservation in the other."[19] The greater the population of slaves, the more whites feared for their "self-preservation" and the greater they imagined emancipation's social cost.

Racial slavery had developed in the early English colonies with little criticism or restraint, indeed less public debate and official effort at restraint than in Spanish America. But beginning in the mid-eighteenth century, there was a shift in norms in both Europe and North America as critics attacked slavery as morally offensive, economically anachronistic, and politically unjust. Religious leaders, especially from the evangelical denominations, played a leading role in initiating the shift in moral values. The British antislavery movement initially focused on the international slave trade without challenging slavery itself in Britain's overseas colonies. Whether slaves could be held within Britain itself became the subject of an important case in 1772, when an enslaved man from Virginia, James Somerset, petitioned for his freedom after being brought along by his owner on a visit to London. England's Chief Justice ruled that slavery was "so odious" that only positive law— that is, a statute—could authorize it, and since Parliament had passed no such law, Somerset had to be freed. The Somerset ruling did not apply to the colonies, but it had wide reverberations.[20]

By the 1770s, sermons and pamphlets in Britain's colonies also increasingly spoke of slavery as an evil. In the words of the historian Winthrop Jordan, a "generalized sense of slavery as a communal sin" prevailed in New England. An especially strong impetus for emancipation came from the Quakers, who called upon their members to free their slaves and provided much of the leadership for antislavery efforts, including the founding of the first antislavery organization in

1775. The voices demanding freedom for slaves included those of free blacks as well, who rightly saw the revolutionary cause as an opportunity. Political theories of natural rights complemented religious beliefs: What legitimate place could slavery have under a government whose leaders pledged that all men had equal rights to life, liberty, and the pursuit of happiness? Many of the Revolution's leaders admitted the inconsistency but were unable to confront it. The first draft of the Declaration of Independence included a paragraph—cut, Jefferson later said, in deference to South Carolina and Georgia—accusing King George of violating the "most sacred rights of life and liberty in the persons of a distant people who never offended him, captivating & carrying them into slavery in another hemisphere, or to incur miserable death in their transportation hither." A French general who traveled through Virginia in 1782, the Marquis de Chastellux, reported that Virginians "grieved at having slaves, and are constantly talking about abolishing slavery and of seeking another means of exploiting their lands."[21]

It is precisely periods like this, when both values and political systems change, that test how deeply institutions are entrenched. Slavery did retreat in the face of changed sentiment, but only in some states. Though it took decades for the process to play out in full, the colonial divergence in slavery's development became a sharp split between Northern free-soil and Southern slave states—indeed, it was this very process that created the "North" and "South" as distinct sectional interests. By 1784, Pennsylvania, Connecticut, and Rhode Island had passed gradual emancipation laws, and during the next two decades New York and New Jersey would do the same. None of these states freed slaves currently in bondage; they emancipated the children of slaves born after passage of the laws but required those children to remain in servitude until ages ranging from eighteen to twenty-eight. Three other states— Vermont, New Hampshire, and Massachusetts—ended slavery through their constitutions and state judicial rulings. The decision by the Massachusetts Superior Court in 1783 that slavery violated rights enshrined in the state's recently ratified constitution was particularly notable.[22]

The southern states did not emancipate their slaves, but they did relax their limits on private manumission. By 1790, Virginia,

Maryland, and Delaware as well as states in the lower South, except for North Carolina, had given masters the power to free their slaves individually. Between 1782 and 1806, when manumission was limited again, slaveholders in Virginia freed about 10,000 slaves out of an enslaved population that, in 1790, numbered 293,000.[23]

Could the Revolutionary era have gone further and even abolished slavery? If the Continental Army in the Revolutionary War had enlisted slaves in significant numbers, it might have made a difference—or so Alexander Hamilton argued in 1779, when he supported a proposal to pay slaveholders $1,000 per slave to create several battalions of black soldiers who would be freed on completion of their service. Giving Negroes "their freedom with their muskets," Hamilton wrote, will "secure their *fidelity*, animate their courage, and I believe will have a *good influence* on those that remain, *by opening a door to their emancipation*."[24] Military emancipation has a long history. To the outrage of the Revolutionary leaders, the British promised freedom to slaves who defected, and about 20,000 did, more than fought on the American side. Southern opposition to arming slaves defeated the proposal endorsed by Hamilton and limited black participation in the Continental Army to around 5,000, not enough to bring about the transformative effects that the role of black soldiers in the Civil War would have.[25]

While the legitimacy of slavery eroded in the 1770s and 1780s, the economic interests in the institution remained powerful and, in the South, overwhelming. Regional differences in the costs of change help to explain the differences in steps toward emancipation. Adam Smith was not entirely unfair in 1776 when he wrote sardonically, "The late resolution of the Quakers in Pennsylvania to set at liberty all their negro slaves may satisfy us that their number cannot be very great. Had they made any considerable part of [the Quakers'] property, such a resolution could never have been agreed to."[26] The gradual emancipation laws in the North, according to an economic analysis by Stanley Engerman and Robert Fogel, did not impose a significant cost on slave-owners or, for that matter, on non-slaveholders: The additional years of labor of living slaves and their children provided nearly full compensation for the slaves' market value at the time of the laws' enactment. In the same

sardonic spirit as Smith, Fogel and Engerman observe that northern whites arrived at a "felicitous compromise" by imposing the
cost of emancipation on a group excluded from politics—the slaves
themselves—a solution that the authors call "philanthropy at
bargain prices."[27]

"Free womb" emancipation was also the solution to the problem of compensating slaveholders after independence movements
in Latin America. Between 1811 and 1831, Chile, Argentina, Co-
lombia, Ecuador, Uruguay, Peru, Venezuela, and Bolivia passed
laws formally freeing the children of slave mothers but requiring
them to remain under slave-owners' tutelage for some fixed period
of time.[28] In 1833, when Britain enacted legislation to end slavery
in its colonies, it provided for compensation to slaveholders in two
forms—half from continued labor by slaves for a limited period,
and half from £20 million in cash compensation paid by British
taxpayers.[29]

Except for Britain, all these governments were unwilling to ask
taxpayers to bear compensation costs, but they did put slavery on a
path to extinction. So why did the U.S. South not accept gradual
emancipation through "free womb" laws at the time of the nation's
founding? Here the social costs of emancipation were critical. The
South's slave population had grown spectacularly in the eighteenth
century, primarily from a much higher rate of natural increase than
elsewhere in the Americas. As a result, whites in the South lived
amid black majorities or near-majorities. Like Jefferson, the southerners who conceded the injustice of slavery believed that emancipated slaves would have to be moved somewhere else, but they were
never able to resolve how to remove them, much less how to replace
their labor. Since Indians had never been enslaved in large numbers,
their removal to the West caused whites no economic problems—
indeed, it gave them additional property—whereas black removal
would have cost slaveholders both capital and income. Even if there
had been an agreement to offer compensation (for example, through
proceeds from the sale of western lands), the labor and social costs
of emancipating black slaves were greater than southern slaveholders and other whites would have been willing to bear.

Economic and demographic concerns also help to explain the
early, though only partially successful, efforts to exclude slavery

from the western territories. Excluding slaves did not impose an immediate cost on slaveholders, and it would make the new territories' populations overwhelmingly white, a key objective for Jefferson. In 1784, the Confederation Congress narrowly defeated a bill supported by Jefferson to ban slavery from the western lands. A single additional vote, he later said, "would have prevented this abominable crime from spreading itself across the country." If a slight shift in one close political decision might have averted the extension of slavery, this may have been it—except that slaveholders had already made their way into the territories, especially south of the Ohio River, and if the measure Jefferson sought had passed, those slave-owning settlers might have agitated successfully to reverse it, if not immediately, then after the cotton kingdom beckoned. But on July 13, 1787, in one of its final actions under the Articles of Confederation, Congress passed the Northwest Ordinance, excluding slavery from the territory north of the Ohio River, and that ban ultimately did prevail over settler opposition.[30]

When the Constitutional Convention met in Philadelphia in the spring and summer of 1787, it represented an opportunity as well as a danger to the southern states. The opportunity was to create a national government capable of overcoming the economic and political crisis in the 1780s that put southern and northern interests alike in jeopardy. As a league of sovereign states rather than a single nation, the United States under the Articles of Confederation had no national executive or judicial branch and only limited legislative powers. Its weakness had left it vulnerable to external threats and domestic disorder, and the economy was in shambles. Unable to pass taxes and conscript soldiers, the Confederation was for all practical purposes bankrupt and impotent. It depended on requisitions of money and soldiers from the states and was powerless to do anything when the states failed to comply, as many of them had in the struggle against Britain. The Confederation was similarly powerless when individual states failed to fulfill U.S. obligations under the Treaty of Paris ending the Revolutionary War. Nor could it deter European powers from closing their ports to U.S. trade or respond effectively when Spain closed the Mississippi at New Orleans, potentially leading western settlers to secede. These developments directly implicated southern interests. As a region dependent on exports of its agricultural products, still struggling to defeat powerful native tribes, and looking toward opportunities beyond the Appalachians, the South would benefit from a stronger federal government. Like their northern counterparts, southern elites were also concerned about threats to property that they discerned in the movements among hard-pressed farmers, who sought to weaken obligations to repay debts under state law.[31]

Compared with the Articles of Confederation, the Constitution vastly increased the national government's fiscal, military, judicial, and other powers. Therein, from the South's standpoint, also lay the danger. A federal government whose laws were supreme might someday give antislavery forces the power to abolish slavery throughout the nation. The rising tide of emancipation in the North also alarmed slaveholders. Consequently, the South's representatives were determined to limit federal authority even as they expanded it, and to obtain sufficient representation in the new government to protect slavery and other sectional interests.

As it turned out, no effort materialized at the Constitutional Convention to emancipate the nation's slaves, though the convention did lay the ground for an end to the international slave trade. Deeming it tactically unwise, Benjamin Franklin, at the time president of the Pennsylvania Abolition Society, decided not to present its petition to the convention. In the interests of forging an agreement, the representatives who personally opposed slavery gave priority to the nationalist aims that northerners and southerners shared. Not for the last time, the interests of black people were sacrificed in the name of compromise and national unity. Consequently, the Constitution does not deal at length with slavery; indeed, the words "slavery" and "slaves" never appear in it. The absence of those words is not an oversight. Delegates opposed to slavery or morally conflicted about it wanted at least to avoid extending it explicit constitutional recognition and thereby entrenching the principle of property in man in national law. But slavery is the unmistakable subject of three major provisions, and it lurks behind others.[32]

The most notorious of these provisions, the "three-fifths" clause, gave southerners more representation in Congress (and consequently more votes in the Electoral College) than they would have had if the apportionment of the House had been based on the free population alone. On the surface, the clause appeared to balance taxation and representation: "Representatives and direct Taxes shall be apportioned among the several States ... according to their respective Numbers, which shall be determined by adding to the whole Number of free Persons ... *three fifths of all other Persons*"—in other words, slaves. Contrary to appearances, however, the clause had almost no bearing on taxes because the new government was expected to be financed, and was financed, through tariffs rather than "direct taxes" (such as capitations and taxes on property). Some historians have argued that by comparison with total population, the three-fifths provision can just as readily be seen as a two-fifths penalty as a three-fifths bonus in apportionment. Counting slaves in any degree, however, added to the power of those who enslaved them, and by no plausible theory of "virtual representation" did slave-owners represent the interests of slaves.[33] The three-fifths rule rewarded slaveholding states with more power if they had more slaves. While insisting that slaves were property, southerners sought to have them counted as persons when it served their interest. The Constitution allowed them to have it both ways.

The two other constitutional provisions dealing directly with slaves effectively treated them as property, although the word "property" never appears in that context. Using another circumlocution in a provision regarding foreign slave imports, Article I barred Congress before 1808 from prohibiting the "Migration or Importation of such Persons as any of the States now existing shall think proper to admit" (Article V further barred any amendment of that provision). The Constitution here did not impose a ban on slave importation after two decades; it only allowed Congress to ban it at that time, but in doing so it implicitly acknowledged that Congress would have the power to regulate the slave trade. In 1794, before it could ban slave imports, Congress prohibited Americans from participating in the international slave trade as maritime carriers. Then in 1807, in the only significant action against slavery while Jefferson was president, it overwhelmingly approved legislation he proposed to bar slave imports (ten days before Parliament prohibited the slave trade throughout the British empire).[34]

These measures against the international slave trade, while applauded by opponents of slavery, also had the support of most southern representatives, particularly those from the Upper South. Limiting importation raised the prices of slaves domestically, increasing slaveholders' wealth. Moreover, since Virginia's slaveholders had a surplus of slaves whom they were selling into the Lower South, they profited from protectionist legislation. White support for a ban on foreign slave imports, without any similar restriction on interstate traffic, also reflected anxiety about the number of blacks rising to levels that might lead to insurrections. Even during the late colonial period, Virginia had sought to limit slave imports. Britain denied it that power, a point that became part of the indictment of George III in the Declaration of Independence. After independence, nearly all the states had individually limited slave imports. But the deferral of any federal ban proved significant; South Carolina reopened the slave trade from 1803 to 1807. That the Constitution denied the federal government the power to ban slave imports for twenty years was a measure of the willingness of northern delegates in Philadelphia to make concessions on slavery even when only South Carolina and Georgia were emphatically demanding the trade be kept open.

The third clause specifically about slavery dealt with fugitive slaves, and it was unambiguously a gain for slave-owners. Under the Articles of Confederation, slaveholders in one state had had no legal basis for obtaining cooperation in seizing runaways in another state. The Constitution, however, gave slaveholders a legal basis for that power, denying free-soil states the right to award freedom to a slave who escaped into their territory: "No persons held to service or labour in one state under the laws therefor, escaping into another, shall, in consequence of any law or regulation therein, be discharged from such service or labour, but shall be delivered up on claim of the party to whom such service or labour may be due."

Beyond these three provisions, the Constitution's bearing on slavery came mostly from clauses that had wider application. For example, the federal government was authorized to mobilize the militia to "suppress insurrections," a power it could use against slave revolts, thereby making them a national rather than a local matter. But the government could invoke the same clause to suppress revolts of other kinds, and the most important use it would ever make of that authority would be against the South in the Civil War.

Ultimately, the single most important change wrought by the Constitution was the entrenchment of the union itself. Unlike the Articles of Confederation, the Constitution bound the slave and free states together within the same sovereign power. In a confederation, not only does each state remain sovereign, its continued membership is voluntary. That was no longer true under the Constitution, which explicitly derived its power not from the states but from the people themselves, as its first words, "We the People," made clear. During the debate over ratification, Madison stressed that "the Constitution requires an adoption *in toto*, and *for ever*." It created an "indissoluble Union" and included no provision for legal exit.[35]

Since the Constitution was mostly silent on slavery, it left open how a union of free and slave states would ultimately resolve the conflicts between them. The general principles of the nation's founding mostly pointed one way, while the specific and practical implications of the Constitution pointed the other. The Declaration of Independence had identified the United States with the idea that all men have inviolable rights to life, liberty, and the pursuit of happiness. Likewise, the Constitution's "We the People" rested the government on a principle of popular sovereignty that seemingly included all people, or at least allowed that interpretation. The Guarantee Clause—guaranteeing the states a "Republican Form of Government"—could similarly be interpreted as precluding oligarchic control of a state, though exactly what "republican" meant was ambiguous. For their part, slaveholders would claim that the nation's founding ensured the inviolability of private property and that it therefore guaranteed property in slaves—an inference that antislavery constitutionalists would never grant. The specific provisions relevant to slavery, however, did protect it. And perhaps most important, the machinery of government the Constitution created gave the South the power to ensure slavery's continued protection.

One sleeper provision would eventually weaken that political protection. Every ten years, the federal government was to conduct a census, the results of which would be used to reapportion representation among the states in the House (and therefore the Electoral College). Southern states had no reason to think they would be disadvantaged by this provision, and their representatives actively sought it at the Constitutional Convention.[36] Before the Revolution, the colonies below the Mason and Dixon line received two-thirds of white immigrants as well as nearly all slaves.[37] Far from wanting to limit white immigration, representatives from all regions hoped to encourage it. Little did southern leaders anticipate the political consequences that decennial reapportionment would have once economic growth and immigration shifted to the North.

The conflicts among founding principles and rules related to slavery and the power of the South raise a fundamental, theoretical question about constitutional entrenchment: *What, if anything, does a constitution entrench when its provisions may later be interpreted in conflicting ways?* Formal provisions of constitutions do not enforce themselves, but neither are they without consequence. Their significance may depend on the interplay between them, particularly as they affect the allocation of power. The express rules regarding the machinery of government, such as those for apportioning representatives, are less open to interpretation than more abstract principles, such as the guarantee to the states of a "republican" form of government. If the machinery created by a constitution tilts power in one direction, it may tilt the subsequent interpretation of more abstract provisions in the same direction. That is not to say that general principles are inconsequential. Political leaders and social movements may seize on them to inspire changes in constitutional and political understanding, as Abraham Lincoln did.[38] By the 1840s, abolitionists were trying to inspire that kind of change with regard to slavery, though they were understandably divided in their view of the Constitution in light of how Congress and the courts had interpreted it in the intervening years. William Lloyd Garrison called the Constitution a "covenant with death" and held it responsible for the nation's failure to end slavery, whereas Frederick Douglass insisted the nation's founding principles were a charter of freedom. Up to and during the Civil War, abolitionists continued to debate whether the Constitution authorized Congress to end slavery or had to be amended to bring about emancipation.

During the debate over ratification of the Constitution between the fall of 1787 and spring of 1788, southern leaders were mostly satisfied that it would protect slavery. Madison said slaveholders would have "a better security than any that now exists"; Charles Cotesworth Pinckney told his fellow South Carolinians that the "Eastern States allowed us a representation for a specie of property which they have not among them." Still, some antifederalists in the South thought slavery was insufficiently protected; Patrick Henry warned that the federal government could use its new tax and war powers to emancipate slaves. Lincoln eventually proved Henry right: war powers were the legal basis claimed by Lincoln for the Emancipation Proclamation.[39]

The increased powers of the national government, as Dan Fehrenbacher observes, gave the Constitution both "greater proslavery potential and greater antislavery potential than the Articles of Confederation."[40] But in the early republic, the express rules and machinery established by the Constitution moved the balance to the proslavery side. Since slavery was the antecedent condition in the states and territories, it continued as the default, wherever action was not taken to end it. Under Britain's Somerset decision, the silence of the law meant that slavery was impermissible, but in the United States the silence of the Constitution meant that slavery continued. Furthermore, while the Constitution did not explicitly entrench slavery, it entrenched protections for slaveholders. Those protections might have shielded slavery from attack even longer if the economy, population, and geographic boundaries of the United States had changed more slowly. Instead, the dynamic growth of the country threw off the calculations that went into the founding compact. Slavery grew and antislavery grew too, and with the intensification of interests and sentiments on both sides, the contradiction that had been built into the nation's founding became impossible to contain.

SLAVEHOLDERS AND NATIONAL POWER

Although two different societies and property-rights regimes emerged in the North and South, the differences between them did not immediately lead to confrontation. The constitutional agreements about slavery held the nation together for more than seventy years and at the same time allowed slavery to deepen its hold on the South. From 700,000 in 1790, the number of slaves increased to nearly four million in 1860. By that time, slaveholders had about $3 billion invested in slaves—more than the total national investment in railroads and manufacturing combined. Planters, conventionally defined as owners of twenty or more slaves, held slaves worth about $1.5 billion.[41] Slavery was so thoroughly entrenched that many in public life thought it not only pointless but dangerous to discuss its abolition. Until the late 1850s, the South's political leaders typically found enough northern allies to support the same strategies of silence and compromise that the Constitutional Convention had followed to prevent conflicts over slavery from upending the national project. Wherever possible, Congress avoided direct engagement with antislavery protest and slavery itself—tabling petitions, gagging debate, silencing dissent, suppressing doubt.

In the early years of the Republic, the basic compromise was the "federal consensus," which held that slavery was a state matter, beyond federal authority, except for the few questions directly addressed in the Constitution.[42] As Americans moved west, however, the acquisition of new territories and accession of new states led to new conflicts and, until the end of the 1850s, new compromises. Far from preferring the federal government to stay out of decisions affecting slavery, slaveholders wanted and at key moments received the government's active support. Increasingly, the two systems could not simply coexist without impinging on each other. The transformation of slavery from a local to a national institution—the "nationalization" of slavery as a political issue and potentially as a legal form of property throughout the entire nation—locked opposed interests into a struggle for national power that eventually turned to war.

The South's national political power was crucial to the development of the southern plantation economy. Beginning in the

1780s, the expansion of cotton textile manufacturing in Britain had created a surging demand for cotton that India, Brazil, and other regions in the world were also in a position to satisfy. What distinguished the United States from virtually all other cotton-growing areas, Sven Beckert writes in his global history of cotton, was "planters' command of nearly unlimited supplies of land, labor, and capital, and their unparalleled political power."[43] That unparalleled power played a central role in the expansion of each of the factors of production and the development of supporting transportation and communications infrastructure. Comparative advantage was as much the result of politics as of natural endowments.

Unencumbered land was the foundation. Southern planters were able to move into millions of acres of empty land because it was deliberately emptied of inhabitants. Indian removal was a massive and violent political project that by 1840 had reduced the native population east of the Mississippi to a few thousand. "Never has such a prodigious development been seen among the nations," Tocqueville observed, "nor a destruction so rapid."[44] This was strategic entrenchment of the most primitive kind, the coerced displacement of an indigenous population by settlers and their slaves, creating irreversible facts on the ground—what today would be called ethnic cleansing and genocide. After surging into the interior of South Carolina and Georgia, the "cotton rush" moved on to Alabama and other territories to the west. The federal government played a crucial role in this process through the Louisiana Purchase (1803), the Indian Removal Act (1830), and the annexation of Texas (1845) and the ensuing war with Mexico. The new land added in the first half of the nineteenth century accounted for half the cotton that Americans grew in 1850.[45]

Just as important was the government's role in upholding and enforcing the labor regime in plantation agriculture. Slave markets came with cotton markets, and neither federal nor state law impeded the domestic sale of slaves or regulated the conditions of their enslavement. Roughly one million black people were forcibly uprooted from Virginia and other areas and sent further south, splitting families to satisfy cotton's thirst for labor. Like the sugar planters of the Caribbean, the South's cotton planters organized work in the fields according to an intensely supervised gang system.

According to Robert Fogel, it was "the enormous, almost unconstrained degree of force available to masters" that enabled them "to
transform ancient modes of labor into a new industrial discipline"
and raise productivity to higher levels than would have been possible with free labor.[46] White workers would not easily submit to that
regimentation, but black slaves could be forced to do so, and the
American law of slavery backed up the use of force. In an infamous
decision in 1830 overturning the conviction of a slaveholder for an
assault on a female slave, the North Carolina Supreme Court declared, "The slave, to remain a slave, must be made sensible that
there is no appeal from his master."[47]

Like land and labor, capital in the slave economy ultimately depended on political power, partly because so much of a slaveholder's capital was invested in slaves, whose entire economic value
depended on their being legally recognized as property. Since
cotton was produced for distant markets, it also required complementary investment in infrastructure. Public investment in canals
and railroads as well as the federal post office and post roads provided transportation and communications systems unmatched in
the world's other cotton-growing regions. Cotton farming itself
was capital-intensive, and cotton plantations were some of the
largest and least flexible enterprises of their time. With much of
their capital invested in the people they owned, planters could not
just lay off workers when demand was slack. They also had no
equivalent alternative crop if demand for cotton fell. When demand was strong, the slave system was exceptionally profitable;
hence a refrain from 1854 that planters "care for nothing but to
buy Negroes to plant cotton & raise cotton to buy Negroes." But
declines in the demand for cotton could be ruinous. So could a loss
of confidence in slave property. If slavery itself came into question,
the market price of slaves might fall precipitously. Who would invest in purchasing slaves if they might be emancipated, possibly
without compensation? The value of all capital depends on beliefs
about the future. To the usual economic anxieties, slavery added
another: fear that the capital itself might rise in revolt and seek
vengeance on its owners.[48]

Just as insecurity about terrorism today is not proportional to
the actual risk people face, so insecurity in a slave society was not

proportional to the occurrence of slave rebellions. White panics followed distant uprisings and rumored slave conspiracies as well as the rare insurrections that slaves in the South were able to carry out. The revolution that began in the French colony of Saint-Domingue in 1791 and resulted thirteen years later in the establishment of the Republic of Haiti, the first black government in the New World, terrified slaveholders in the United States. In 1800, Virginians uncovered a plot by a slave blacksmith named Gabriel to take over Richmond; in 1811, Louisiana authorities defeated a large slave insurrection on plantations north of New Orleans; in 1822, South Carolinians prevented a group led by a free black man, Denmark Vesey, from carrying out a rebellion in Charleston; in 1831, Nat Turner's Rebellion swept through Southampton County, Virginia, killing more than fifty whites. These and other plots, real and imagined, led to the torture and mass executions of blacks and to the tightening of restrictions on manumission, heightened policing of free blacks, and hardening of southern opposition to emancipation.

In most slave societies, the possibility of manumission encouraged slaves to cooperate and thus reinforced their masters' control. Individually freed slaves were also often allies of their former masters in fighting slave rebellions and catching runaways. But in the American South, except in the quarter century beginning around 1780, lawmakers were generally too fearful of an enlarged population of free blacks to allow masters discretion in freeing their slaves. Restricting manumission kept down the size of the free black population, whose mere presence violated the binary caste system in which race corresponded to slave status. Panicked about slave conspiracies and revolts, southern lawmakers in the early 1800s increasingly treated free as well as enslaved blacks as security risks. After the Denmark Vesey plot, for example, South Carolina passed the Negro Seamen's Act, requiring all free black sailors on visiting ships to be locked up while they were in port. Nat Turner's Rebellion led to a wave of restrictions on the rights of free blacks across the South.[49]

Southern anxieties about unrest were also reflected in general restrictions of freedom of speech and hostility to an open public sphere. Southerners blamed slave resistance on the ideas in northern antislavery publications that reached Vesey and other literate blacks and then diffused by word of mouth. In the eyes of the South's leaders, any public support for emancipation was an incitement of slave unrest, and abolitionist literature was by definition "incendiary" and therefore properly banned. Alarmed by the rise and eventual triumph of Britain's antislavery movement, southern politicians were determined to stop abolitionists from taking the United States down the same road. No longer ambivalently defending slavery as a "necessary evil," from the 1830s on they increasingly defended it as a "positive good," the very basis of an orderly civilization, and attacked northern capitalism as slavery in a disguised but more brutal form.

The South was unquestionably an economic success from the slaveowners' standpoint. Counting slaves as wealth, the South had as much wealth per capita as the North. The richest counties in the country and the largest agricultural establishments were to be found in the South. As Fogel and his colleagues have argued, the slave plantations may have been more efficient than small family farms with free labor in the production of cotton and certain other crops that lent themselves to the gang system.[50] Compared with most of the rest of the world, the South was also relatively advanced technologically and economically.

But compared to the North, the South was a laggard. The southern states, unlike those in the North, generally made no provision for public education even for whites. As a closed society concerned to keep out dangerous ideas, the South was inhospitable to diversity and innovation. Technological innovation, as measured by data on patents, was far lower in the South. The North had a booming internal market for new consumer goods that absorbed much of its growing industrial production, whereas the South had neither the internal market nor the new industry. While the South solved its labor problems through slavery, the North addressed its perennial shortage of labor through immigration, new technology, and education—all of which positioned it for stronger economic growth in the coming transition to an industrial society.[51] But although the entire social and economic regime that came with slavery would likely have limited the South's development in the long run—and in that sense was an institutional trap—the slave economy in the antebellum era was an engine of wealth creation and an oligarchical powerhouse.

In the previous chapter, I suggested that wealth may be translated into power in four ways: through the control of a particular domain (in the case of slavery, the plantation), the concentration of ownership, privileged political representation, and the structural indispensability of specific assets. I also observed that in a preindustrial society, the power of landed wealth depends primarily on the first three of these. The antebellum South conforms to this view, though it proved to be of great consequence that on the eve of the Civil War, the South's planters suffered from an illusion of structural indispensability, the belief that the North's economy, and indeed the entire world's, would come crashing down without the South's cotton.

The domain control exercised by owners depends on the rights and powers held by other parties, and plantation slavery gave singularly few rights or powers to labor. In the antebellum South, masters not only could regulate their slaves' lives, they also had quasi-judicial powers that only the government itself could exercise over free persons. "We try, decide, and execute the sentences, in thousands of cases, which in other countries would go into the courts," wrote the planter-politician James Henry Hammond, a South Carolina governor and senator who owned twenty-two square miles and more than three hundred slaves and famously justified slavery on the grounds that every society requires a "mudsill" class to do the menial work. Sexual prerogatives were part of the package that Hammond enjoyed: he took one of his slaves as a mistress, and when that woman's daughter turned twelve, he took the daughter as a concubine too.[52]

Although slaveholding had a broad base of support in the white population, planters like Hammond held a singular position at the top of the social hierarchy. During the first half of the nineteenth century, about a third of white families in the South owned slaves, a proportion that declined before the Civil War, though never below one-fourth. Yet slave ownership was always highly concentrated, as was overall wealth. In 1860, the richest 10 percent of free males in the South owned 86 percent of the slaves.[53] With their wealth and high social standing, the planters dominated southern politics, even after most states in the South, like those in the North, expanded white male voting rights in the early nineteenth century. Southern elections were often hotly contested by candidates who differed sharply over economic policy—but not over slavery. Whether because they hoped to own slaves, feared an emancipated black population, or accepted the leadership of the slaveholding elite out of traditional habits of deference, non-slaveholding whites did not oppose slavery as an institution or slave-owning planters as their political leaders. Two-thirds of all southern state legislators in 1860 were slave-owners. The proportion of slaveholders among southern representatives in Congress may have been even higher, although data are limited. At least forty-eight of the fifty-two members of Mississippi's congressional delegations before 1861 owned slaves.[54]

Planter domination was closely related to the kind of government states had. The planters had no interest in paying taxes for public schools when they could educate their children with private tutors. From the colonial era, governments tended to be "more aristocratic, weaker, and less competent" where slavery was dominant.[55] Among the southern states, South Carolina stands out for its resistance to the trend toward popular government in the early nineteenth century and for its political leaders' singular role in the defense of slavery and periodic threats of secession. Although it had a near-universal white male franchise for legislative elections, the state maintained steep property qualifications for holding office, and many legislative seats went uncontested. The South Carolina legislature in turn appointed the governor, senators, and local officials. While wealthy planters generally controlled southern politics, South Carolina was the extreme case of an exclusive slaveholding oligarchy.[56]

Maintaining slavery required federal as well as state power. Of the first eleven presidents, seven were slaveholders, as were nineteen of the thirty-four men appointed to the Supreme Court from Washington to Lincoln. Until 1860, the three-fifths rule and the equal representation of states in the Senate made it impossible for any political party to win power nationally while bypassing the South. The major parties had southern wings that were controlled by slaveholders, and in deference to those wings, the parties followed a general rule of non-interference with southern slavery. The three-fifths rule was especially important in the nation's early decades. In 1800, the extra votes it gave Jefferson in the Electoral College enabled him to defeat John Adams; in 1808, the additional votes it gave Madison in the Republican caucus made him the party's presidential nominee. Even though the South never had a majority in the House, it often had a majority in the majority party. Moreover, while southern representatives were united in defending slavery, northern representatives were typically divided. Northern commercial interests had ties to southern planters, and northern politicians often had ties to the southern-dominated administrations and an interest in the patronage they dispensed. The North also had plenty of race-baiting politicians who sided with the South and who tended by the 1820s to gravitate to the Jacksonian Democratic Party.[57]

As the North's population grew faster, the South's share of House seats fell, but the Senate still gave the South a veto on crucial questions. After the War of 1812, Congress admitted a slave state whenever it admitted a free state to preserve the sectional balance. The prospect of Missouri's admission as a slave state in 1819 (when there were eleven free and eleven slave states) precipitated a crisis because no other part of the Louisiana Territory had enough white settlers to be admitted as a free state. In the compromise reached the following year, Congress paired the admission of Missouri with that of Maine (previously a district of Massachusetts) and prohibited slavery in all the rest of the Louisiana Territory north of 36°30′ latitude (Missouri's southern border).[58]

But while the Missouri Compromise resolved the immediate conflict in 1820, it threatened in the long run to deprive the South of its power in the Senate. The territory north of 36°30′ from which Congress had agreed to ban slavery could accommodate many additional states (eleven, as it later turned out). From the 1820s on, not only would the North grow more rapidly in population than the South; northerners would also dominate settlement in the West. The South's slaveholders found themselves "fighting the census returns," as the saying went at the time. If the South were to retain the national political power essential to slavery and the plantation economy, it would need ways of offsetting the edge that the North was gaining.

OVERCOMING SLAVERY'S ENTRENCHMENT

Throughout the first half of the nineteenth century, the entrenchment of a slave society in the South, together with the South's political power in the federal government, effectively made slavery impossible to dislodge. Nonetheless, after the adoption of emancipation measures in the North, efforts to end slavery throughout the country continued.

The most prominent, respectable line of thought called for gradual, compensated emancipation and the removal of black Americans to colonies in Africa. The American Colonization Society, established in 1817, counted Jefferson, Madison, Henry Clay, and Daniel Webster among its leaders and supporters. The colonization movement was divided between those who wanted to expatriate only free blacks and those who saw colonization as a necessary complement to emancipation. Since slave-owners suspected that starting with free blacks would lead to the release of their slaves, they generally opposed the entire movement. Colonization long had its distinguished advocates (including Abraham Lincoln), but it never made any headway in the face of the opposition of free blacks and slaveholders alike and the staggering costs that compensation to slaveholders and a black exodus would have imposed.

Rejecting the premises of the colonizationists, the more radical, religiously inspired abolitionists who formed the American Anti-Slavery Society in 1833 insisted that blacks and whites could live together in America on terms of equality and that slavery had to be ended immediately without any compensation. But while abolitionism profoundly affected northern religion and public opinion, it also elicited intense racist opposition and mob violence in the North as well as outright suppression in the South and remained marginal to electoral politics for the next two decades.

Only in the wake of the Mexican War and the ensuing struggles over slavery's western expansion did antislavery finally become the basis of an electoral politics with the potential to win control of the federal government. After several abortive efforts, political antislavery coalesced around the new Republican Party in the mid-1850s. While including a range of views from conservative to radical, the Republicans were united on one central tenet: opposition to the extension of slavery. Instead of directly attacking it where it was entrenched in the South, Republican leaders attacked slavery where it was not entrenched—in the West—thereby achieving two results that had eluded the colonizationists and abolitionists. First, they won fervent support from northern white farmers and workers, who feared the competition from slavery's expansion as a direct threat to their own interests in pursuing land and economic opportunity in the West. The Republicans, for example, supported homestead legislation that provided land for family farms at no cost to white settlers, while the South saw free homesteads as inimical to its interests in expanding slavery in the territories. Second, by opposing the addition of any further slave states, political antislavery threatened to alter forever the sectional balance, enabling the North to control the nation's destiny.[59]

For the South, the westward expansion of slavery was both a critical vulnerability and a political imperative. With the area north of 36°30´ forbidden to slavery under the Missouri Compromise, the South needed the federal government to swing development in its favor, which it could do in three ways—by acquiring new territory for new slave states, repealing the Missouri Compromise, and creating a constitutional guarantee for the property rights of slaveholders wherever they took their slaves. For more than a decade—from the annexation of Texas in 1845 through the Kansas-Nebraska Act in 1854 and the Supreme Court's *Dred Scott* decision in 1857—the South seemed to get its way on all three fronts. On each one, southern interests called for nationalizing slavery in the sense of making the federal government the instrument of slavery's preservation and extension. All three raised the specter of what Republicans called the "Slave Power," the South's undue sway over the federal government. Conversely, southerners saw Republican opposition to slavery's extension as a plot to gain national power and impose steep protective tariffs and other policies favored by northern manufacturing and finance.

The Texas annexation and Mexican War brought the nation new territory that could potentially be turned into several more slave states. With the help of northern allies in the Senate, southerners defeated a proviso sponsored by a congressman from Pennsylvania,

David Wilmot, that would have banned slavery from the territory acquired from Mexico. But the legislative package settling the territorial issues created by the war (the Compromise of 1850) did not deliver the South the gain in slave states it needed. California was admitted as a single free state, instead of being divided in two, with a separate state in southern California open to slavery. Although slavery was left up to voters in the Utah and New Mexico territories, neither was likely to adopt it (Mexico having previously prohibited slavery in those areas). Four years later, the South scored a major victory with the Kansas-Nebraska Act, which repealed the Missouri Compromise and opened Kansas to slavery, depending on a territorial election. But the effort to impose the proslavery Lecompton Constitution on Kansas through a fraudulent vote ended in failure in 1858.

Southerners also sought new territory beyond the continental bounds of the United States, envisioning a slave empire extending into the Caribbean, Mexico, and Central and South America. Expeditions of freelance invaders ("filibusters") went to Cuba, Honduras, and Ecuador; in 1855, one of those filibusters, William Walker, seized Nicaragua and briefly legalized slavery. In 1858, Mississippi Senator Albert Gallatin Brown declared: "I want a foothold in Central America ... because I want to plant slavery there. ... I want Cuba, ... Tamaulipas, Potosi, and one or two other Mexican States; and I want them all for the same reason—for the planting and spreading of slavery."[60] But the acquisition of territory for slavery depended on holding national power and being able to use it aggressively for that purpose, and by the late 1850s the odds the South would have that power were receding. The North was growing more rapidly in population and electoral votes and becoming more united in its opposition to slavery's expansion.

The South's view of federal powers varied according to their implications for slavery. As representatives of the minority section, John C. Calhoun and other antebellum southern leaders generally insisted on states' rights and a narrow construction of federal powers, for fear those powers might someday be used to limit or abolish slavery. But they also favored the strongest possible use of federal power on behalf of slavery, in catching fugitive slaves, defending slave-owner interests on the high seas, and most of all, expanding slavery through the seizure of territory. It was a slave-holder president, Andrew Jackson, who pushed for Indian removal, and another slaveholder president, James Polk, who led America into the war with Mexico. "Whenever a question arose of extending or protecting slavery," the historian Henry Adams later wrote, "the slave-holders became friends of centralized power, and used that dangerous weapon with a kind of frenzy."[61]

The South sought not only to nationalize slavery but also to constitutionalize it—to entrench slavery by giving it the full protection of the Constitution. The old federal consensus, which treated slavery as a state matter except in those respects expressly addressed in the Constitution, was insufficient to advance slavery in the territories or in foreign relations. Southerners now insisted that the Constitution required the federal government to protect slave-owners' property rights not just in the states where slavery existed but in areas where the federal government enjoyed full jurisdiction, including the territories and the District of Columbia. Indeed, slaveowners charged, under the Constitution the federal government had no power over slavery except the power to protect it. In contrast, according to the constitutional interpretation that came to dominate in the new Republican Party, slavery was a wholly local institution that the framers of the Constitution had refused to admit into national law. In the concise formulation of Salmon P. Chase, "Freedom is national; slavery is only local and sectional." Chase argued that because the Fifth Amendment barred Congress from depriving any "person" of "life, liberty, or property" without due process of law, Congress had no authority to enforce enslavement in any area where the federal government exercised exclusive jurisdiction.[62]

The constitutional issue came to a head in the 1857 *Dred Scott* case, which concerned a slave in Missouri who sought freedom for himself and his family on the grounds that their owner had taken them to live for years on free soil. In a decision supported by seven justices (six from slaveholding states), Chief Justice Roger Taney ruled that the Scotts remained slaves, and furthermore that black people were not citizens of the United States regardless of whether they were enslaved or free. The nation's founders, Taney wrote, regarded blacks as "beings of an inferior order, and altogether unfit to associate with the white race ... and so far inferior, that they had no rights which the white man was bound to respect." The Constitution, in Taney's reading, "distinctly and expressly affirmed" the right to property in slaves. Consequently, Congress had no authority to bar slavery from the territories and the Missouri Compromise had been unconstitutional. Since barring slavery from the territories was the Republican Party's central tenet, the Court effectively declared the party's cause to be futile.[63]

With *Dred Scott*, the Supreme Court entrenched both slavery and racism more profoundly in American law than ever before. The logic of the decision, according to Lincoln and other Republicans, threatened to introduce slavery not just into the territories but into the North as well. If the federal Constitution guaranteed the rights of slaveholders outside the states that permitted slavery, what was to prevent them from bringing slaves into the free states? In October 1857, an appellate court ruled that eight slaves brought to New York for shipment to Texas were free as soon as they stepped on free soil. But the Supreme Court might now overturn the New York decision, in which case there would be nothing to stop slave traders from setting up slave markets in the North. This was the context for Lincoln's declaration in June 1858 that "a house divided against itself" could not stand and that either the opponents of slavery would arrest its spread and set it on a "course of ultimate extinction," or its advocates would "push it forward, till it shall become alike lawful in all the States, old as well as new— North as well as South."[64]

The political strategies and ideas of southern slaveholders, as they confronted the threats to their national power from the growth of the free states, fit into a general pattern. Whenever a dominant, propertied class faces the prospect of political decline in a representative system, it has an incentive to use its power over the system's rules to entrench itself in two ways: first, by engineering electoral advantage and, second, by creating constitutional barriers against hostile electoral majorities. The South's efforts to increase the number of slave states fall into the first type of entrenchment strategy. The constitutional theories favored by the South, from states' rights to the federal protection of slaveholder property rights in *Dred Scott*, correspond to the second type.

But instead of working as the South and its northern supporters hoped, these efforts to entrench slavery backfired, stirring up northern opposition to the Slave Power and contributing to a historic political realignment that crystallized in 1858. Not only did the Whigs collapse; the Democrats suffered huge losses in the North and then split into separate northern and southern parties for the 1860 presidential election. As the Republican nominee that year, Lincoln received only 40 percent of the national vote, but he won the presidency by triumphing in the most populous region with a majority of votes in the Electoral College. For the first time, the United States had a president who owed nothing to the South.

From the founding to the 1850s, the South had always had a final card to play in blocking antislavery measures: it could threaten to secede if the North did not make a credible commitment to respect southern interests in slavery. The calculation that lay behind this threat was that northern political leaders (and the voters who chose them) cared more about other goals, including the survival of the Union itself, than about ending or limiting slavery. At the Constitutional Convention, Charles Pinckney threatened to walk out if slavery came up for discussion. Beginning in the late 1820s, South Carolinians, led by Calhoun, repeatedly made strategic use of the disunion threat in conflicts over the tariff and slavery. Southern fire-eaters threatened secession all through the controversies over the territories in the 1850s. The demand for credible commitments had always worked. But with the Republican victory, southern leaders concluded that their only option for dominating a nation-state was to create their own. Seven states across the Lower South, from South Carolina to Texas, had already seceded and formed a Confederate government by the time Lincoln was sworn in on March 4, 1861. Supremely confident of their position, Confederate leaders expected to have support in the North and abroad because of the indispensability of cotton. In 1858, when he proclaimed "Cotton is king," Senator Hammond gave perfect expression to that illusion of structural indispensability. "I firmly believe," he declared, "that the slave-holding South is now the controlling power in the world."[65]

The southern states did not secede because of any specific action Lincoln was poised to take but because of the signal his victory sent. He was not calling for slavery's abolition in the South and could not have carried out such a policy; the Republicans had only pluralities in both houses of Congress (though those pluralities became majorities when southerners left). But his victory signaled that the long-term erosion of southern power had reached a tipping point and that slavery's federal protection had ended. Ultimately, secession was a response to a cause that the South saw it was already losing—national power.

Lincoln was willing to conciliate the South on some issues, but as he wrote after the election, he was "inflexible" on the question of slavery's expansion. That alone was decisive for the South, because slaveholder wealth depended on controlling enough states to control national policy. A month after Lincoln's inauguration, the new president of the Confederacy, Jefferson Davis, said that Republican measures excluding slavery from the territories would have the effect of "rendering the property in slaves so insecure as to be comparatively worthless, and thereby annihilating in effect property worth thousands of millions of dollars." Southern leaders believed, furthermore, that just as antislavery forces in France and Britain had incited slave uprisings in Haiti and elsewhere in the Caribbean, so the Republicans, once in power in Washington, would incite slave uprisings in the South.[66]

The irony is that Lincoln and other Republicans had never figured out a way to end slavery. Although they had talked vaguely about putting it on a path toward "ultimate extinction," they had not arrived at a policy or strategy for bringing about that distant goal. But it turned out not to matter. By withdrawing from the Union and going to war, the South supplied the answer to a puzzle none of slavery's opponents had been able to solve. War would break down the barriers to abolition posed by the constitutional entrenchment of slavery and the costs of emancipation.

ENTRENCHING ABOLITION—BUT NOT EQUALITY

By the late 1850s, leaders in both the free states and the South were saying that the differences between them could no longer be papered over. Just as a logical contradiction exists when two statements cannot both be true, so a contradictory social condition exists when two forms of organization cannot continue operating in the same system without at least one of them, and therefore the system itself, undergoing fundamental change. That was, in essence, the claim about the United States that Lincoln made in his 1858 "house divided" speech, when he said the country could not continue half slave, half free but would become all one or all the other. Later the same year, William H. Seward—senator from New York and Lincoln's chief rival for the 1860 Republican presidential nomination—also declared that the United States would "sooner or later" necessarily become either "entirely a slaveholding nation, or entirely a free-labor nation."[67]

But what was making the contradictory forces of the slave and free-labor systems impossible to contain? Seward suggested that the underlying cause was the economic integration of the country due to improved transportation and the market revolution. An increasing population, "a new and extended network of railroads and other avenues, and an internal commerce which daily becomes more intimate" were bringing the two systems into "closer contact," producing a "collision" and "an irrepressible conflict between opposing and enduring forces." That collision, however, was not only the result of the knitting together of the national economy, which aroused the fear among northern workers and farmers that slave labor would undercut their earnings and block their opportunities. The collision also stemmed from the expansionary tendencies of both the southern and northern varieties of capitalism. Cotton planters were continually on the hunt for new land, while northern industry and finance sought to expand their markets through policies such as high tariffs and free homesteads that the South opposed. As the nation expanded territorially, neither the South nor the North was content to see its system confined within its old geographic limits. Both slavery and free-labor capitalism required the backing of federal law and federal power, and whichever system dominated the West would control the national government.

The contradiction between the slave and free-labor systems could have had other means of resolution besides war. Social contradictions, even entrenched ones, need to be resolved through change, but not necessarily through violence. The contradiction between slave and free labor might have been resolved by secession if the Union had simply let the South go. The Confederacy, unlike the Union, was not born in ambivalence or division about slavery. Its constitution guaranteed "the institution of negro slavery" in all of its states and territories, thereby barring any individual state from abolishing slavery and creating internal conflict of the kind that divided the United States. Nor was there any conflict between the Confederacy's general principles and specific constitutional provisions. Referring to Jefferson's Declaration of Independence, the Confederacy's vice president, Alexander Stephens, declared, "Our new government is founded upon exactly the opposite idea: its foundations are laid, its corner-stone rests upon the great truth, that the negro is not equal to the white man; that slavery—subordination to the superior race—is his natural and normal condition."[68]

As I suggested earlier, slavery might eventually have become an institutional trap for the South, limiting its economic growth. But this was not apparent in 1860, when demand for cotton was strong and prices were high. Even if demand weakened, an independent Confederacy might have fulfilled the designs that slaveholders had on Mexico, the Caribbean, and Central America and created a slave empire that would have been equal in wealth and power to the United States and a continuing source of support for slavery elsewhere in the world—perhaps well into the twentieth century, when the Confederacy might have become an ally of Germany and the world wars might have been fought on American soil.

The abolition of slavery in the United States now seems like a logical result of Lincoln's election and the Civil War, but even leaving aside the possibility of the Confederacy's survival, abolition was far from inevitable. Republicans had united around the goal of stopping the expansion of slavery, not abolishing it; they generally acknowledged that the Constitution afforded the southern states the legal right to maintain slavery. After the war began, in April 1861, the steps toward emancipation were not immediate, and the wartime measures Lincoln and Congress adopted could have been reversed afterward. Abolishing slavery permanently through a constitutional amendment was not a self-evident idea; Americans had never before used amendments to the Constitution to bring about large-scale social change.[69]

In fact, the idea of amending the Constitution in regard to slavery first came up after Lincoln's election for the opposite purpose. Hoping to dissuade the southern states from seceding, advocates of compromise suggested dozens of amendments to protect slavery. A package of six amendments offered by Kentucky Senator John Crittenden followed the classic pattern of attempting to placate the South with credible commitments to respect slavery. The Crittenden amendments, which would themselves have been unamendable, included not only protection for slavery within the existing slave states but also the extension of the Missouri Compromise line to the Pacific—a step Republicans would not accept. As Lincoln put it in December, if slavery were guaranteed in all territory acquired to the south, "immediately filibustering and extending slavery recommences."[70]

Led by Seward, however, Republicans did rally behind an alternative that became known as the Corwin amendment (after Thomas Corwin, who headed the committee that sent the amendment to the floor of the House). Passed by both houses of Congress by the necessary two-thirds vote just before Lincoln took office in March, the Corwin amendment prohibited any future amendment that would authorize Congress to "abolish or interfere" with any state's "domestic institutions," including "that of persons held to labor or service by the laws of said State." In his inaugural address, Lincoln said that he regarded this provision protecting slavery within the slave states to be "implied constitutional law" and therefore had "no objection to its being made express, and irrevocable." Making it express and irrevocable, however, was hardly insignificant, as it would have given state-sanctioned slavery the unamendable status that the Constitution extends to only one other provision, the equal representation of states in the Senate. If the South had been thereby dissuaded from secession, or if the war had been quickly settled on the basis of the ratification of what would have been the Thirteenth Amendment, slavery would have become expressly entrenched in the Constitution and more difficult to overturn later. But in the month after the Corwin amendment passed Congress, only two states ratified it, and the outbreak of war then deprived the amendment of its rationale.[71]

The war itself did what antislavery agitation had long been unable to do. The longer it went on, the more it broke down the reluctance of Lincoln and the Republicans to attack slavery. Step by step, Congress and the president adopted a strategy of military emancipation, offering freedom to slaves as a way of both weakening the South economically and strengthening the Union militarily. The direct effect of the war was to encourage slaves—by 1864, more than 400,000 of them—to flee to Union lines. Although some Union generals at first returned runaways, Congress in March 1862 approved an article of war forbidding officers under penalty of court-martial from returning escaped slaves to their former masters. Two Confiscation Acts also moved in the direction of military emancipation—the first, in August 1861, authorizing the confiscation of slaves used by the Confederacy for military purposes; the second, in July 1862, emancipating all rebel-owned slaves who escaped to areas held by Union troops. Perhaps most important, the Second Confiscation Act gave Lincoln the authority to employ blacks in whatever way he saw as "necessary and proper for the suppression of the rebellion," which opened the way to enrolling blacks into the military effort not just as laborers but as soldiers.[72]

Still, through the first sixteen months of the war, Lincoln refrained from endorsing stronger measures against slavery, much less adopting emancipation as a war aim, for fear of getting too far ahead of public opinion, violating constitutional limitations, and driving the non-seceding slave states (Kentucky, Maryland, Delaware, and Missouri) into the arms of the Confederacy. Only in mid-1862, when a quick Union victory was no longer likely, did Lincoln begin considering the Emancipation Proclamation that he would issue in final form on January 1, 1863. Grounded on "military necessity" and therefore on the president's powers as commander-in-chief, Lincoln declared "all persons held as slaves" in the Confederacy to be free and authorized the active recruitment of blacks into the "armed service" of the Union. By this point, Congress had abolished slavery in the District of Columbia and the federal territories, important symbolic steps even though they affected only a few thousand enslaved people. The presidential Emancipation Proclamation applied to about three million slaves, omitting roughly 800,000 in the border states, the soon-to-be-admitted state of West Virginia, and certain exempt areas of the Confederacy under Union control. The proclamation could be carried out only with a Union victory, but it turned the Civil War into a war of liberation.[73]

Military emancipation proved as crucial to the black struggle for freedom as it did to the Union's triumph. By the end of the war, more than 180,000 blacks served in the Union army, about one of every five adult black males under age forty-five. If it were not for the black soldiers, Lincoln told two Wisconsin Republicans in August 1864, "we would be compelled to abandon the war in 3 weeks." The recruitment of blacks signaled a shift in public attitudes; an Ohio congressman called it "a recognition of the Negro's manhood such as has never before been made by this nation." The heroic sacrifices of those soldiers then contributed to a new respect for the dignity and courage of black Americans among many whites who, for the first time, recognized them as their fellow countrymen.[74]

The role that slaves in the Americas played in bringing about their own emancipation has long been a subject of international scholarly contention.[75] The Haitian Revolution is the one unambiguous case of a violent uprising by slaves directly bringing about abolition. In the United States, slave revolts did not weaken the southern resolve to maintain slavery, though they affected white opinion in the North by undermining the claim that slaves were contented. Frederick Douglass and others who escaped from slavery played a role in informing and arousing the religious and moral movements against slavery. It was the war, however, that finally enabled slaves en masse to make the most direct contribution to their own freedom, both by fleeing the South (a movement that the sociologist W. E. B. Du Bois later likened to a "general strike") and by fighting on the side of the North. Black soldiers carrying guns symbolized a transformation of their status in a society that had long denied blacks the right to bear arms. The soldiers' experience in the Union army, where many of them learned to read and write and gained leadership experience, also had effects after the war when, as veterans, they played notable roles in the organization and politics of black communities.[76]

Once the war was over, however, there was no guarantee slavery would be permanently abolished. After the French Republic abolished slavery in its Caribbean colonies in 1794, Napoleon reestablished it eight years later, and colonial slavery then survived until France had another revolution in 1848. Lincoln and the Republicans had good reason to think that wartime emancipation might later be reversed. After long granting that slavery was within the power of the states, they could not be certain that the Supreme Court would uphold either the Emancipation Proclamation or any federal abolitionist legislation. As part of his Reconstruction policy, therefore, Lincoln sought to have the slave states themselves adopt new constitutions abolishing slavery. Since those constitutions might be changed, however, the more secure strategy for entrenching abolition was an amendment to the U.S. Constitution.

Parties and other groups typically favor the constitutional entrenchment of a rule or policy when they hold power but are uncertain whether they will keep it. Before the Civil War, the South's efforts to constitutionalize slavery and entrench it politically stemmed from growing uncertainty about its own power. As the war ended, the Republican effort to entrench abolition in the Constitution reflected an interest in seizing the historical opportunity presented by the war and the destruction of the Old South. The war had increased both antislavery and anti-southern sentiment. Many in the North saw abolition as both a fitting reward for black service to the Union and a fitting punishment for slaveholders for the destruction and death they had brought upon the nation. After so bloody a war, why leave its original cause in place and perhaps have to fight over it again? As Union armies advanced, moreover, and much of the former Confederacy came under military occupation, voters there and in the border states were subject to loyalty tests. Constitutional emancipation had previously been inconceivable because it would have to be ratified by three-fourths of the states, but in the war's aftermath the governments of the occupied southern states would help reach that threshold.[77]

What became the Thirteenth Amendment was the diametric opposite of the Corwin amendment. Passed first by the Senate in April 1864, the amendment prohibited slavery and involuntary servitude, except as a punishment for crime, and authorized Congress to enforce that prohibition by appropriate legislation. After its initial defeat in the House, the amendment became part of the Republican Party platform in 1864, and upon their reelection Lincoln and congressional Republicans claimed a mandate to pass it. The president did not hesitate to use all the powers at his disposal to push it through the House in January 1865, and it became part of the Constitution that December, when Georgia became the twenty-seventh state to ratify.[78]

Although later overshadowed by the Fourteenth Amendment, the Thirteenth was striking for its radicalism. Before the war, most Republican leaders saw immediate abolition as an unreasonable goal, and well into the war, Lincoln had remained committed to the ideas of gradualism, compensation, and colonization. Even after the Emancipation Proclamation, he was still trying to persuade representatives of the border states to accept gradual emancipation, with compensation to slaveholders to be financed by the federal government. With the Thirteenth Amendment applying to the entire country, not just the former Confederacy, emancipation was both immediate and complete, slave-owners went uncompensated, and colonization was forgotten.

In its immediacy and lack of compensation, the Thirteenth Amendment was more radical than earlier northern emancipation laws or Britain's emancipation of West Indian slaves in 1833. The £20 million in compensation that Britain paid to colonial slaveholders for half the market value of their slaves was no small commitment by British taxpayers: it equaled 40 percent of Britain's public expenditure that year.[79] Providing southern slaveholders equivalent compensation for the roughly $3 billion in market value of slaves in 1860 would have cost twenty-four times that year's total U.S. federal outlays.[80] To be sure, paying that compensation would have been cheaper in the long run than fighting the Civil War. But no one could have made that calculation beforehand, and slaveholders never showed any interest in compensated emancipation.

Slavery in the early republic had become entrenched through the political power of the South, constitutional law, and the staggering costs of emancipation, as those costs appeared at the time. By 1865, each of these obstacles had been overcome. Lincoln's election demonstrated the South's loss of power over the national government. The secession and defeat of the Confederacy removed the obstacles to changing the Constitution, and blacks' own sacrifices in blood contributed to the support for making abolition an irrevocable constitutional commitment. The immediate costs of emancipation fell once again on a class that, at least for the moment, had no power—the former slaveholders. Together, the Emancipation Proclamation and Thirteenth Amendment represented the greatest liquidation of concentrated wealth in American history—"the most stupendous act of sequestration in the history of Anglo-Saxon jurisprudence," Charles and Mary Beard wrote, referring to the Emancipation Proclamation alone. This is what violent revolutions do, and by any reasonable definition the Civil War and Reconstruction qualify for the designation the Beards gave it, the "Second American Revolution."[81]

The abolition of slavery in the United States may now be remembered more for its limitations than for its radicalism. But the subsequent history of white supremacy and Jim Crow should not obscure the significance of abolition and the early thrust of Reconstruction, or lead us to think that no other outcome was possible.

The Thirteenth Amendment itself was limited or at least ambiguous in its reach. In the interests of maximizing support, the sponsors of the amendment were deliberately vague about the rights the amendment conveyed to former slaves. According to the free-labor thought of the time, self-ownership included the right to enter freely into contracts and to receive the "fruits" of one's labor, but not necessarily full civil and political equality. The limitations of that minimal definition of freedom became clear as the war ended, when some of the new southern state governments enacted Black Codes that threatened to reduce the newly freed people to a condition close to slavery. Seizing national leadership from Lincoln's successor, Andrew Johnson, the radical Republicans in Congress responded with a series of measures, including the Civil Rights Act of 1866. Then they took advantage of the singular political opportunity of Reconstruction (including reimposed military rule) to pass the Fourteenth and Fifteenth Amendments, ratified successively in 1868 and 1870. Reversing the *Dred Scott* decision, the Fourteenth established that all those born in the United States are citizens (the principle of birthright citizenship) and prohibited any state from abridging "the privileges and immunities of citizens" or depriving any person "of life, liberty, or property, without due process of law" or of "the equal protection of the laws." The Fifteenth Amendment extended the suffrage to black men, barring citizens from being denied the right to vote "on account of race, color, or previous condition of servitude."[82]

The passage of the Reconstruction amendments was part of a wide-ranging effort to transform southern society. Among the countries that ended slavery in the nineteenth century, the United States stands out as the only one that, at least briefly, gave former slaves some genuine power as part of an effort to replace the plantation order with a society based on free labor and equal rights.[83] The failure to carry out those changes in full and make them stick—in other words, to entrench them—was due in part to the enormous obstacles Reconstruction faced. As difficult as it was to end slavery as a property-rights regime, it was even more difficult to change the social relations that had developed under it. Abolishing slavery did not abolish the racial caste system. It would have taken a thoroughgoing governmental commitment sustained over decades even to begin mitigating the many deprivations that slavery imposed. According to one line of analysis, the de facto power of whites, stemming from their advantages in education and capacities for collective action, explains the persistence of racial hierarchy and the resilience of old elites after the Civil War.[84] But the advantages whites enjoyed are only part of the explanation. Transforming southern society after the war would have required the active power of the national government, and federal intervention in the South was limited in both depth and duration.

In post-emancipation societies, the position of former slaves depended on their real economic alternatives. In the U.S. South, they might have had two alternatives to a labor regime controlled by their former masters: working in the North's growing industrial economy or obtaining their own land and becoming independent farmers. Racism in the North closed off the first of these possibilities. As long as industrial employers preferred white immigrants and could rely on large numbers of them arriving every year, opportunities for blacks to move north were limited. Freedpeople were also unable to obtain their own farms, although they were led to believe the government would help them do so. On establishing the Freedmen's Bureau in March 1865 to provide aid to former slaves, Congress authorized the agency to create forty-acre plots out of abandoned and confiscated land and to rent those homesteads and eventually sell them with "such title as the United States can convey." Some federal officials did begin settling freedpeople on farms, and with 850,000 acres under its control, the bureau might have created a substantial class of black freeholders. Later in 1865, however, President Johnson issued pardons to former Confederates and restored their land, unilaterally reversing the bureau's legal mandate and leading the army to evict tens of thousands of blacks from lands they had expected would be theirs. No land reform ever took place. After abrogating property in slaves, Republicans were not willing to take the further step of expropriating land, even when the owners had taken up arms against the government. An attempt to make land available from the public domain, the Southwest Homestead Act, resulted in only four thousand applications; the land being offered was generally of poor quality and often inaccessible, and hence would have taken capital to develop. Sustainable land reform would have required not just land itself but capital, credit, and other forms of assistance. Instead, federal officials forced former slaves to sign annual contracts for plantation labor. While slavery ended, it gave way to a form of economic entrapment. Even so, the share of plantation income going to blacks did increase substantially in the period after the war compared with the in-kind goods they had received as slaves.[85]

Slavery, moreover, had been a system not just of labor relations but of comprehensive power relations—"the permanent, violent domination of natally alienated and generally dishonored persons," in Orlando Patterson's definition.[86] The end of slavery enabled black men and women to enter into legal marriages and form families without the risk of being sold. It enabled them to create churches and mutual aid societies under their own control and to see many of their children educated. (Between 1860 and 1880, the proportion of school-age children attending school increased from 2 percent to 34 percent among blacks, in a period when the percentage among whites rose from 60 percent to 62 percent.) While facing persistent violence by whites, blacks were also able to organize politically during Reconstruction and assume roles in government. But federal intervention in the South failed to change the "balance of property" or to prevent a wave of terror from snuffing out black political organization. And so when the federal government pulled out its troops and the last of the Republican governments in the South fell in 1877, the planter class reimposed its political domination in what was, in effect, a counterrevolution.[87]

The outcome of Reconstruction highlights again both the importance and limitations of constitutionally entrenched principles. Reconstruction introduced into the Constitution general principles of civil and political equality nowhere to be found in the original text or the Bill of Rights. The constitutional entrenchment of those principles has been undeniably significant. Long afterward, the civil rights movement would successfully invoke them to mobilize both popular support and the weight of federal authority on behalf of equal rights for African Americans and other minorities.

But general principles depend for their efficacy on the machinery of power. After the Civil War, southern planters lost their sway over national politics and the Supreme Court, but they nonetheless became once again locally entrenched as a dominant class and were able to nullify the Fourteenth and Fifteenth Amendments in their home region. At the national level too, the Reconstruction amendments long proved ineffectual in advancing their original intent in assuring equal civil and political rights. The Fourteenth Amendment became the basis for strengthening the rights of property against state intervention. In 1912, a study of the 604 Fourteenth Amendment cases decided by the Supreme Court up to that point showed that only 28 of the cases, or less than 5 percent, had concerned African Americans—who lost nearly every case they brought. But 312 cases had involved corporations, and in those the Court used the amendment to strike down regulation of business, including child labor and minimum wage laws.[88] There is no better example than the Reconstruction amendments of how general principles can be put to different purposes if contrary interests dominate.

But precisely because constitutional rights are at least textually entrenched, they lie ready to be reactivated. The overthrow of slavery turned upside down the old constitutional understanding of the relationship between the national government and freedom. According to the earlier understanding, restrictions on federal power protected liberty, even though much of the impetus for those restrictions actually came from an interest in protecting slavery. With the abolition of slavery, a more powerful national government became the means of advancing freedom. The New Deal and the civil rights revolution would take up that model in the twentieth century.

Reconstruction failed to bring the South fully into line with northern society, but the war did put to rest the challenge that the South's peculiar institution posed to the North. The United States had contained two expansionary economic systems, each of which demanded the backing of the national government. With the Civil War, the North gained firm control, while the white South surrendered its greater ambitions and was left to rule at home. The Civil War did not end the moral inconsistencies between equality and white supremacy in America, but it subdued, for a time, the contradictory relation between the South and the nation.

The drive of the antebellum southern planter class to dominate national institutions was not a peculiar phenomenon. Concentrated wealth fits uneasily into representative governments. Modern democracies arose amid the propertied classes' fear that if given the vote, popular majorities would use it to redistribute wealth. In some cases, that fear has led the propertied to support military dictatorships and other forms of authoritarian rule. Many on the left have also believed that concentrated wealth cannot coexist with democracy. Nonetheless, capitalism and democracy have proved a surprisingly stable combination, in part due to the uses of entrenched rules in the design of democratic institutions, which we turn to next.

CHAPTER FOUR

The Conservative Design of
Liberal Democracy

D EMOCRACY IS SUPPOSED TO prevent the entrenchment
of power. Unlike autocrats, the leaders of a functioning
democracy know that the voters may remove them at
the next election, and it is this insecurity that is expected to make the government responsive and accountable to the
people. If political incumbents can manipulate at will the rules governing elections, their own authority, and individual liberties, they
may be able to insulate themselves from challenge. So democracy
ideally uses entrenchment of one kind (rules) to prevent entrenchment of another kind (power).

That ideal, however, is not easy to achieve. When rules have
calculable effects, they often have calculating authors. Those who
fashion rules are rationally interested in their consequences, not
least for themselves and the policies they favor. Democracies therefore have an inescapable internal tension between their reliance on
elections as a method for ensuring accountability and the interest
of incumbents in crafting rules for elections and other features of
government that enable them to stay in office or at least prevent
their policies from being reversed.

Democratic governments provide opportunities for the strategic entrenchment of power and policy for another reason. There is

no single design for democracy that unambiguously, and without bias, puts democratic principles into practice and provides the one true expression of the people's will. Liberal protections of individual rights put boundaries on the range of alternatives. But without necessarily violating liberal democratic principles, those in power at moments of institutional design have great leeway in crafting electoral rules and the architecture of government. Some choices are typically spelled out in a constitution, while others are left to legislative and executive decision. Both constitutional and ordinary political moments present opportunities for political engineering—that is, for choosing rules likely to bring about particular results. If the rules are spelled out in a constitution, they may be hard to change because amending the constitution is difficult. If they are left to elected officials, they may be hard to change because those officials have an interest in maintaining rules that may have enabled them to win in the first place. When they agree to new rules, it may be because the old ones no longer serve their purposes.

Constitutionally entrenched rules are an attempt to solve one problem for democracy—how to prevent incumbents from continually recasting political institutions to their own advantage—but they are also the source of a democratic dilemma: Why should the living be bound by the decisions of their ancestors? Like the entails that the British aristocracy imposed on their heirs, a constitution is a type of perpetuity since its provisions usually have no sunset date. Just as Adam Smith objected to entail on the grounds that it was absurd for "the present generation [to] be restrained and regulated according to the fancy of those who died" long before, some democratic critics of constitutions have objected to being bound by the "dead hand of the past." The most famous of these critics was Smith's contemporary Thomas Jefferson, who declared in a letter to James Madison in 1789 that "the earth belongs in usufruct to the living" and "the dead have neither powers nor rights over it." Later he ridiculed people who "look at constitutions with sanctimonious reverence, and deem them like the ark of the covenant, too sacred to be touched." Jefferson was an original but not an originalist. Constitutions, he wrote to Madison, should expire every nineteen years, a proposal many people would find terrifying.[1] Whoever had the upper hand at the point of a constitution's expiration could then reset the rules for their own benefit, a prospect that could regularly ignite destructive conflicts.

But while Jefferson's idea for an expiration date on constitutions was no solution, the problem is genuine. Constitutions not only reflect the ideas of the dead; they often impose on the living the preferences that the rich and powerful had in the past. The provisions in the U.S. Constitution that protected slavery are only the most egregious example. Democratic constitutions written during political transitions or periods of intense social change often incorporate provisions sought by elite interests, sometimes those associated with the prior regime, who are willing to accept a democratic government provided their vital interests are protected. The uncertainties surrounding social and political upheavals heighten the interest in entrenched rules; anxious about their possible successors, those with influence at times of institutional design understandably want to increase their chances of retaining power and reducing the damage if they lose it. Consequently, what I earlier called "rules of change"— the rules of the game that govern changes in other rules—are often framed not only to allow for change but also to limit it.

These interests in controlling risk and uncertainty during democratization have repeatedly led to the adoption of rules of change that serve as "safeguards" against what elite groups and predemocratic parties see as the dangerous potential of popular majorities or the political leaders who claim to represent them. This chapter focuses on three such types of rules: electoral rules that affect party systems and the basic understanding of democracy; rules that limit the authority of elected leaders and assign certain areas of decision-making to constitutional courts, central banks, and other independent, ostensibly nonpolitical institutions; and rules entrenched in international treaties and transnational institutions that limit the policies of individual nation-states. Elite interests have sought to use all three types to entrench their power. They have used electoral rules to reduce the ability of radical parties to win power, countermajoritarian institutions to circumscribe the choices of the parties and leaders that do win elections, and international agreements to provide a backup level of protection against wayward states.

But while elite interests in entrenching power and policy have shaped these rules, they are not the entire explanation for the rules' development and do not necessarily define their ultimate significance. Limiting majoritarian power is a cause that unites minorities of many kinds: not only propertied elites but also marginalized ethnic groups, political dissenters, and others who fear ascendant majorities and the unfettered power of the state. Moreover, while rules have calculating authors, they often outlive both the authors and their calculations. Rules expected to reinforce power may have the opposite effect when economic and demographic conditions change. As we saw in the previous chapter, southerners at the Constitutional Convention in 1787 expected their states to grow more rapidly than others and consequently sought a decennial census to reapportion the House of Representatives and Electoral College. But that provision cost them control over the national government when the North raced ahead in population. By the time it becomes clear that a rule no longer works as expected, it may be too late: The rule may have become so entrenched, perhaps even sacralized, that its originators are stuck with it. What begins as the entrenchment of power through rules may lead to the entrenchment of the rules themselves.

Partly for that reason, even when rules originate in strategic calculations by the powerful, their entrenchment may come to reflect a more general interest. Concessions to elites during democratization may lead them to accept a regime they would otherwise oppose and disrupt. Their acceptance of change may thus produce a more "settled" path of democratization and a stronger and more effective democratic state.[2] Conservative in the sense of maintaining some interests in property and privilege, the design of democratic institutions may be more open-ended in its long-run consequences. It is not just liberal or progressive institutions and policies that have had unanticipated consequences. Strategies for entrenching power and limiting liberal and progressive possibilities also don't always work out as planned.

ENTRENCHMENT OF ELECTORAL RULES

The standard narrative of democracy from the eighteenth to the twentieth centuries is a story of falling barriers—falling barriers to voting participation by the disenfranchised, and to contestation by previously excluded parties and candidates. But the story has another side. During the same period when ruling parties and elites agreed to extend rights, they made other institutional changes that reduced their risks of losing power to radical parties of the left. Some of these changes then became lasting features of democratic governments, albeit not always with the originally expected effects.

Among the lasting innovations were changes in the rules that translate votes into representation. Although electoral systems come in many varieties, by the early twentieth century two types had emerged as the most common. In the system that still prevails in the United States and Britain, voters in a legislative district pick one representative, who needs only a plurality to be elected. These are single-member-district plurality systems, more commonly known as "first past the post." (In an important variant of single-member-district systems, the winner needs to receive a majority, and if no candidate does so in the first round, the top two compete in a runoff.) In contrast, under proportional representation (PR)—the system in use in about 80 percent of democracies with more than one million in population—parties receive a share of seats proportionate to the votes for the parties' candidates in multi-member districts.[3]

The two principal electoral systems are associated with different party systems. Single-member plurality creates an incentive for voters to choose a candidate of one of the two leading parties instead of "wasting" their vote on a third-party candidate, whereas PR allows voters to choose smaller parties without wasting their votes because the *electoral threshold*—the threshold for winning a seat—is lower. As a result, countries with single-member plurality typically have a two-party system (or one dominant party), while countries with PR generally have multiple parties—a pattern known as Duverger's law. Even though candidates under "first past the post" may win elections with less than a majority of votes, such systems are generally called "majoritarian" because elections usually deliver a majority of legislative seats to one party. In contrast, by providing more seats to minority parties, PR often yields no majority for any single party and requires the formation of governing coalitions.

The difference between majoritarian and proportional election rules influences a society's dominant understanding of democracy. The majoritarian conception sees democracy as a series of contests in which voters choose between two rival parties and give power to one or to the other, whereas voters in PR systems—"consensus democracies," in Arend Lijphart's phrase—generally understand that elections often lead to post-election bargaining and may enable minority parties to hold a share of power.[4] Social movements develop differently as well. In a majoritarian system, movements typically aim to influence at least one of the two major parties, if not both, while under PR they may more readily take the form of parties and compete in elections directly. The high threshold for unseating one of the two major parties in a majoritarian system means that the parties themselves tend to become more entrenched than parties do under PR. Even without any explicit constitutional recognition, much less protection, party systems may become highly resistant to change because of the forces set in motion by the choice of electoral rules.

It was during the nineteenth and early twentieth centuries that single-member plurality came to predominate in the United States and Britain, while proportional election rules spread in continental Europe. The first country to adopt PR was Belgium, in 1899, followed by Finland in 1906, Sweden in 1907, and a large number of western European countries shortly after World War I. The timing of these developments suggests a causal relationship between democratization and electoral system change, and indeed in some countries the same legislation expanded suffrage and changed electoral rules. The regional spread of PR, as well as the concentration of first-past-the-post in the English-speaking democracies, also suggests mutual influence among political parties and governments with cultural and political connections. Countries with electorally viable socialist parties were especially likely to shift to PR, though exactly why they did so is a matter of dispute. According to one view, just as elites agreed to expand voting rights as a concession to popular demands, so they adopted proportional rules as a concession to socialists. That view seems to fit with evidence that countries with PR later developed more highly redistributive welfare states.[5] But in fact, many socialist parties were opposed to PR or indifferent to it when it was first proposed. No single factor explains all the cases of electoral system change, and more than one set of conditions may lead to the same rules. In the most common pattern, PR was originally adopted by ruling elites as an exclusionary "safeguard" to reduce the impact of inclusive reforms.[6]

Before they had established universal manhood suffrage, most emerging democracies in western Europe contained a mix of multi-member and single-member districts, electing legislators under either plurality or majority rules. In many countries, as cities grew, governments added seats to existing urban districts, often leaving rural districts as the only ones with a single representative. But while increasing the number of seats per district in urban areas—sometimes up to a dozen or more—governments initially retained the rule that the party winning the district received all its seats.[7] This winner-take-all system took on special significance with the change in the electorate. The extension of the franchise to working-class voters and the rise of socialist parties posed a risk to governing elites that radical forces could gain power by sweeping winner-take-all urban districts.

In this context, a shift to either single-member districts or PR could help the existing elites maintain their power. Both systems would divide up representatives of urban areas. With single-member districts, the preexisting parties could prevail in the middle- and upper-class parts of a city, and under PR they would also win a share of a city's seats. In both cases, given their support outside of metropolitan areas, the established parties could prevent the socialists from taking power at the national level.[8]

The adoption of new electoral rules was part of a more general strategic shift by ruling elites in Europe in the nineteenth century. Just as they often banned unions, strikes, and radical publications, so they at first sought to exclude socialists altogether from legislative representation. When finally agreeing to expand voting rights, many leaders of established parties thought that they could win over workers, as the major parties in the United States had done. But as efforts to repress socialism failed and workers' parties entered the electoral arena on their own, the established parties shifted to strategies that would enable them to outcompete the insurgents. Initially, the winner-take-all multi-member districts had offered an optimal strategy for shutting out socialists entirely. Later, with the mass enfranchisement of working-class voters, winner-take-all in urban areas became too risky, and the established parties did away with it.

Belgium exemplifies how strategic considerations led to changes in electoral systems. Like the other early adopters of PR, the Belgian government was in the midst of democratization at the time it introduced new electoral rules. Although its 1831 constitution called for a representative government, as of the early 1890s Belgium still limited voting rights to only about one-tenth of adult men. The electoral system included single- as well as multi-member districts, the latter with up to eighteen representatives; elections were held under a winner-take-all majority rule, requiring a runoff if no party received a majority in the first round. In 1894, amid labor unrest, the government agreed to constitutional changes, giving nearly all adult men the right to vote while establishing a system of plural voting that awarded up to three votes each to men with more property or education—a measure plainly intended to limit the number of seats won by the radical, socialist Belgian Workers' Party. The assembly that approved this change also debated the merits of single-member districts and PR but could not agree on either one. In the first election under the new rules, the Catholic Party won 103 seats, while the Workers' Party won 28, displacing the Liberals as the second largest. By edging out the Liberals in urban areas in the first round, the Workers' Party became the main opposition party, and under the winner-take-all rules, it stood a chance some day of taking power. By 1898, with the Liberals close to extinction, the Catholic Party—still with an overwhelming majority—enacted a PR system (including the plural vote for the more affluent) that had the effect of restoring the Liberals as the principal opposition and enlarging the antisocialist legislative majority. The diminished Liberals naturally supported the measure, which brought them back to life, while the socialists voted unanimously against it. In effect, the Catholic Party sacrificed some of its own seats to revive an ideological ally in resisting the radical left.[9]

Aside from having rising socialist parties, all but two of the European countries that opted for PR shared another characteristic.

Like Belgium, they had single-member *majority* systems with run-offs, not single-member plurality. A system with a majority rule and runoffs initially helped deny seats to socialists by raising the electoral threshold and allowing supporters of the antisocialist parties to join together in the second round. But the interests of established parties flipped when the socialist opposition reached the point of winning majorities; now the antisocialist parties stood the risk of being shut out and saw PR as preferable. But unlike first-past-the-post, a majority rule with a second round had already fostered a multiparty system. When there is a runoff, smaller parties have an incentive to run in the first round and then try to obtain concessions in return for their endorsement in the second round. As of 1898, countries with majority rules and runoffs had on average more parties and were more likely to have coalition governments than countries with single-member plurality. These countries moved more readily to PR because they already had multiparty systems.[10] Historically, as one analyst of electoral rules points out, rather than rules determining party systems (Duverger's law), it was the other way around: "multi-party systems already existed in most countries when electoral systems of proportional representation were chosen."[11]

In the early twentieth century, a variety of minority parties supported PR in the hope of gaining a share of power. Consequently, PR often gained support from diverse coalitions, sometimes including socialists. Switzerland, one of the many countries to adopt PR in the wave that followed World War I, exemplifies this pattern. In the face of a long-standing Liberal Party monopoly on power in the national government, two minority parties—Socialists and conservative Catholics—joined together in a strange-bedfellows alliance to support PR and finally succeeded in establishing it through a popular referendum in 1919.[12]

PR's attraction to minority groups and minority parties is that it offers them a direct parliamentary voice and a chance of holding power in a coalition government. Not only do multiparty systems incline countries toward PR; the parties have strong incentives to resist shifting to majoritarianism. But the politics that results from PR may also change the parties. While PR did not succeed in excluding socialists from government, it helped moderate their revolutionary ambitions. The coalition governments that grew up under PR in western Europe often fostered cross-class alliances and economic arrangements for collaboration between business and labor.[13] The historical evidence does not suggest these were factors in the origin of PR, but they were significant in its entrenchment and in the reconciliation of capitalism and democracy in many countries.

So why did majoritarianism and two-party systems become entrenched in the United States, Britain, and many other English-speaking democracies? The diffusion of institutional models and mutual influence among countries with a shared political heritage may help explain the adoption of similar electoral rules, but such considerations can take us only so far with the countries that have served as primary exemplars—the United States and Britain.

Although Americans now take single-member districts for granted, the Constitution does not prescribe any system for elections to the U.S. House of Representatives. From 1790 to 1840, states had a combination of single- and multi-member districts, and one-quarter of the states used the "general ticket"—that is, a state's representatives to the House were all elected at large on a party ticket in a winner-take-all election (the method still used for the Electoral College by all but two states). Not until 1842 did Congress require states to elect representatives from single-member districts. At the time, the Whigs were in control of Congress but were staring at a likely defeat in the midterm elections. With single-member districts, they could at least hope to win some of the seats in what would otherwise be solid Democratic delegations. As it turned out, this short-term political engineering was a failure: The Whigs were crushed in 1842, with some of the Democratic states still using the general ticket in defiance of the federal law and able to get their representatives seated in the new Congress thanks to its Democratic majority. But when the House changed hands again, the recalcitrant states fell into line for fear of having their representatives turned away.[14]

Although parties with congressional majorities in later years might have gained advantage by eliminating the single-member district system, it has had powerful self-reinforcing effects. Unlike the at-large representatives elected on a "general ticket," the representatives of single-member districts have incentives to perform local constituent services and may be better able to accumulate seniority, thanks in part to the states' use of gerrymandering in periodic redistricting. These considerations may help explain why states adopted different rules for the Electoral College than for Congress. Neither constituent service nor seniority is relevant in the Electoral College, where nearly all states have kept the general ticket, winner-take-all system to maximize their influence in presidential elections. If a radical, socialist party in nineteenth-century America had threatened to win pluralities across the country in enough congressional districts and states, and if instead of first-past-the-post, American elections had followed a majority rule with runoffs, the United States might have developed a multiparty system and then responded as those parties did in Europe by introducing PR. But the established parties never faced a serious socialist threat, and only a few jurisdictions adopted a majority rule with runoff elections, so no pressure arose for PR.

In Britain, as in the United States, the single-member-district system also owes its modern form to short-term political engineering in the 1800s, although Britain has come close to changing its election rules several times. Until 1885, it had a mix of single- and multi-member parliamentary districts, the latter having up to four representatives. When a Conservative government in 1867 expanded the franchise, it included a provision for the "limited ballot" in multi-member districts (fewer ballots per voter than seats available). The ostensible reason was to give fair representation to minority parties, but the legislation applied the limited ballot only to urban constituencies typically dominated by Liberals, thereby giving Conservatives a better chance to win some seats. Meanwhile, the limited ballot did not apply to rural constituencies, which were held by Conservatives. In 1885, when it was the Liberals' turn to expand the franchise, they used the opportunity to abolish multi-member districts entirely. By this time, PR had prominent advocates in Britain, who argued for it chiefly as a means of improving minority representation. But it was rejected in the 1885 and several subsequent electoral reforms, often on the grounds that single-member plurality produces more decisive and effective government precisely because it turns a narrow edge in votes into a clear majority of seats.[15]

The established parties in Britain, unlike the United States, did face a challenge from an electorally viable socialist party. After an alliance with the Liberals, the trade union movement entered the electoral arena with its own candidates just after the turn of the twentieth century, and in the early 1920s, the Labour Party overtook the Liberals without triggering a move away from single-member plurality. Two factors help explain the persistence of the old electoral rules. Compared with the more radical socialist parties in continental Europe, Labour presented less of a threat to the existing order. The Liberals also simply miscalculated. They could have instituted PR while in power, but they suffered a catastrophic split and an unexpected, precipitous decline after World War I. What happened at that point illustrates how single-member plurality rules can withstand party change. Although Labour had previously supported PR, it reneged on its commitment once the party moved ahead of the Liberals in the 1922 election and Labour's leaders saw how they could benefit from a majoritarian system. In 1924, when the Liberals in Parliament finally voted nearly unanimously in favor of PR, Labour provided the margin of defeat by voting by more than three to one against it.[16] Reneging on commitments to electoral reform has been a recurrent pattern in British parties after they have won parliamentary majorities.[17]

Just as the multiple parties under PR oppose any shift to majoritarianism, so the top two parties under majoritarian rules typically have no interest in changing to PR, which would enable third and fourth parties to gain traction or dissatisfied groups in their own ranks to split off and run on their own. It should not be surprising, therefore, that change in electoral systems is relatively infrequent, though not impossible. Data on democratic governments over the past two centuries suggest that shifts from majoritarianism to proportional representation are more common than the reverse.[18] In recent years, mixed-member proportional systems (with elements of both single-member districts and proportional representation) have spread, and most of the countries adopting these hybrid arrangements have previously had majoritarian systems (or in some cases dictatorships).[19] As a result, the proportional principle has gained at the expense of majoritarianism.

This shift toward proportionality may reflect several developments. The first is a wider acceptance of minority rights and an effort to avert conflict in ethnically divided societies by giving minorities direct legislative representation. A second factor is risk aversion among leaders of political parties during transitions from authoritarianism. Single-member plurality is a high-stakes bet: Parties can win or lose in a big way because the system tends to exaggerate wins and losses. If three or more parties are electorally viable with roughly equal prospects at the moment a democratic constitution is being drafted, a majoritarian system is risky for all of them because of the sharp fall-off in seats for any party that comes in third or lower, possibly because of how its support is spread geographically. Under those conditions, PR is safer from the standpoint of political survival.[20] Widespread public dissatisfaction with two dominant parties can also destabilize a majoritarian system, as it did in New Zealand, which in 1993 replaced single-member plurality with a mixed-member proportional system through a popular referendum.[21]

The United States is a curious case. The American political system has been plagued by a variety of rules regarding ballot access, districting, primaries, and other features of elections that have helped protect incumbents.[22] As in New Zealand before its change-over, public opinion polls register high levels of dissatisfaction with both major parties, but Americans have virtually no experience with PR at any level of government. If proportional and mixed systems continue to spread around the world, including possibly to Britain, the United States could someday be the last great redoubt of first-past-the-post.

The entrenchment of electoral systems illustrates a larger point. Although parties historically used changes in electoral systems for strategic purposes in efforts to entrench themselves in power, they were not wholly successful. In the United States, the Whigs in 1842 failed to prevent electoral disaster; European conservative parties failed to keep socialists out of government. What has become entrenched has primarily been the structure of electoral and party systems and prevailing conceptions of democracy. It is the entire complex of institutions and corresponding norms and beliefs that makes an electoral system resistant to change. If partisan advantage alone led to changes in electoral systems, governing parties would have changed the systems far more often than they have. At least in this respect, the long-established democracies have fulfilled liberal democracy's demand for the entrenchment of rules rather than power.

COUNTER-MAJORITARIAN ENTRENCHMENT: SUPREME COURTS AND CENTRAL BANKS

Not every aspect of a democratic government is up for grabs in elections, at least not immediately. In exercising their powers, elected leaders usually face limits entrenched in constitutions, independent or semiautonomous branches and agencies of government, and international agreements. These limits are instances of strategic entrenchment insofar as they stem from earlier decisions about institutional design that deliberately made certain rules, powers, and structures hard to undo. In liberal states, some of these entrenched limits serve as counter-majoritarian safeguards—that is, efforts to protect minorities from the unfettered power of the majority. The minorities in question are again a heterogeneous category that may include propertied elites as well as ethnic or political minorities. Partly for this reason, some of the factors that enter into the choice of proportional electoral systems also affect the development of counter-majoritarian institutions.

In the standard narrative of democracy, constitutional protections of minority rights emerged as part of the general expansion of rights, including the right to vote. But as with electoral rules, the story has another side. Just as incumbent parties responded to uncertainty and threats of decline by changing electoral rules, so they have adopted counter-majoritarian safeguards to reduce the risks to privilege and power posed by ascendant majorities. The historical development of two institutions—constitutional courts and independent central banks—exemplifies the logic of counter-majoritarian entrenchment.

If it is solely up to political leaders to determine what a constitution means, they face no institutional impediment to interpreting it however they wish. A supreme or constitutional court with powers of judicial review is supposed to impose constitutional fidelity and restraint, and thereby fulfill the promise of an entrenched constitution and rule of law. Constitutional rules are more firmly entrenched where amendments require the approval not just of one legislative chamber but of two, and not just by a majority but by a supermajority; and where they must also be approved by majorities or supermajorities of constituent state or provincial legislatures or by popular referendum. The greater the number of veto players, the greater is the rigidity of a constitution.[23] Requiring a legislative body to approve amendments in two successive sessions has some of the same effect in constraining constitutional change. To be sure, constitutional entrenchment doesn't always prevent rules from being reinterpreted (especially where, as I suggested in the previous chapter, they concern general principles rather than express procedures for the machinery of government). In countries with constitutional courts and judicial review, judges may be able to change constitutional doctrine, and political leaders may do so through judicial appointments. As in other areas, entrenched rules impede or constrain political change but do not necessarily stop it.

Like judicial review, the independence of central banks takes decisions out of political hands and depends critically on the rules governing the appointment and tenure of the institution's decision-makers, as well as their authority to make policy without being politically overruled. In the case of central banks, that authority primarily involves monetary policy. The banks' legal mandate often commits them solely to the goal of price stability, and even where it includes other aims, such as full employment (as it does in the United States), central bankers tend to give higher priority than do political leaders to low inflation. Central bank independence entrenches that preference.

The origins of constitutional entrenchment and central bank independence date to late seventeenth- and eighteenth-century England and America and are closely connected to the emergence of constitutional liberalism. Internationally, however, the spread of constitutional courts and independent central banks took place mainly in the twentieth century during the wave of democratization after World War II, and especially during the larger wave from the late 1970s to the 1990s. In the international diffusion of any institution, the causes are not necessarily the same for the early and late adopters, in part because of the influence of countries in the lead on those that follow. In the cases of judicial review and central bank independence, the late adopters were influenced not only by the early adopters' example but by the pressure of international institutions.

Until World War II, the only countries with flourishing systems of judicial review were the United States, Canada, and Australia, a pattern that led some observers to identify judicial review with federalism. On this theory, a supreme court's distinctive function was to referee conflicts between a national government and its subdivisions. Judicial review later spread, however, to non-federal governments. After 1945, four major countries adopted it—three of them (Japan, West Germany, and Italy) as a direct consequence of being defeated by the United States and its allies, and one of them (India) in the process of decolonization. In the last third of the twentieth century, judicial review expanded worldwide. During the transitions from authoritarianism and communism between the 1970s and early 1990s, many new governments and some older ones adopted constitutional courts in a global trend toward constitutional entrenchment of rights and greater judicial power.[24]

In the same period, an increase in central bank independence paralleled the rise of constitutional courts. Central banks date to the seventeenth century; Sweden's was founded in 1668, followed by the Bank of England in 1694. The United States saw two early national banks overturned in the nineteenth century before Congress established the Federal Reserve in 1913. Until the late twentieth century, most governments lodged central banking functions in finance or treasury departments under direct executive control. The shift to greater central bank independence began in the late 1980s; during the 1990s, fifty-four countries adopted laws making their central banks more independent, while only one (Malta) did the opposite.[25] Between 1989 and 2003, according to the widely used Cukierman index (based on statutes), the average level of central bank independence doubled from 0.3 to 0.6.[26]

The similarities in the history of judicial review and central bank independence suggest a two-level process: first, their development in a few countries on the basis of internal processes, and then the international diffusion of those models. The internal conditions that led to judicial review and central bank independence have generally been explained in two ways. One of these sees counter-majoritarian entrenchment as a form of *political insurance* for elites facing risk and uncertainty. The other views counter-majoritarian institutions as a means of *credible commitment* that fosters mutual gains and general benefits to a society.

The reduction of political risks is central to both of these theories. In the political insurance theory, the risks are to a party or elite that is uncertain of its future power. The logic here is similar to the rationale for changing electoral rules during democratization. At moments of political change, entrenchment through constitutional courts and central banks insures against the risk that the opposition will gain power through elections. The basic argument goes as follows: If a party or elite believes its power to be insecure and sees its potential successors as a threat, it is more likely to seek to entrench its power and policies through the redesign of institutions that critically affect its own interests and those of its supporters. In contrast, if an elite or party is confident of remaining in power through ordinary politics, it is less likely to seek to create constitutional or other institutional mechanisms to impede ordinary political processes. Indeed, if the incumbent party remains in office, its leaders would sacrifice the advantages of direct political control by empowering potentially troublesome independent decision-makers in courts and central banks.

Versions of the insurance theory appear in analyses of both judicial review and central bank independence. The adoption of new constitutions with judicial review during transitions from authoritarianism to democracy fits readily into this framework. Explicitly formulating the insurance theory, Tom Ginsburg points to the "time horizons of those politicians drafting the constitution" as the critical factor. Those who see themselves as winning elections are "likely to design institutions without encumbrance," whereas prospective losers will prefer to "entrench judicial review as a form of political insurance." The appeal of judicial review is that it offers "an alternative forum to challenge government action."[27] The same logic applies to shifts toward judicial entrenchment in countries experiencing transfers of political power short of a regime change. In a study of four such cases—Canada, Israel, New Zealand, and

South Africa—Ran Hirschl argues that after previously rejecting a formal constitution or judicial review, elites altered their positions as their electoral prospects fell. The South African case is a good example. Under apartheid, the dominant National Party had no interest in establishing a constitution with a bill of rights; it preferred a system of parliamentary sovereignty, exclusively under white control. But as the party saw its electoral fortunes decline, it discovered the virtues of constitutional entrenchment.[28]

The same patterns appear in analyses of the sources of central bank independence. Even conservative leaders prefer direct control when their power is secure, but when they fear for their future, they are inclined to favor an independent central bank to "bind the hands of their inflation-prone successors."[29] In Chile during the 1970s and early 1980s, the Pinochet government retained control over monetary policy even though the free-market economists who influenced the government's other economic policies advocated an independent central bank. Not until a 1988 plebiscite confronted the government with a future when it would "no longer be in charge" did it seek to "safeguard its interests by enacting a constitutional amendment to create a highly autonomous central bank."[30]

While the insurance theory sees parties and elites adopting counter-majoritarian institutions to limit the risks of losing power, the credible-commitment theory views the state, or a dominant party, as rationally tying its own hands for the sake of larger gains. The basic argument is that constitutions and other entrenched constraints on political leaders serve as credible commitments to stable legal rules and are therefore conducive to economic development. In the paradigmatic historical case study developing the theory, Douglass North and Barry Weingast argue that the political institutions that emerged from the Revolution of 1688 fostered England's economic growth. Before 1688, in a pattern typical of unconstrained sovereigns, the Stuart monarchs opportunistically reneged on commitments to repay loans and arbitrarily seized assets, undermining the security of property rights and limiting the government's access to capital markets. The 1688 revolution, however, established parliamentary supremacy and the independence of the judiciary, credibly committing the government to limits on the use of its power. The Crown was barred from raising taxes without

Parliament's approval, and judges, instead of serving at the king's pleasure, could be removed only for a criminal offense or by action of Parliament. Not only did the division of powers among branches of government increase the number of veto players capable of checking abuses of power; the government also created a private constraint on itself by establishing an independent central bank. In 1694, seeking subscribers for a new loan, the government invited them to incorporate as a bank—the Bank of England—which then became responsible for handling all loans to the government. If the government failed to meet its obligations, it would have difficulty getting access to funds from a current loan. The new institutional structure enabled the English state to raise far more money than before on the capital markets, which were, in turn, greatly stimulated in private lending as well. Stable legal rules thereby reduced the interest rates paid by the English state and contributed to the private economy's expansion.[31] Without a doubt, England would not have enjoyed such good credit if it had not also raised taxes substantially (in fact, by 600 percent from 1688 to 1783) to meet its obligations, but the state's ability to collect those taxes partly reflected the legitimacy it gained from parliamentary approval of taxes and scrutiny of the public accounts.[32]

The political-insurance and credible-commitment theories overlap in that both see counter-majoritarian institutions as a response to political uncertainty. They differ in their predictions, however, when a dominant party does not need the cooperation of other parties and expects to remain in power. Under those circumstances, the insurance theory predicts a low likelihood of entrenchment (why should the dominant party accept any constraints?), whereas the credible-commitment theory may plausibly predict a higher probability of entrenchment (the dominant party may be more likely to capture systemic benefits than when power is diffused). Cross-national data on judicial review provide modest support for the insurance position.[33] In addition, several of the case studies that highlight the *timing* of decisions about central bank independence and judicial review favor the political-insurance position: Regimes or parties with a firm grip on power have repeatedly shown no interest in creating independent central banks or constitutional courts until their power begins slipping away.

But while the political-insurance theory may better explain the decision to establish counter-majoritarian institution, the credible-commitment theory may be highly relevant to their reinforcement and spread. In the English case, lower interest rates contributed to the state's ability to carry more debt, most of it war-related. Credible commitments to self-restraint (in relation to asset holders at home, not necessarily anyone else!) thereby augmented England's military power as well as its economy, enabling it to extend its empire and institutions around the world. Constitutional limitation can become a formula for increasing state power: limited power is sometimes more powerful than unlimited power. Just as individuals may increase their overall power by committing to certain rules of conduct (thereby foregoing opportunistic gains at the expense of others), so governments can become more powerful through enforced self-restraint.[34] To be sure, even after the Revolution of 1688, England was not a democracy, so its institutional innovations cannot be described as counter-majoritarian (the entire government was counter-majoritarian). But by strengthening judges' independence, creating a central bank, and passing a Declaration of Rights, England established a model for counter-majoritarian entrenchment in democratic regimes. Not only did the entrenchment of power lead to the entrenchment of rules, the reverse occurred as well: constitutionally entrenched rules furthered the entrenchment of power, with consequences that extended beyond a single nation-state.

Judicial review and central bank independence have also spread worldwide through international processes. Institutions may diffuse from one country to another because the first coerces the second, or the second learns from the first. States may adopt the same institutions as they compete with rivals for investment, or because transnational organizations or professional communities elevate a model into a universal standard and make adhering to it a condition for membership, loans, and other benefits.[35]

Counter-majoritarian institutions have spread through all these mechanisms, especially through chains of influence. The United States sought to copy the Bank of England in the early development of national banks. Later, the American development of judicial review and central bank independence influenced their adoption in other countries, including Germany while it was under military occupation after World War II. The Bundesbank and the German constitutional court in turn influenced the establishment of the European Central Bank and constitutional review in the European Court of Justice. Competitive and normative pressures came especially into play in the accelerated spread of these institutional forms late in the twentieth century. During the 1990s, the constitutions drawn up for post-communist countries all included "at least a paper provision for a constitutional court with the power of judicial review."[36] Central bank independence followed a similar pattern as it became widely accepted by the early 1990s, even by left-wing parties. By then, the prevailing view among economists was that independence for a central bank increases price stability without impairing economic growth.[37] International financial institutions came to expect central bank independence as a sign of creditworthiness.[38] Global and regional factors dominated domestic ones in this "revolution" in monetary policy-making institutions.[39]

Political uncertainty in the late twentieth century was strongly related to the timing of counter-majoritarian entrenchment. During transitions from authoritarianism to democracy, when the design of institutions is in play, neither the departing elites nor any of the new groups forming parties may be entirely confident that they will emerge and remain the winners.[40] A stable, dominant party at that point—the condition leading to no counter-majoritarian entrenchment, according to the insurance theory—is therefore relatively unlikely. Entrenching a bargain among the various parties may satisfy them when they peer into the future through the veil of ignorance that large-scale political change often creates.

Uncertainty alone, however, cannot explain the specific institutions that spread in the late twentieth century. Earlier periods of high political uncertainty did not typically result in the entrenchment of judicial review and central bank independence. At times of institutional choice—constitutive moments—ideas become critically important, and in the late twentieth century, the ideas were liberal democratic with a distinct neoliberal slant. Although not exclusively American, they reflected the legitimacy that these responses to political uncertainty enjoyed in an era when the United States was the dominant international power and exerted influence (and sometimes pressure) both directly and via international organizations.[41]

In that global context, both high levels of internal political uncertainty and high exposure to foreign influences through trade, investment, and linkages to transnational civil society created favorable conditions for the establishment of counter-majoritarian institutions. Many regimes that had been hostile to internal constraints now accepted them as a necessary precondition of international legitimacy. Like the internal interest in counter-majoritarian entrenchment, the external interest originated from a concern about threats posed by ascendant majorities and leaders claiming to represent them. Domestic political elites in the late twentieth century were not alone in insisting on credible commitments to political rights, property rights, and price stability and to the establishment of judicial review and central banks as insurance policies against electoral uncertainties and limits on decision-making by elected leaders.[42] Of course, many governments made only "paper provisions" for counter-majoritarian domestic institutions. But international treaties and other agreements backed up these institutions, serving as yet another level of entrenchment.

ENTRENCHMENT THROUGH INTERNATIONAL TREATIES

Just as elected political leaders face limits to their power entrenched in constitutions and agencies of their own government, so too they face limits created by international regimes. Treaties, transnational organizations, and trade and loan agreements impose conditions and obligations on states that often make specific policies hard to reverse and thereby constrain political leaders. Some of these conditions are imposed one-sidedly on weaker states by a hegemon or alliance of dominant powers, sometimes at the end of a war. Other constraints arise through more evenly balanced agreements that are structured to be difficult to undo by all parties. Constraints also arise out of a third situation: the very insecurity of a government may lead it to seek binding international agreements. A nation's leaders may enter into international agreements or organizations in a deliberate effort to entrench a policy or institutional arrangement at home, knowing that once their government signs and ratifies a treaty it will become difficult for their successors to get out of it. In other words, rather than just being unwillingly subject to pressure, political leaders may invite constraints as a means of entrenching policies against potential domestic opposition or subsequent political change. As Robert Keohane writes, "A major strategic problem that any programmatically committed democratic government faces ... is how to ensure that its policies are perpetuated after it has left office. ... Policies that are incorporated in international agreements are much more difficult for future governments to alter." A policy is entrenched through an international institution if the latter prevents a government from abandoning a policy when the government or its preferences change—for example, because of new circumstances that lead those in power to see the policy as no longer in their interest.[43]

International agreements vary in their legal status, from statements of mutual understanding with no legal force to treaties that are incorporated into a country's domestic law. What begins as a treaty may evolve historically into a constitution. The Articles of Confederation, ratified in 1781 as the United States was still fighting for its independence, was more like a treaty among the states than a constitution. In contrast, the agreement signed in Philadelphia in 1787 and ratified the following year was a constitution by virtue of the stronger government it created for the "Union," as it properly came to be known. Western European countries started down a similar path after World War II, when they established the Common Market and common standards of human rights, which led to the Treaty on European Union in 1993 and the creation of European citizenship and European law. But the EU is not a union in the American sense; exit is an option if a country is willing to bear the costs (as Britain may if it carries out its 2016 referendum to leave). Although the provisions entrenched in the European constitutional order represent constraints on the policies of individual member states, they are much weaker constraints than in a unified federal government.[44]

The origins of European human-rights law illustrate how entrenchment through treaties serves as political insurance, providing a backup to domestic constitutional guarantees and an additional forum beyond the nation for groups that see their rights as threatened domestically. Negotiated under the Council of Europe during 1949–50, the European Convention on Human Rights (ECHR) is the source of authority for the European Court of Human Rights, established in 1959. Most of the Council of Europe's forty-seven member states have not only accepted the ECHR but made it part of their domestic law. Contrary to what one might expect, its leading proponents were not the dominant powers and long-standing liberal governments but instead new democracies attempting to entrench preferred policies in the face of uncertainty.[45]

Most international agreements, however, are not entrenched through constitutionalization. A nation's leaders may nonetheless still observe an agreement that no longer serves their interests if the costs of abrogating it are enough of a deterrent. Those costs may come from direct retaliation by other parties for breaching the agreement, indirect costs of noncompliance such as costs to reputation, and adverse domestic reactions. Indeed, these three responses may follow in sequence—retaliation for breaches creating immediate direct costs and stirring up adverse reactions at home.

The development of free-trade agreements from the 1930s to the 1980s illustrates this entrenchment process. In the United States during the nineteenth and early twentieth centuries, trade policy divided the two major parties. The Republicans favored protectionist policies and, as the dominant party after the Civil War, were able to entrench a high-tariff regime; the Democrats, as the party of free trade, sought to cut tariffs but could make only small modifications. High tariffs were self-reinforcing; they favored the growth of industries that benefited from protection, and those industries then exerted pressure to maintain the policy. The regime was entrenched until 1933, when a unified Democratic government under Franklin D. Roosevelt passed the Reciprocal Trade Agreements Act, giving the executive branch power to reduce certain tariffs in exchange for other countries' reductions of trade barriers. Though its effects were initially limited, the legislation set in motion a series of institutional changes that ultimately entrenched a free-trade regime. From then on, abrogating reciprocal agreements would have significant economic and political costs: retaliatory protectionist measures by trading partners and domestic mobilization of export-oriented interests, which grew stronger over time as a result of free-trade agreements.[46] Multilateral trade agreements impose greater constraints on reversibility. As Keohane writes of the post–World War II General Agreement on Tariffs and Trade: "One effect of reaching multilateral trade agreements is to bind mutual concessions, thus making these tariff-cutting exercises difficult for future governments to reverse."[47]

By the 1980s, however, the development of free trade had entered a distinctly different phase as governments began to use trade agreements as a means of entrenching market-oriented domestic economic policies. International trade had grown steadily and substantially under the Bretton Woods Agreement negotiated in 1948, but the terms of that agreement excluded major industries and gave individual countries the means of limiting the domestic impact of trade. Under the influence of the views variously known as the Washington Consensus, market fundamentalism, and neoliberalism, these continuing limits on free trade came under attack in new rounds of trade negotiations. The advent of the World Trade Organization (WTO) in 1995 signaled a major shift from "shallow" to "deep" economic integration. Shallow integration had not demanded much of domestic policy, but under deep integration, government regulations could be ruled an impermissible restriction on trade. Trade policy trumped domestic policy. Now it became not only more difficult for individual countries to erect trade barriers to protect domestic interests; corporations seeking the elimination of environmental and other forms of regulation could use the WTO to do an end-run around their domestic political opponents. Entrenching rules at the international level made them difficult to reverse through electoral politics.[48]

The interaction between developments abroad and those at home is critical for international human-rights law as well, though here the prospects for entrenchment have depended on domestic support. Unlike treaties that regulate the conduct of states toward one another, human rights treaties regulate the conduct of states toward their own citizens or other persons under their power. Consequently, direct retaliation by other states for failure to comply is far less likely than with trade or security agreements. Though often dismissed as lacking enforcement, the human rights treaties pose the same question as constitutional protections: Why do governments accept such limits, and when do they observe them? Under traditional concepts of national sovereignty, governments were not internationally accountable for their human rights abuses. The Universal Declaration of Human Rights, adopted by the United Nations in 1948, marked the beginning of a shift, though it was not legally enforceable. But a series of treaties regarding genocide, torture, civil rights, women's rights, and children's rights adopted since World War II are legally binding on nations that ratify them. Like constitutional rights and judicial review, formal commitments to international human-rights treaties have spread to governments that ratify them as a matter of "window dressing." But the more a nation is tied into the global economy and civil society, the more likely a treaty commitment results in improved human rights practices. A key factor is the effect of such treaties on transnational organizations and domestic political mobilization.[49]

Entrenchment at the international level favors liberal democratic values only insofar as liberal democracies dominate international institutions and promote abroad the principles they are constitutionally bound to uphold at home. Those commitments have been eroding for nearly two decades. In contrast to the earlier pressures on governments to protect human rights, the new international security regime established after the attacks on the United States on September 11, 2001, required governments to expand surveillance and control. A United Nations Security Council resolution requiring member states to criminalize terrorism and to change their laws accordingly became a convenient way for some countries to justify repression.[50] With the election of Donald Trump in 2016, the United States has effectively reversed even the limited previous efforts it took to uphold liberal democratic values elsewhere in the world.

The use of international institutions to entrench free-market policies has also grown weaker and even backfired, damaging the very idea of a rules-based international order. Populist parties and governments in many countries have portrayed the policies as violations of their national sovereignty and denounced the civil-society and political groups that supported them as puppets of foreign powers. The rise of populist and illiberal governments is now putting both liberal internationalism and neoliberal economic policies to a test that will determine just how deeply entrenched they are.

The path to a consolidated democracy—the entrenchment of democracy itself—is strewn with obstacles. Even after a democratic government is established, elite and popular discontent may bring back authoritarianism by any of several means, including the seizure of power by a single leader or party, a revolutionary insurgency, or a military coup. Democracies die from internal conflicts along racial, ethnic, and religious lines and from opposition fanned by old elites unreconciled to the new regime. Consequently, democracies not only use constitutionally entrenched rules to limit the entrenchment of power; they also, to some degree, entrench the power of minority interests to minimize the risk that those interests will disrupt or undo a democratic settlement. All the institutions discussed in this chapter can be understood in this light.

Here a comparison with the consolidation of revolutionary dictatorships, such as those in the Soviet Union, China, and North Korea, may be instructive. Revolutionary regimes, Steven Levitsky and Lucan Way write, "can survive for many decades despite intense external pressure, poor economic performance, and large-scale policy failures." One source of their durability is that the violent struggles at their origin resulted in "the destruction (or substantial weakening) of alternative centers of power," including the killing, exile, or expropriation of previous ruling elites.[51] Since democratic regimes, in contrast, generally do not emerge from violent struggles that eliminate prior elites, they often face a continued challenge from those elites and the alternative centers of power they represent.

The prospects for democratic consolidation hinge in significant degree on whether those elites accept the new regime or at least do not try to reverse democratic changes. Reassurance of the right has therefore often been crucial to successful transitions from authoritarianism. To state it plainly: If conservative elites believe left-wing radicals are under control and their own conservative party has a reasonable chance of electoral success, they may decide to live with democracy; if not, they turn to authoritarianism.[52] Concessions to property have been the price for democracy.

During the late twentieth century, liberalizing movements and parties often used guarantees to privileged elites to win support from an authoritarian regime's "soft-liners" and to discourage them from defecting back to authoritarianism later on. In their work on transitions in southern Europe and Latin America in the 1970s and early 1980s, Guillermo O'Donnell and Philippe Schmitter argue that prospects for democracy improved when the opposition proceeded "on the installment plan" through bargaining that elicited cooperation from authoritarian elites, often through "pacts" that protected their "vital interests." When those agreements led to founding elections, according to O'Donnell and Schmitter, democracy was more likely if the left did not win a smashing victory.[53] In general, others argue, democratic consolidation is more likely when there are "institutions that place limits on pro-majoritarian policies."[54] Guarantees to elites associated with a prior authoritarian regime include both "diffuse" protections such as constitutionally entrenched property rights and "targeted" protections to elites such as the military, affording them institutional autonomy and power as well as immunity from prosecution for earlier crimes.[55]

Similarly, constitutional guarantees contribute to democratic consolidation if they offer protection to ethnic minorities and minority parties fearful of majoritarian power. Proportional representation makes it easier for minorities to win legislative representation and gain a direct political voice. An independent judiciary to enforce constitutional rights may be especially important if the electoral system is majoritarian. When ethnic or religious minorities are geographically concentrated, federalism may serve to protect their rights.[56] In all these cases, constitutionally entrenched inclusiveness offers minorities—whether propertied elites or historically disadvantaged groups—a guarantee against the risk that the majority will renege on its promises to respect minority rights. When a government signs a human rights treaty or joins a transnational organization such as the EU, it may provide a further guarantee. Elected democratic leaders may use international agreements to ensure that liberal principles are entrenched domestically when they are no longer in office.

But the use of any of these mechanisms has mixed possibilities. The entrenchment of policies in international agreements may undermine democratic government by hamstringing economic policy in damaging ways, or merely by lending plausibility to populist accusations that a liberal government has conceded sovereignty to foreign powers or international financial interests. The central bank, courts, and other autonomous agencies may become so powerful as to confine democratic institutions to a narrow range of policies. In the extreme case, the elites that dominated an old regime may exercise de facto control over the new one and make a sham of democracy.

As much as democracies need counter-majoritarian institutions, they also need counter-oligarchic ones. No problem is more difficult for democracies than the entrenched power of concentrated wealth. Eighteenth-century republicans believed that by changing the rules of inheritance, they could bring the political power of concentrated landed wealth under control. The opponents of slavery in antebellum America sought to deny the Slave Power its sway over the nation. Both of those groups succeeded in their immediate goals, yet the fundamental problem remained. Limiting the political power of wealth may seem to present endless difficulties—but wealth has not always had its way. In the next chapter, I turn to the historical developments in the mid-twentieth century that limited the power of concentrated wealth and, in some respects, entrenched progressive and egalitarian policies.

CHAPTER FIVE

Entrenching Progressive Change

CAPITALISM AND DEMOCRACY CONTINUALLY pose stress tests for each other. Economic crises unsettle politics, while popular movements and charismatic or merely capricious leaders unsettle the stable conditions that business counts on government to provide. Pressure for guarantees of security has come from both directions. Just as elites have sought to entrench property rights and other safeguards of their interests in constitutional law and counter-majoritarian institutions, so the advocates of egalitarian policies have sought to make social rights and protections irrevocable. Neither side has entirely had its way: Entrenched wealth has frustrated progressives, as entrenched forms of redistribution have frustrated conservatives. But for a time in the mid-twentieth century, it seemed as though the tensions between capitalism and democracy had found a resolution. During the thirty years of prosperity after World War II, many observers pronounced the modern welfare state to be an irreversible fact, conclusive refutation of the old dire predictions of increasing misery and relentless class strife under capitalism.

The decades from the 1940s to the early 1970s now stand out as a time of peak economic equality in the advanced capitalist democracies, when "growth with equity" was more than a slogan. While inequalities narrowed, governments took on responsibilities for economic performance and maintained high taxes on top incomes. With rising productivity, low unemployment, and the maturing of modern welfare state programs, conditions improved substantially for people who previously were counted among the poor. Beginning in the mid-1970s, however, as the advanced economies confronted spiraling inflation, reduced growth, and de-industrialization, political power shifted to the right. Market incomes became more unequal, governments cut taxes on the top brackets, and welfare policies came under attack.

Accounts of this reversal have generally followed two lines of analysis. One emphasizes the structural economic and social changes associated with the shift toward a post-industrial economy; the other foregrounds the ideological changes associated with neoliberalism. The two are not mutually exclusive, even though they may be presented that way. In the first view, de-industrialization and the shift toward a post-industrial economy undermined the political foundations of the welfare state. The turn toward neoliberalism, according to some versions of the second account, has been nothing short of a transformation in "the world's political economic framework," in which markets have supplanted the state through policies favoring privatization, deregulation, and welfare-state retrenchment.[1] In this view, ideological change has driven a radical political shift undermining social protection and increasing inequality.

Yet the trends since the mid-1970s have been more varied than this picture of a neoliberal revolution suggests. Rather than falling as a percentage of gross domestic product (GDP), public expenditures in the advanced capitalist societies have either leveled off or risen. According to estimates by the economic historian Peter Lindert, the net impact of taxes and spending has become more progressive.[2] While deregulating their economies in some respects, both the United States and European Union have seen considerable increases in other forms of regulation, much of it in the interest of greater social equality, such as rules barring discrimination by race, gender, sexual orientation, age, or disability. Regulation of the environment and of consumer health and safety, only minimally developed as of the mid-1970s, has vastly expanded.

These mixed developments pose a challenge for understanding the entrenchment of progressive policy ("progressive" in a distributive sense, favoring greater equality). On the whole, capital has gained power relative to labor over the past forty years. After rising during the early postwar decades, labor's average share of national income fell from 73 percent in 1980 to 64 percent in 2005, according to a study of sixteen leading economies.[3] Yet many of the forms of redistribution established in the heyday of the twentieth-century welfare state have survived or even grown. The entrenchment of progressive institutions only in part reflects strategic choices made by earlier political leaders with the conscious intention of making their reforms difficult to undo. Most such policies have been enacted through ordinary legislation and could be changed or repealed the same way. Although many countries, as well as the European Union, have written social rights into their constitutions, those constitutional provisions have not been the primary source of institutional stability. Rights need remedies, and governments have provided only limited legal remedies to enforce social rights even when they have constitutionalized them.

The entrenchment of redistributive change has more often been the result of emergent effects that raised the political cost of switching to alternatives. At their origin, the policies have been contingent on historical circumstances and political choices. Once established, however, redistributive policies have generated constituencies and popular expectations that have made it difficult to take away benefits, even as these have grown in cost to far higher levels than earlier anticipated. Varying choices in the early design of these institutions have consequently often become hard to undo. These are chiefly cases, in other words, of path dependence, though as I emphasized in Chapter 1, path dependence does not necessarily lead to lock-in (and even where an element becomes locked in, it does not preclude an institution from evolving in other respects). In the sphere of politics, lock-in depends on the magnitude of the costs of change and the power of those who stand to gain or lose, as filtered through cultural and ideological frames that may themselves have become entrenched.

A complete account of change with distributive implications would have to deal with nearly every facet of law and institutions, including credit and debt, antitrust, trade, and immigration. This chapter focuses primarily on taxation and social policy. Both have shown strong tendencies toward path dependence and lock-in. Macroeconomic policy and labor organization serve as points of contrast. During the late twentieth-century shift to the right, Keynesian policies and unionization proved more vulnerable to reversal than did tax and welfare-state institutions.

The imposition of a tax on a large scale is not a common event. When governments do make such a change, it is often during a crisis or emergency, such as a war, that relaxes the ordinary constraints. Consequently, a country's tax system may depend on the configuration of power at critical junctures in the past when the state went down one path in taxation rather than another. To be sure, governments often change tax rates and other provisions; it is the fiscal regime—consisting of the principal forms of taxation and their constitutive features—that tends to resist change. Fiscal regimes become locked in partly because of increasing returns (for example, the initial setup costs for administering a tax are often high, and the more a state relies on a tax, the more it can spread those costs and achieve greater tax efficiency, that is, higher net revenue relative to the cost of collection). But power considerations are usually crucial. Switching to a different type of revenue would shift costs to new groups, and the resisting power of those groups may be decisive in locking in a particular type of taxation. Instituting a new tax is also a highly visible decision. Political leaders in search of more revenue are more likely to minimize blame by enacting marginal changes in an existing tax than by adopting a new one.[4] Often, governments can simply let a tax drift upward (for example, by not indexing or adjusting graduated rates in an inflationary period). All these considerations, economic and political, help explain an adage of public finance, "An old tax is a good tax"— good in the sense of being unlikely to disturb private plans and decisions and stir up political trouble.[5]

Much the same logic helps to entrench redistributive spending policies. From the eighteenth to the twentieth centuries, industrialization, economic growth, and related political changes spurred diverse interests in expanding the public provision of services, including the extension of schooling and protection against the risks of lost wage income from industrial accidents, disability, sickness, and old age. The particular form those measures took, however, depended on the configuration of power at moments of reform and on the available institutional models, either from a society's own historical repertoire or from another country that reformers deemed to be successful. The early decision-makers could not have foreseen the scale such commitments would reach or the difficulties of reversing them, once beneficiaries incorporated their gains into their understanding of the status quo. Loss aversion—people's tendency to resist losses even more strongly than they seek gains—has made it hard for governments to back out of commitments.

The obstacles to reversal, moreover, have arisen not just from individual psychological responses. Redistributive policies have fostered the growth, collective awareness, and political organization of beneficiaries and related interest groups, including both private service providers and public bureaucracies. The policies have also influenced how people plan their lives (for example, by institutionalizing retirement) and shaped the formation of whole industries, such as health care. The creation of new beneficiary groups and changes in complementary institutions create powerful pressure to maintain commitments ("positive feedback").[6] In the economically advanced societies, public opinion polls show that overwhelming majorities favor upholding the central, social insurance functions of the welfare state, and that high approval is an important proximate cause of welfare-state entrenchment.[7] But public opinion cannot be taken as a sufficient explanation in itself; it reflects how deeply welfare-state policies have transformed people's lives and their expectations of government. Public opinion today registers past political choices that have come to be seen as natural and necessary and therefore irreversible.

The entrenchment of fiscal and social-policy regimes, however, does not mean their development simply stops. Modern societies have undergone fundamental economic and demographic changes since the late nineteenth and early twentieth centuries, when they established social insurance systems and related measures. Those systems typically had industrial origins, and much of that industrial base has disappeared. They reflected the assumption that families would have male breadwinners while wives stayed at home, and new patterns in gender relations and family structure have made those assumptions obsolete. The aging of populations and the expansion of health care have enormously enlarged what were originally limited programs of retirement security and health insurance. Rather than just reinforcing the status quo, the policies themselves have contributed to pressures for change.

The growing costs of social programs have also raised questions about their broader functions. Support for welfare-state policies was never entirely or even mainly about redistribution. Social insurance, as the term "insurance" implies, helps people maintain their standard of living in the face of adversity; it primarily redistributes income within the middle and working classes—for example, from the healthy to the sick—but not necessarily from the rich to the poor. During recessions, unemployment insurance and other programs bolster consumer demand, serving as automatic stabilizers and promoting recovery. The case for social spending, particularly on education and health care, has always rested in large part on the proposition that it contributes to increased productivity and long-term economic growth. But when the performance of the advanced economies deteriorated in the 1970s after decades of rising social expenditures, what had previously seemed settled about the welfare state became unsettled.

Like all institutions, policy regimes provide platforms for adaptation as well as continuity. Some of the adaptations come through express political and administrative decisions, while others come through less visible choices not to act (so-called non-decisions). Just as governments have often allowed taxes to drift up to generate revenue, so they have also let social protections drift down by failing to adjust for changes in society, thereby economizing on expenditures and avoiding blame for either tax increases or explicit benefit cuts. In recent decades, as part-time, temporary, and other forms of precarious work have increased, the people who do those jobs have often not received the benefits and protections accorded standard employment. Downward drift is one of several ways in which redistribution may erode without being expressly reversed.[8] Low-visibility decisions and non-decisions—sometimes raising revenue, sometimes limiting benefits—do not erase established policy regimes. They testify to the continued popularity of welfare-state policies and how hard governments find it to directly undo earlier commitments, even as they may substantially weaken them.

Entrenchment, as I've suggested earlier, rather than being a form of stasis, should be understood as involving two kinds of constraints—limiting the reversibility of earlier decisions and channeling change in particular directions. As pressures to roll back the welfare state rose in the late twentieth century, its defenders faced not one but two sets of challenges: Could they adjust inherited policies to survive the new stress tests? And could they also respond to new sources of inequality and insecurity? The pressures on the welfare state from the post-industrial transition and neoliberalism raised questions not just of minor revision but also of fundamental change in the constitution of society. The scope of rights and obligations, the distribution of life chances, full membership in society—all these were at issue in the conflicts over the constitutive rules of fiscal and social-policy regimes. Early choices about those regimes would have important effects on both the reversibility of earlier policies and the response to new demands.

VARIETIES OF SOCIAL PROTECTION

The rise of redistributive institutions and policies in the industrialized capitalist societies occurred, broadly speaking, in two stages. The first phase consisted of varying national developments in the nineteenth and early twentieth centuries, when countries began developing systems of publicly financed education, social insurance, and income taxation. Before World War I, however, no country devoted more than 2 or 3 percent of its GDP to social spending, and income tax rates even on top incomes generally stayed in the single digits.[9] The second phase, when these policies were expanded and entrenched, was a more global process. It was the succession of crises in the international system, from World War I through the Great Depression, World War II, and the Cold War, that saw governments in the advanced economies take on a large-scale role, including macroeconomic management, substantially higher levels of taxation, and broadened systems of social protection (that is, non-market guarantees of income and services). The prolonged global crisis of the twentieth century produced tendencies toward convergence—all the industrialized, capitalist countries adopted policies in roughly the same areas—without erasing the differences among different families of nations.

Many people today associate redistribution and the welfare state with socialism, and during the second phase of development, the socialist parties of western Europe were an important force in welfare-state expansion. But those parties had no role in government at the origin of welfare-state policies, in the period before World War I, when many socialists regarded such policies with suspicion as efforts to coopt workers. Insofar as labor movements and socialist parties affected the welfare state's emergence, it was through the challenge they posed to parties in power and the varying strategies that employers and governments took in response.[10]

Although the pre-1914 phase of redistributive policy was limited in scale, it critically affected national paths of development. Different countries adopted institutions that varied in their rules for determining the dimensions and organization of social protection: who would be eligible for support, the level of benefits, how those benefits would be financed, and how they would be administered.

Four general types of institutional structures have been particularly important in the history of social protection.[11] *Targeted aid* to the poor, whether financed through charity or taxes, reflects the assumption that most people can and should manage on their own and that assistance therefore can be limited to the residual population who cannot. Traditional poor relief, as well as later systems of "public assistance," "social assistance," or "welfare," are all examples of targeted aid, conditioned on demonstrated need and often on morally acceptable behavior. Poor relief traditionally came with a distinct stigma as well as the loss of political rights and sometimes personal freedom (through confinement in a workhouse); the modern forms of targeted aid are generally less punitive, though still often associated with moral opprobrium. The level of assistance is typically low, and recipients enjoy limited, if any, legal rights to benefits and have no control over their administration.

Associational aid consists of forms of mutual support. Though it began on a voluntary basis independent of government, associational aid often became the foundation of public provision insofar as states mandated or subsidized it (or did both). Medieval guilds and corporations provided a historical model for associations that grew during industrialization, such as the German *Hilfskassen*, French *sociétés de secours mutuelles*, English friendly societies, and American fraternal lodges. Early trade unions took on these functions as well. Members paid contributions, and they or surviving family members received support in the event of ill fortune. Such systems offered benefits in relation to occupational status and earnings, without the stigma of poor relief.

The final two institutional structures for social protection have extended it on a more universal basis, often to all citizens or even to all persons regardless of citizenship. In a *basic security* system, the government provides benefits or services at a more or less adequate level but expects the more affluent to use private savings, employer benefits, or other private means (possibly subsidized through the tax system) to supplement or substitute for the public system. A *comprehensive security system* includes both basic and higher-level protections under the aegis of government, with a marginal role, or perhaps none at all, for private markets. Although such systems require high levels of taxation, the taxes may be levied on consumption or solely on wages (excluding capital income) and are not necessarily progressive in themselves.

In practice, these ideal types come in many variations. Nothing, moreover, requires a country to adopt the same institutional models in different policy domains. Nations have varied not only in the models they use but in the consistency with which they have applied those models across policy areas. Between the late nineteenth and mid-twentieth centuries, many countries did adopt the same approach in various forms of social insurance, and these "welfare regimes," according to a widely used schema developed by Gøsta Esping-Andersen, fall into three types.[12] Two of the three fit the historical cases reasonably well: the conservative, corporatist policy regime pioneered by Germany that spread across continental Europe, and the more universalistic, social democratic regime in the Nordic countries. Esping-Andersen's third type, a "liberal" regime supposedly characteristic of Great Britain, Canada, Australia, New Zealand, and the United States, is less useful because the institutions have been so varied, both within and across those countries and over time.

The constitutive moment for the conservative corporatist model of social protection came in the 1880s, when Germany adopted a series of legislative measures for compulsory insurance against sickness, industrial accidents, and old age and permanent disability. As a late but rapid industrializer, Germany continued to reflect premodern status hierarchies, while the newly consolidated German state confronted a growing labor movement and an avowedly revolutionary socialist party. The chancellor, Otto von Bismarck, was not coy about his motives for introducing social insurance. After passing antisocialist legislation, he sought social insurance laws to secure the loyalty of industrial workers to the existing order. Bismarck's original program was limited to those workers. Rather than create a system out of whole cloth, it extended the existing occupationally based associational aid and made it compulsory. Social insurance primarily helped the stronger elements of the German working class; it did not end poor relief, which continued at the local level and often supplemented insurance benefits. Bismarck himself would have preferred a greater state role in administering social insurance, but partly as a result of concessions to conservative and Catholic forces, the final legislation ceded administrative control to employer and occupational groups. The corporatist model thus carried over into modern welfare capitalism elements of traditional society in the form of separate insurance funds, differentiated in their organization and benefits according to occupational status.[13]

The Nordic model, though later identified with social democracy, originated chiefly through other political forces at the turn of the twentieth century in Denmark and Sweden. The Scandinavian countries still remained primarily agrarian, and the advent of a more democratic politics gave farmers new influence. Bismarckian proposals for old-age pensions and insurance against work accidents that focused exclusively on industrial workers did not address farmers' problems. Not only did agrarian groups resist policies exclusively for industry; they also saw an opportunity to shift the burden for local poor relief, financed by property taxes, to a national program financed by consumption taxes that would spread much of the fiscal burden to cities. This was the beginning of universalist, tax-financed benefits in the Nordic countries. Sweden, which introduced "people's pensions" in 1913, was the first to provide a minimum benefit to all citizens without respect to income. What began as a basic security system only later evolved into a comprehensive system after the Social Democrats came to power, beginning in the 1930s.[14]

Great Britain took even more substantial steps toward a modern welfare state before World War I than Sweden did. By the turn of the twentieth century, the Liberal Party had moved well beyond laissez-faire; the New Liberalism of the period rejected the old insistence on self-reliance and favored an expanded government role. The Liberals' interest in reform also reflected their dependence on support from workers at a time when the Labour Party was emerging as a parliamentary rival. It was under a Liberal government in 1908 that Britain adopted a limited system of old-age pensions financed out of general tax revenue. Three years later, in the National Insurance Act, the Liberals passed a system of compulsory social insurance for sickness and invalidity and even went beyond Germany in providing unemployment insurance. The German influence was direct. David Lloyd George, the central figure in the reforms as chancellor of the exchequer, became a convert to compulsory insurance after a trip to Germany. The young Winston Churchill, then the Liberal minister for trade, privately advised that the government needed to "thrust a big slice of Bismarckianism over the whole underside of our industrial system."[15]

In contrast, before World War I, the United States did not move significantly in the direction of Bismarckianism, though it did expand redistributive policy more substantially in one respect than European countries did. This was an era when the courts at both the federal and state levels regularly struck down minimum wages, maximum working hours, and other labor laws on the grounds that they violated freedom of contract and due process rights under the Fourteenth Amendment. Nearly every form of national economic regulation was at the mercy of a judicial veto. Under reigning doctrine on the Supreme Court, the Constitution barred the federal government from extending social rights (except for veterans, the recipients of a massive disability and old-age pension system after the Civil War). The early campaigns for social insurance consequently took place in the states, where the only substantial achievement was insurance for industrial accidents, the one case where employers gave their support. The states' interest in maintaining incentives for investment made it difficult to pass social legislation that business opposed. Between 1915 and 1919, reformers tried to pass compulsory health insurance in the industrial states but uniformly met defeat.[16]

In public education, however, the United States had long been a leader, at least for its white population. Decentralization here worked in favor of social rights, allowing communities in the North and West to develop public schools in the early nineteenth century when the southern states largely opposed public spending even to educate white children, let alone slaves. Not only did local communities in the free states vote the taxes to support their schools; many northern and western states entrenched a right to education in their state constitutions. Although some European countries began financing primary education as early as the late eighteenth century, conservative elites often opposed educating the children of the poor on the grounds that schooling would only make them discontented with their assigned lot in life. Except in regard to slaves, this argument failed to win support in the United States. Americans saw primary education as a means of achieving widely shared goals: self-discipline, individual advancement, economic growth, citizenship, and the assimilation of immigrants. Somehow the traditions of individualism and "patronage democracy"—often cited as the reasons for America's failure to follow European examples in social protection—did not prevent Americans from enacting compulsory school attendance laws and creating bureaucratic school systems. When there was the requisite political support, Americans built the needed state capacity, as they did with remarkable speed in wartime, and as they did in schooling. By the turn of the twentieth century, European countries were catching up to the United States in primary education, but with the growth of high schools, America took the lead in education at the secondary level.[17]

The early establishment of social insurance in Germany, Sweden, Great Britain, and other European countries reflected a diversity of political interests. These measures drew support from political leaders who hoped to coopt radical movements and foster a loyal and healthy working class that would be better prepared to defend national and imperial interests. At the same time, social reformers saw compulsory insurance as a means of superseding the poor laws and providing protection against destitution in circumstances that individuals could not control. Social insurance turned what had been stigmatized charity into a legal right. Originally limited in scale and scope, the new policies established institutional structures that would be vastly enlarged in the following decades.

THE GREAT CONJUNCTURE

The succession of global crises beginning with World War I and continuing through the Great Depression, World War II, and the Cold War led to an expansion in the role of the state and a contraction in economic inequality. In the era after World War II, many social scientists overgeneralized from these trends, identifying the decline in inequality as an intrinsic aspect of economic growth and the rise of the welfare state as a functional imperative of industrial society.[18] Marxists similarly explained the state's expanded social and economic role as part of the logic of capitalism.[19] Neither view anticipated the political and institutional reversals that began in the 1970s. The idea that the Great Depression had launched industrial societies onto an epochal shift away from a free-market regime was also a central theme of *The Great Transformation*, a widely influential 1944 book by the economic anthropologist Karl Polanyi. Polanyi developed the concept of "social protection" as a limit on the market's treatment of labor, land, and money as pure commodities. Like many others at the time, he saw history as moving in only one direction, with no mechanism that could produce a return to a market orientation.[20]

It now seems clear, with the benefit of a longer historical perspective, that rather than being inexorable aspects of modernization or other linear developments, the redistributive changes of the mid-twentieth century are better understood as effects of a singular historical conjuncture. The industrialized societies confronted the shocks of war and depression in the context of growing working-class and radical movements at home and the challenge of Soviet communism internationally. The adoption of higher taxes, large-scale social programs, and related policies is impossible to understand without taking into account the larger risks that governing parties and business confronted at home and abroad, and the crises' impact in discrediting received ideas and opening politics to alternatives.

Some of the national shifts in response to the Great Depression had an almost random character, depending on the party that happened to be in office when the crisis struck. The Depression discredited incumbent governments of all kinds, whether conservative, liberal, or socialist, and often produced reactive movements toward alternatives on either the right or the left. Benefiting from recoveries that were not entirely their own doing, the new parties and governments that came to power were sometimes able to entrench themselves.[21]

This pattern of historical chance and political entrenchment was a crucial element of mid-twentieth-century developments, but it was not the whole story. The Depression was followed by World War II, and the victors in that war overturned the losers' regimes and spread their own institutions and policies. In the United States, the Democratic Party benefited from being out of power when the economy went into a tailspin in the late 1920s. But while Franklin Roosevelt's election in 1932 fits the reactive pattern of Depression-era changes in government, the New Deal he led had far-ranging consequences. It disproved doubts about the resilience of democracies and their capacity for reform, and it took on global significance because of the role the United States played in the war and in the forging of a new international order afterwards. While economic downturns discredit incumbent parties, wars generally empower the incumbents who end up on the winning side. Crises do not always divert institutions from their previous path; the shocks open up moments of choice for political leaders (and in a democracy also for voters), and even if the choice is to adopt an alternative, its adoption may last only as long as the emergency. But once adopted, policies and institutions with large-scale redistributive consequences are not easily undone. The twentieth-century succession of global crises and conflicts, moreover, created sustained pressures to expand redistributive policies, not just introduce them temporarily.

The shocks of depression and war tended to equalize incomes—indeed, they did so even before taking into account taxes and transfers (that is, payments from government programs like Social Security). In an analysis of changes in inequality in France applicable to much of Europe, Thomas Piketty notes that inherited wealth between 1914 and 1945 suffered devastating losses as a result of the "destruction caused by two world wars, bankruptcies caused by the Great Depression, and above all new public policies enacted in this period (from rent control to nationalizations and the inflation-induced euthanasia of the rentier class that lived on government debt)." While wage inequality in France was stable, total market income—that is, income from both labor and capital—became more equally distributed "due entirely to diminished top incomes from capital." Inequalities in market income also declined in the United States during that period, though in a different way. Capital losses were not as great in the United States as in Europe, but during the 1940s there was a narrowing of differences in labor earnings ("the great compression," Claudia Goldin and Robert Margo call it).[22]

The shocks, especially the world wars, also led to higher levels of taxation and redistributive public programs, and therefore to still greater equalization of income after taxes and transfers. The "total wars" of the twentieth century demanded the mobilization not only of mass armies but of entire civilian populations. Needing popular commitment, governments faced pressure to be more accommodating to labor and grant broader social rights. The scope of the conflicts and breadth of sacrifice diminished distinctions between soldiers and civilians and served to justify postwar benefits to all citizens, not just to veterans. World War II had particularly notable effects on norms of solidarity in the liberal Allied countries. Summing up the shift in Britain at the war's beginning, the sociologist Richard M. Titmuss later recalled the dawning realization that "war strategy" required that "millions of ordinary people, in Britain and overseas, [be] convinced that we had something better to offer than had our enemies—not only during but after the war."[23] The Atlantic Charter, the statement of war aims signed by Roosevelt and Churchill in 1941, included commitments to social welfare. Britain took important progressive steps under the wartime coalition government, including a report in 1942 that came to be seen internationally as a manifesto of the welfare state. The Beveridge Report—named after its author, William Beveridge, a senior government official—called for a free health service, universal family allowances, and a government commitment to full employment.[24] The fiscal demands of the world wars led to dramatically higher taxes in Britain and other countries, and when peace returned, taxes did not fall to their prewar levels. The wars accustomed people to higher levels of taxation and allowed governments to assume broader social functions afterward.[25]

Shorter, more confined wars with lower levels of mobilization have often not had these effects, and even World War II might not have proved such a turning point in the scale of state intervention had it not been followed by the Cold War. The postwar period extended the configuration of forces that underlay greater equality; the existential conflict with fascism became an existential conflict with communism, creating pressures for accommodation between business and labor and among the major political parties. Four areas of institutional change were central to the pattern of relatively equitable economic growth: the adoption of Keynesian macroeconomic policies, the acceptance of unions and collective bargaining, the expansion of social rights and protection, and progressive taxation.

During the postwar decades, the most important factor in the adoption of Keynesian and welfare state policies was the orientation of governing parties—more particularly, the strength of parties with working-class ties and those parties' ability to forge majority coalitions with other groups.[26] But the process was complicated by other factors. During the Depression and even after the war, many left-wing parties in Europe continued to favor the traditional socialist remedies of economic planning and the nationalization of industry. Just as Germany's Social Democrats resisted social insurance in the late nineteenth century, so Britain's Labour governments in 1929–31 and again in 1945 at first did not pursue Keynesian macroeconomic policies. Labour's leaders came around to Keynesianism only when the more radical, traditional measures either were blocked or failed to generate robust growth.[27] The left's acceptance of Keynesianism and welfare-state policies required at least a tacit acceptance of capitalism, just as the acceptance of those policies by the center and right meant swallowing some redistribution. Both kinds of policies became a basis for political consensus and class compromise in the postwar West because they provided for greater economic equality without interfering with the rights of owners and managers to allocate capital and run their businesses for a profit.

Keynesian ideas were embraced more slowly and were never as widely and fully entrenched as welfare-state policies. Already internationally known in the 1920s, John Maynard Keynes published his major work, *The General Theory of Employment, Interest, and Money*, in 1936 but had only limited influence on government responses to the Depression. Classical laissez-faire doctrine held that markets have a natural tendency toward stability and that in an economic downturn, government could do little to stimulate employment and growth except to cut spending and balance the budget. Keynes held, on the contrary, that the economy could get stuck in an underemployment equilibrium, and to get out of it, the government should run a deficit by increasing expenditures or cutting taxes. Conversely, when unemployment was low, the government should run a surplus by adopting the opposite policies. In short, governments could overcome recessions and depressions and achieve full employment through the countercyclical management of aggregate demand. While the idea of deliberately running deficits was heresy to classical economics and public finance, the priority Keynes gave to full employment made his work especially attractive to labor. Consequently, Peter A. Hall points out, the parties that initially introduced Keynesian policies were generally social democratic, though conservative parties often later maintained them. The reverse sequence—the introduction of Keynesianism by conservatives and its continuance by parties of the left—was rare.[28]

Yet that reverse sequence was common for welfare-state policies, beginning with the introduction of social insurance in the 1880s in Germany and later across continental Europe. In Germany itself, conservative corporatist policies for social insurance outlasted political regimes; the Bismarckian model was expanded under the Weimar government in the 1920s (which added unemployment insurance in 1927) and largely kept in place under the Nazis and the postwar West German government. In 1982, a historian could accurately write, "The history of social insurance in Germany is the history of its expansion." In the 1880s, the system had covered about 40 percent of the employed and 10 percent of the total population; a century later, it covered all the employed and 90 percent of the total population. From providing a minimum protection against destitution, it had evolved to ensuring maintenance of achieved living standards and had become part of a broad system of social protection. In contrast, except for a brief period under the Social Democrats in the late 1960s and early 1970s, postwar German economic policy did not follow Keynesian principles.[29]

Other European countries, including Austria, France, Belgium, the Netherlands, Italy, and Spain, also adopted social policies on the Bismarckian model. In many of these countries, Christian Democratic parties were crucial to the programs' growth. Catholic influence became strongly correlated with expanded welfare-state spending. Although these governments gradually extended social protection on a universal or near-universal basis, they typically conditioned rights to social insurance on employment and contributions, set benefits in relation to earnings, financed them through payroll taxes, and vested administrative responsibility in organizations representing employers and workers.

As Germany had served as the original welfare-state exemplar, so Sweden became the model of the most advanced welfare state, thanks to the rise of the Social Democrats and their success in forging coalitions first with agrarians and later with white-collar workers. Like a number of other European countries, Sweden had seen the advent of universal suffrage and proportional representation immediately after World War I and the first participation of the Social Democrats in government in the 1920s. The socialists had the good fortune, however, to be out of office in the late 1920s, when the Great Depression struck, and then to come to power in 1933 as the economy began to recover. By agreeing to enact price supports for farmers, the Social Democrats were able to form a governing alliance with the Agrarian Party and to push through an aggressive, deficit-financed program of public works, along with unemployment insurance. A 1938 agreement between labor and business representatives created the basis for economy-wide wage bargaining that for decades was a central feature of the Swedish welfare-state model. The Social Democrats' political dominance lasted through World War II (when Sweden remained neutral) and into the 1970s, enabling the party to extend the early social insurance programs into a comprehensive security system that included family allowances, both a universal and an earnings-related pension, universal health care, and a commitment to full employment. This was the model that the other Nordic countries adopted in varying degrees.[30]

In Britain, the postwar era also saw a major expansion of the state's economic and social role. The Labour government that swept into office in July 1945 expanded social insurance for unemployment and old age (though short of the full commitments proposed in the Beveridge Report) and established the National Health Service (NHS), putting voluntary and municipal hospitals under government ownership. These were also the years when the Labour government nationalized the Bank of England as well as coal mining, electricity, and railways and expanded community planning and public housing. When the Conservatives returned to power in 1951, they maintained the various branches of the welfare state.[31]

Comparative studies of social policy typically classify Great Britain as a liberal welfare regime in which the state intervenes only as a last resort, with aid primarily targeted to the poor. That view, however, does not accurately describe Britain (or other British Commonwealth countries) in the postwar era. In important respects it was a welfare state leader. The ideas of two British figures, Keynes and Beveridge, both members of the Liberal Party, were central to the "golden age" of the welfare state internationally. With medical care free for everyone, the British NHS was, if anything, more socialized than the continental European health insurance systems. Partly as a result of the alternation in power of left and right parties and their varying success in entrenching their own policies, liberal governments do not necessarily follow the same institutional design across policy domains, adopting instead a variety of institutional forms, ranging from targeted aid to the poor to basic social security and, in cases like the NHS, comprehensive security.[32]

In the United States, the key constitutive choices about progressive policies and their limits came during the New Deal and reflected the distinctive obstacles created by the multiple veto players in the American constitutional system. The commanding Democratic majorities in Congress after 1932 were not enough to assure passage of Roosevelt's agenda. Under its long-established doctrines, the Supreme Court threatened to block activist, redistributive measures. And to get reforms through Congress in the first place, Roosevelt depended on representatives of the South, who sought to protect the region's racial hierarchy from federal intervention.

Both of these veto players—the Supreme Court and southern Democrats—helped shape the economics of the New Deal. Roosevelt did not come to office as a Keynesian; he turned to Keynesian policies only in his second term, during a severe recession in 1938 after he had tried to balance the federal budget. Initially, he had sought to revive the economy through corporatist planning. The National Recovery Administration (NRA), established in 1933, brought representatives of business and labor together to develop "codes of fair practices," including wages, prices, and production targets for each sector. But the NRA ran into early troubles, and whatever potential it may have had, the Supreme Court struck it down as unconstitutional in 1935. A second effort to establish national planning on an ongoing basis came with the government's increased role in managing the economy during World War II. This time, instead of the Court intervening, southern Democrats defected from the national party to join with Republicans in Congress to put an end to the hopes for planning, eliminating the National Resources Planning Board in 1942 and taking other steps to limit direct federal management of the economy. But the southerners did not object to an activist fiscal policy as long as it did not threaten white supremacy. The 1940s proved decisive for the choice of Keynesianism over planning and corporatist bargaining as the basis of progressive economic policy in the United States.[33]

In addition to facing a southern veto in Congress, the achievement of labor and social rights during the New Deal also faced a potential veto by the Supreme Court. At the height of the New Deal, in 1935, Roosevelt was able to keep the southerners on board and business at bay in passing two landmark laws: the National Labor Relations Act (known as the Wagner Act), codifying the rights of workers to organize unions; and the Social Security Act, providing for unemployment insurance, contributory old-age pensions, and federal aid to the states for targeted relief of the indigent. Both these laws, however, as well as others were at risk of being judicially overturned. Consequently, after his landslide reelection in 1936, Roosevelt proposed enlarging the Supreme Court to give himself more seats to fill. But in 1937, in the "switch in time that saved nine," one conservative justice changed sides, creating five-to-four majorities upholding both the Wagner Act and a state minimum wage law; another conservative justice soon resigned. Even though his court-packing legislation failed, Roosevelt was able to take advantage of openings on the Court to entrench the New Deal's constitutional revolution.[34]

But continued dependence on southern Democrats in Congress proved a limit the New Deal could not escape. To satisfy southern concerns, Social Security excluded domestic servants and agricultural workers, employment groups that were heavily African American. Many New Deal programs were devolved to the states, allowing local officials to discriminate. In 1947, southern Democrats were also instrumental in overcoming a veto by Roosevelt's successor, Harry Truman, and passing the Taft-Hartley Act, which enabled states to adopt "right-to-work" laws banning the union shop and effectively limiting union expansion. The South thereby preserved its low-wage labor regime as well as white supremacy.

At their height in the mid-1950s, labor unions represented about 35 percent of U.S. workers, but the seeds of their later decline had already been sown. A key factor in labor's strength, according to comparative analyses, is the extent of centralization in labor organization and collective bargaining. Unions can represent workers at the level of the plant, enterprise, industry, or nation as a whole. The more centralized the organization, the greater the breadth of interests that unions are likely to take into account in collective bargaining. In the postwar era, corporatist institutions in Scandinavia and continental Europe encouraged high-level coordination between labor and management; unions were also integrated into government decision-making. They flourished under these conditions as the membership grew and the agreements they negotiated covered a growing proportion of the labor force.[35]

Labor organization in the United States, however, developed on a more decentralized basis. Under the Wagner Act, unions had to organize one establishment at a time, and every new firm was born union-free; under Taft-Hartley, twenty states, mostly in the South, enacted right-to-work laws, encouraging the flight of industry from northern states long before jobs were being shipped overseas. Other provisions of Taft-Hartley banned secondary boycotts and excluded even low-level supervisory personnel from unionization, further limiting labor's reach. Together with unrelenting employer opposition, southern anti-unionism helps account not only for the regional limits of unions but also for labor's inability to develop as a national institution in the United States.[36]

Comparative analyses of social policy in Europe and the United States point to constitutional structure and racial and ethnic heterogeneity as key sources of trans-Atlantic differences. Racial heterogeneity tends to limit redistribution only under some circumstances, in particular where minorities are concentrated among the poor, as they have been in the United States.[37] Both constitutional structure and race were clearly at work in constraining the scope and reach of the New Deal. As the comparative studies show, the most favorable institutions for redistributive policy have been systems of proportional representation with few veto points. The United States has first-past-the-post elections and many veto points. Major eras of national reform in American history have typically come at the relatively rare historical moments when at least two of the three branches of the federal government are aligned in favor of transformative change and the third bows to pressure from the other two. The Great Depression created that kind of moment, but the path was open to reform only insofar as the South would agree. This was how race served as a limiting factor. Racial slavery in the United States left behind not only generalized prejudice and institutionalized disadvantage, but also a region of the country whose representatives in Congress effectively limited social rights and protection at the national level. Explanations that attribute the limits of social rights in the United States entirely to liberal individualism miss this political reality.

The policies of the New Deal—significantly compromised at their inception, but substantial nonetheless—became incorporated into the mid-twentieth-century political consensus. The Republicans who returned to power in the 1950s, like Britain's Conservatives in the same period, did not try to reverse their predecessors' innovations in welfare-state policies. President Eisenhower even signed legislation extending Social Security to include disability insurance, and his appointees to the Supreme Court cast historic votes in favor of the rights revolution that began in the 1950s. In the 1960s, under John F. Kennedy and Lyndon B. Johnson, Democrats tried to pick up where the New Deal left off and to make up for what it had left out. Medicare extended social insurance for health care for seniors, while Medicaid and other antipoverty programs provided targeted aid to the poor. Much of the targeted aid enacted as part of Johnson's War on Poverty, such as the "community action" programs aimed at "maximum feasible participation of the poor," did not survive long once Republicans won back the presidency with Richard Nixon in 1968. But like Eisenhower, Nixon accepted social insurance and did not attempt to roll back the New Deal or Medicare.

The contrasting fates of the targeted and broad-based programs suggested a simple rule about the entrenchment of progressive reforms. While social programs for the poor were highly vulnerable to erosion and reversal, programs with universal benefits were protected by their middle-class constituencies and were therefore sturdy and irreversible. The subsequent erosion of universal programs would complicate this understanding, but not entirely disprove it—universal programs have had more staying power. In the early 1970s, it was plausible to believe that all the capitalist democracies would ultimately converge on the universal social protections and relatively high economic equality established in western Europe. After all, even the United States had adopted progressive changes in all four of the areas earlier mentioned as underpinnings of equitable growth: macroeconomic policies, unionization, welfare-state benefits, and progressive taxation. Keynesian policies had become so widely accepted that in 1971 Nixon could say he was "now a Keynesian in economics."[38] While unions did not achieve the position they had in Europe, they had become part of the industrial order in the United States outside the South. America had also adopted most of the principal elements of social insurance, except for health care—but in the early 1970s, Nixon was proposing a national health insurance plan, and it seemed only a matter of time before Republicans and Democrats settled on a compromise. On the whole, welfare-state measures were less comprehensive than in much of western Europe. But just as the United States had earlier led the way in mass public education, so it had also become a leader in another area of redistributive policy—progressive taxation.

THE CURIOUS CASE OF PROGRESSIVE TAXATION

In the mid-twentieth century, the United States maintained tax rates on top incomes that in retrospect seem astonishingly high. From 1932 to 1981, the top income tax rate averaged 81 percent; from 1936 to 1981, the top tax rate on estates never fell below 70 percent.[39] Other industrialized countries also turned to progressive taxes, but generally not to the same extent. In twenty countries in Europe and North America, the average top income tax rate rose to just over 60 percent at midcentury, where it remained until the early 1970s.[40] These are statutory marginal rates—the rates applied to the next dollar earned above a given threshold—not the average rates the rich actually paid. In the United States, a significant gap opened between the top statutory rates and the effective rates after 1945, but when corporate income and estate taxes are taken into account, it remains true that the United States taxed top incomes at comparatively high levels.[41]

To be sure, in the postwar era (and still today), the western European states had higher levels of taxation overall than the United States, but they relied more on regressive taxes (mainly the value-added tax and payroll taxes). This contrast seems difficult to reconcile with any of the arguments about American exceptionalism offered to explain why the United States has had a more limited welfare state.[42] General cultural and ideological differences between Americans and Europeans cannot simultaneously explain why the United States developed less comprehensive social protections and a more progressive tax system.

The seeming anomaly of America's progressive taxes becomes more understandable when we recall the tendency of fiscal regimes toward path dependence and lock-in. For the reasons I suggested at the outset of this chapter, major forms of taxation are often difficult to undo, so the fiscal institutions established by political leaders and parties at critical junctures may persist long after they lose power and the original motivating interests and political configurations have disappeared. In the United States, Democrats were able to reshape federal taxation when they were in power during the world wars and Depression. In Europe, labor and social democratic parties generally had more power than in the United States, which might have resulted in greater reliance on progressive taxes. But in countries with corporatist institutions, the left struck bargains with business and conservative parties that, in effect, traded regressive taxes and moderation on wages for a comprehensive welfare state.

In economically advanced societies, tax progressivity depends largely on choices about consumption and income taxes, the two forms of taxation that have generated the greatest revenue. Consumption taxes, including tariffs, excises, sales taxes, and value-added taxes, tend to be regressive because people with low or middle incomes generally spend all or most of what they make, while the rich can more easily reserve income for savings. Although consumption taxes on luxury goods may be progressive, the revenue they produce is limited.[43] Taxes on income, in contrast, can produce substantial revenue on a progressive basis. The incidence of personal income taxes is progressive if the rates rise with higher incomes and the taxes capture income from capital such as corporate dividends and capital gains, whereas payroll taxes are regressive because the rates are flat and apply only to wages (even the employer-side payments ultimately come out of workers' earnings).[44]

Mass democracy might be expected to bring high taxes on the rich, and that is certainly what conservative elites long feared. Expanded suffrage, a mid-nineteenth-century British Conservative wrote, would mean "that the rich pay all the taxes, and the poor shall make all the laws."[45] Yet the extension of suffrage to working-class voters did not bring about massive redistribution, at least not right away, partly because of the strategic choices in electoral and constitutional design I described in the previous chapter, which were adopted with the aim of safeguarding the propertied classes' interests. When European countries first enacted the income tax in the nineteenth century, the rates were low, and the support came, perhaps counterintuitively, from conservative landed elites who wanted to spread more of the cost of government to the urban commercial classes.[46] A positive relationship between democratization and progressive taxes did not emerge until the twentieth century.

Great Britain was the original pioneer in income taxation. Parliament imposed an income tax with varying rates on different types of income to meet the costs of the Napoleonic Wars between 1799 and 1816. Reenacted in 1842 in response to a fiscal crisis, the tax remained in force until 1909, when the Liberal Party introduced a modern, progressive income tax with a top rate of 8.3 percent. By then, several other European countries, including Denmark and Sweden, had also introduced income taxes. In the early twentieth century, progressive taxation became an international movement, increasingly accepted by liberals and even by some conservatives as legitimate and necessary, if only to combat the more dangerous alternatives of socialism and communism. But before 1914, the tax rates remained low.[47]

The American breakthrough in progressive taxation came in the same period. Since its founding, the United States has had two fiscal regimes at the federal level. The first was a consumption tax regime centered on the tariff, established initially by the Federalists in 1789, expanded by the Republicans after the Civil War, and lasting into the early twentieth century. The second has been an income tax regime established chiefly by the Democrats and entrenched in the era that began with World War I and extended through the Depression, World War II, and the Cold War.[48] Under the first tax regime, except during the Civil War, the tariff generally provided about 90 percent of federal revenue; under the second regime, income-related taxes (including payroll taxes) have likewise provided about 90 percent of federal revenue. Which parties were in power at critical junctures greatly affected choices about taxation. That the Democrats were the governing party during the world wars and Depression is the primary historical contingency explaining the shift of the United States from a consumption-tax to an income-tax regime.

From the founding of the United States, war and its aftermath have shaped choices about taxation. The Federalists' institution of the tariff in 1789 came in response to the infant republic's debilitated condition after the Revolutionary War and the growing contention over taxes in the states as they tried to cope with their war debts. Under Hamilton's financial program, the new federal government combined the wartime debt of the Confederation and the states into a single, funded national debt, allowing the states to return to the low taxes of the colonial era and relieve a potential source of political instability. To meet its obligations, the federal government relied chiefly on tariffs, which it could collect efficiently in a few ports. The tariff was thus a strategic solution both to the early republic's fiscal crisis and to its limited administrative capacities. After winning the presidency in 1800, Jefferson reversed some excise taxes the Federalists passed, but the basic features of Hamilton's financial policy had become entrenched.[49]

Tariffs nonetheless became a flashpoint of sectional conflict in the nineteenth century. Northern manufacturing interests sought high protective tariffs, while the agrarian South and West objected to the costs they bore as a result. During the Civil War, unable to produce enough revenue out of tariffs, the federal government turned for the first time to an income tax, but after the war was over, compliance with the tax declined precipitously, and Congress repealed it in 1872. As the dominant party in the following decades, the Republicans raised tariffs on manufactured goods and other items to levels that significantly limited foreign competition. As I pointed out in Chapter 4, high tariffs had self-reinforcing effects because they enlarged protected industries, which then lobbied to maintain them. Through their control of tariff rates on different commodities and the revenue the tariff generated (used in large part to finance the pensions for Civil War veterans), the Republicans were able to create a powerful coalition sustaining a consumption-tax regime.[50]

The shift to an income-tax regime came in two steps: a campaign in the late 1800s and early 1900s to institute a limited income tax that would apply only to the rich, and the subsequent transformation of the income tax into a progressive form of mass taxation. Initially, the politics of the income tax were the reverse of the politics of the tariff. Southern and western representatives, chiefly Populists and Democrats, favored a federal income tax, whereas representatives of the North, especially the Northeast, opposed it. The South and West saw a graduated income tax as a way of reducing the tariff and as an alternative that would fall mainly on the Northeast, where wealth was concentrated; farmer and labor groups expected the tax to be paid by corporations and the rich. In 1894, while Democrats briefly controlled the presidency and Congress, they passed an income tax of 2 percent applicable to individuals with high incomes and to business corporations. But the Supreme Court struck it down the following year, holding for the first time, contrary to precedents, that an income tax was a "direct tax," which under the Constitution must be levied in proportion to each state's population.[51]

Despite that setback, the movement for a federal income tax continued to gather support from progressive Republicans as well as Democrats. In 1909, Congress approved a constitutional amendment expressly allowing taxes on incomes "from whatever source derived" without apportionment among the states. Congress sent the amendment to the states for ratification only because of Republican defections. While opposing income-tax legislation, some Republicans—including President William Howard Taft—endorsed the amendment on the grounds that the government needed the power to tax income in the event of war. Rising international tensions had already led to an arms race in Europe; Britain passed its progressive income tax in 1909 partly in anticipation of the need to finance a larger military budget. The United States was also building up its military, especially the navy, and engaging in increased military action abroad. The political coalition supporting the Sixteenth Amendment drew in other groups, such as the temperance movement, which favored an income tax as a way to wean the federal government off taxes on alcohol and prepare the way for Prohibition. Some Republican congressional opponents of the tax also appear to have miscalculated, going along with the amendment in the expectation that it would fail (no amendment had met the requirement of ratification by three-fourths of the states since 1870). But in 1910 and 1912, Democrats won sweeping victories, taking control of state legislatures as well as Congress, and by 1913 more than enough states had voted to ratify the Sixteenth Amendment. That same year, after Woodrow Wilson took office as president, Congress passed legislation imposing an income tax that applied only to the richest 3 percent, with marginal tax rates from 1 to 7 percent.[52]

The Sixteenth Amendment entrenched only the federal power to tax incomes, not a fiscal regime centered on the income tax. "Virtually none of the income-tax proponents within the government," writes the fiscal historian W. Elliot Brownlee, "believed that the income tax would become a major, let alone the dominant, permanent source of revenue within the consumption-based federal tax system."[53] So while the Sixteenth Amendment is an example of strategic entrenchment, it did not reflect a deliberate effort to change the tax regime in as dramatic a fashion as later took place.

The world wars and Depression precipitated changes in taxation that, like the era's changes in welfare-state policies, tended to promote economic equality, but the shocks alone did not produce that result. Even in a crisis, governments have alternatives; major wars have to be financed, but there is more than one way to do it. The main options for modern war finance have been increased debt, monetary expansion, and taxes of different kinds. War consequently provides an occasion for political leaders to choose among policies with drastically different economic and social consequences.

The combatants in World War I chose their financing methods depending on whether they mobilized heavily for the fighting and what kind of government they had. On the eve of the war, the top income tax rates were just 8.3 percent in Great Britain, 7 percent in the United States, 12 percent in Sweden, 3.2 percent in the Netherlands, and 3 percent in Germany. France introduced an income tax in the run-up to the war, but the top rate was only 2 percent. In a comparative analysis of seventeen countries in Europe and North America, Kenneth Scheve and David Stasavage find a huge shift toward progressive income taxes among ten countries that mobilized at least 2 percent of their population, and only a small shift in that direction among seven countries that remained neutral or did not mobilize heavily. Before the war, the heavily mobilized countries had slightly lower top income tax rates on average; by 1920, their top tax rates exceeded those of the non-mobilization countries by

34 percentage points. Among the mobilizing countries, top rates rose far more in the democracies than in other countries.[54] There was also substantial variation in the proportion of war costs financed through taxes as opposed to debt. The United States financed the highest share through taxes, nearly a quarter; France, 15 percent; Germany and Austria-Hungary, less than 2 percent.[55]

The sharp increases in progressive taxes during World War II suggest that a similar process was at work in changing the politics of taxation. Scheve and Stasavage distinguish between two types of arguments for progressivity. The more familiar argument is that a person's ability to pay increases with income and that a graduated tax is fair because it tends to equalize the sacrifice asked of rich and poor. The less familiar argument—but the one that Scheve and Stasavage point to as crucial to the rise of progressive taxation—is compensatory: Higher taxes on the rich compensate for the advantages the rich enjoy from government policy. With millions of men being conscripted to fight, the argument became more compelling that those who stayed home—and often prospered from the war economy—ought to pay more in taxes. The "conscription of income," some called it.[56]

Postwar difficulties coping with debt and inflation also prompted change in fiscal regimes. Both France and Germany saw major shifts in taxation during and immediately after World War I. Both raised income tax rates and introduced new consumption taxes. France raised its top income tax rate to 20 percent in 1918 and as high as 72 percent in the mid-1920s before cutting it back to 30 percent.[57] Germany raised its top rate to 40 percent in 1919–20. A European movement toward national sales taxes began in Germany in 1918 and France in 1920, and a decade later, the Depression set off another wave of sales taxes across Europe. State governments in the United States also introduced sales taxes in the 1930s.[58]

At the national level in the United States, the world wars and Depression provided an unanticipated opening for a new tax regime. During World War I, with the Democrats in power, the federal government not only financed a higher proportion of expenditures from taxes than did the other major powers; it did so through increased taxes on corporate and personal income. Two-thirds of wartime revenue came from an excess-profits tax; the Wilson administration and Congress also raised income tax rates (with a top marginal rate of 77 percent), increased the proportion of people paying income taxes (up to 15 percent), and enacted an estate tax.[59] When the Republicans returned to power in the 1920s, they eliminated the excess-profits tax and reduced both income and estate tax rates—but those taxes survived, with income taxes ratcheted up from prewar levels and outpacing the tariff as a revenue source. Republican protectionism would have its last gasp with the infamous Smoot-Hawley bill in 1930, which set the highest tariffs in a century. Two years later, trying to balance the budget amid plunging federal revenues, President Herbert Hoover and the Republicans passed what was then the largest peacetime tax increase in American history. Rates on the top bracket went back up, from 25 percent to 63 percent.[60]

Progressive taxation rose even higher under Roosevelt between 1933 and 1945. Initially, the changes were mixed; although the Democrats raised income and estate taxes on the rich in 1935, they also passed a regressive payroll tax that year to finance Social Security. Only with World War II did the income tax became a mass tax on a sharply progressive scale. Like Wilson, Roosevelt decided to use taxes to pay for a high proportion of wartime costs—about half, far more than any of the other belligerents—and to do so through levies on corporations and the rich; in 1942, he even called for a cap of $25,000 on after-tax incomes. Although Congress rejected that idea, it raised the top marginal rate on incomes over $200,000 to 82 percent (and ultimately to 94 percent) and approved a temporary excess profits tax of 90 percent. World War II led to change on a larger scale than World War I partly because it was a far larger economic undertaking. The government for the first time introduced income-tax withholding to facilitate the extension of the tax to working- and middle-class people, who would have found it difficult to pay their taxes in a single lump sum. Between 1939 and 1945, the number of taxpayers rose from 3.9 million to 42.6 million, and total tax collections went from $2.2 billion to $35.1 billion. Together, personal and corporate income taxes provided three-quarters of federal revenue.[61]

Any effort to impose high taxes runs the risk of resistance and evasion. The war gave high progressive income taxes a legitimacy they would otherwise not have had and helped create habits and mechanisms of compliance that lasted into peacetime. These changes served to entrench the income tax regime, not merely to smooth its introduction. Explaining the ratchet effect of World War II in raising tax levels in postwar Britain, Alan Peacock and Jack Wiseman emphasize a psychological factor: "People will accept, in times of crisis, methods of raising revenue formerly thought intolerable, and the acceptance of new tax levels remains when the disturbance has disappeared. It is harder to get the saddle on the horse than to keep it there."[62] Public acceptance of higher taxes, however, did not emerge spontaneously; it involved strategic cultural and institutional policy choices that exemplify what I called "institutional deepening" in Chapter 1. In the United States, besides introducing income-tax withholding to routinize payment and take it out of the hands of individual taxpayers, the Roosevelt administration actively sought to instill tax-paying norms. Calling on wartime patriotism, it conducted a massive public relations campaign to foster a mass culture of tax compliance. The Cold War battle against communism maintained the national-security rationale for fiscal citizenship and high marginal tax rates for decades thereafter.[63]

The American turn toward progressive taxation was path dependent in two respects. It depended on the enactment of the Sixteenth Amendment before World War I and on the Democrats' being in power in both world wars. Consider what might have happened if the Sixteenth Amendment had not passed when it did. Throughout American history, decisions about war finance have depended on the attitude of the party in power toward the available forms of taxation. Governing parties with core constituencies that oppose the tax regime—as the Democrats did during the Mexican War, or the Republicans did during the Iraq War—avoid raising taxes.[64] Without the option of raising income taxes, the Wilson administration might have relied more on debt. If Republicans had been in power, they might have sought to increase consumption taxes, as Germany and France did in the same period. Indeed, the first American effort to establish a national sales tax came from Republicans in 1921.[65] If Congress had enacted a sales tax during World War I or immediately after, it might have become locked in as a source of federal revenue before the states were able to claim sales taxes as their own in the 1930s. Once they did so, however, they posed an additional obstacle to a federal sales tax (or later, a value-added tax). Leaving sales taxes to the states then had self-reinforcing effects in keeping down the level of consumption taxation. Tax competition—the states' interest in not raising sales taxes too much above their neighbors', for fear of driving out business—has helped keep total consumption-tax revenues to a lower percentage of GDP in the United States than in Europe.[66]

To finance the postwar expansion of public spending, European governments could have relied on either progressive income taxes or more regressive consumption and payroll taxes. Social democratic and other left-wing parties did increase progressive taxes, but only to a degree; they accepted a bargain with business that preserved incentives for investment and growth and limited the use of taxes on income and capital as a means of redistribution. Instead, they relied more on consumption taxes and, in taxing income, agreed to increase taxes on labor rather than capital. Even with regressive taxes, welfare-state programs still had a net progressive effect because of the distribution of benefits.[67]

The legacies of earlier tax policies also influenced choices in Europe. The earlier a country introduced a value-added tax (VAT), the greater has been the ratio of public expenditures to GDP—another example of path dependence.[68] Originating in France, the value-added tax proved attractive to parties on both the right and left because it is low in visibility, hidden along the chain of production, and therefore a relatively painless way of raising revenue. Economists also endorsed the value-added tax as the consumption tax that is least likely to distort markets. In the 1960s, the predecessor of the European Union adopted it as the common form of sales tax in the larger movement to harmonize economic policies.[69] By making the VAT a requirement for membership and effectively setting its minimum level, the EU limited the tax competition that might otherwise have kept down rates. The EU's role exemplifies my earlier argument about the use of transnational organizations as a way of strategically entrenching policies against possible domestic opposition.[70]

Several analysts have argued that the reliance of the United States on highly visible, redistributive taxation has intensified opposition to the welfare state and therefore helps explain America's less comprehensive social protection.[71] Like Social Security, however, the defeated proposals for national health insurance from the 1940s to the early 1970s called for regressive payroll taxes. Since health care was the biggest difference in welfare-state development between the United States and Europe, it seems unlikely that progressive taxation stood in the way of closing that gap.

But for other reasons, the U.S. tax system helped limit public social programs, and particularly undercut support for national health insurance. Social protection in America developed on a dual basis, not only through direct public spending but also through employer-provided benefits subsidized through tax exemptions and deductions. One such tax expenditure—that is, a subsidy channeled through the tax code—was for employer-sponsored health insurance. Federal law was originally unclear during the 1940s as to whether employer payments for health insurance represented taxable income, but a revision to the tax code under Eisenhower in 1954 provided a blanket exclusion for all employer health insurance contributions. Labor leaders, intent on winning health benefits for their members through collective bargaining, supported the policy, as did conservatives who saw the tax benefit for employer-sponsored coverage as undermining the drive for a government program. No one at the time paid attention to the cost of the tax expenditure, which became one of the most expensive federal health policies.[72]

By making compensation in the form of health benefits more valuable than cash wages, the tax policy encouraged the expansion of employee coverage and reduced consumer sensitivity to costs. It also raised costs by promoting the fragmentation of health-care finance among multiple payers, instead of the more unified payment systems European countries developed. Nonetheless, the tax expenditure for employer-sponsored health insurance became locked in as its effects increased: It contributed to the lavish growth of the health-care industry and helped create what I have elsewhere called a "protected public." Employees with generous coverage, together with Medicare beneficiaries and veterans, believed they had earned their health care and were often opposed to covering the remaining uninsured through a universal program that would raise their taxes and possibly jeopardize their protected position. Not just the tax expenditure for private insurance, but the whole fragmented, inflationary financing system became locked in.[73]

While taking for granted their own tax benefits for employer-sponsored health care and pensions, middle-class and affluent voters became more conscious of their tax burdens in the late 1970s, when inflation pushed many of them into higher income tax brackets and raised their property tax assessments. It was at this point that America's reliance on highly visible taxes helped spur opposition to welfare-state programs. If the United States had earlier adopted the combined tax and spending policies of many European countries—more universal programs financed by a VAT as well as payroll taxes—taxes and "welfare" might not have become targets of public anger. The American middle class's peculiar mix of high-visibility taxes and low-visibility benefits set the country up for an especially sharp backlash when the era of expansion ended.

LOCK-IN AND LOCK-OUT

Stress Tests and the Survival of the Welfare State

When economic growth slowed and inflation spiked in the mid-1970s, the Keynesian welfare state faced a stress test: Would governments maintain mid-twentieth-century redistributive policies or abandon them? During the postwar decades, the dividends of growth had financed the expansion of public programs, and prosperity encouraged consensus and accommodation. Now taxes began to bite, inflation eroded the value of savings, and public confidence in governing parties, governing ideas, and government itself declined.

It is often a hypothetical question whether institutions are well enough entrenched to survive challenges, but here we have no need for hypotheticals. The stagflation of the 1970s broke the political consensus in favor of the welfare state and led to direct attacks on the institutions and policies of the postwar settlement. The standard remedies associated with Keynesianism—countercyclical adjustments of fiscal and monetary policy—seemed irrelevant in the face of both rising inflation and rising unemployment, a combination that Keynesian theory had not recognized as a possibility. As in other contexts, the political outcome of an economic crisis did not follow from objective circumstances alone. Responses depended on who came to power and the ideas they brought with them—in this case, especially ideas about economic growth.[74] But entrenched forms of social protection set limits on how far the reversal of earlier policies could go.

The support for progressive taxation and increased social spending had, in fact, never entirely been a consensus during the postwar decades. Advocates of free markets and lower taxes had been waiting in the wings for their opportunity; from the early postwar years, a group of conservative intellectuals was making the case for what some of them termed "neoliberalism," the deliberate use of the state to reconstruct free markets. Neoliberalism is not just a rehash of nineteenth-century economic liberalism. It is one thing to oppose government programs and policies before they are introduced; it is another thing to undo them later. While the first requires only a blocking power, the second requires a constitutive power—the paradoxically active use of the state to shrink the state and create markets. Neoliberalism, unlike laissez-faire, demands a strong state as the foundation of a liberalized capitalism. The conservative thinkers who pursued this agenda were not just marginal intellectuals confined to study groups; Friedrich von Hayek and Milton Friedman, to take two of the most prominent, were effective popularizers with strong institutional backing.[75] But their arguments did not get traction during the postwar decades until the economic shocks of the 1970s. At that point, the case for radical free-market innovation found a ready audience in parties on the right where moderates long implicated in compromise were losing influence to leaders who promised a return to true principles. Such was the pattern in Britain with the election that brought Margaret Thatcher to power in 1979 and in the United States with the election of Ronald Reagan as president in 1980. In both countries, a conservative party not only returned to office but underwent a radical awakening of a particular kind, combining a dedication to markets and tax cuts with social traditionalism and a hardline foreign policy.

The 1970s also saw increased questioning of the role of government on the center left, though this had a different inspiration. The movement for deregulation in the United States enjoyed influential support from progressive-minded liberals such as Senator Ted Kennedy and Ralph Nader, who attacked traditional forms of price regulation on the grounds that the responsible agencies had been captured by industry and were no longer protecting consumers. Price deregulation had appeal as a progressive strategy for attacking inflation. Nader and Kennedy were not generally devoted to free markets; they favored stronger regulation of consumer products, workplace safety, and the environment. Nonetheless, price deregulation in airlines, railroads, and interstate trucking in the late 1970s under Reagan's Democratic predecessor, Jimmy Carter, contributed to a general trend toward economic liberalization.[76]

The neoliberal turn in the late twentieth century partly reflected the fading away of the peculiar conditions of the Great Conjuncture. The world wars, Depression, and early Cold War tended both to enlarge the state and to reduce inequality. As communism faded as a threat, welfare-state policies lost some of their earlier rationale from the standpoint of business interests that had gone along with moderately redistributive government for fear of worse. The old dynamics of capitalism and accompanying imbalances of political power returned, not exactly as they had been before World War I, but with many similarities.[77]

That the first attack on the postwar settlement in the United States came against taxes should be no surprise. When prices seem out of control, as they did in the 1970s, voters do have control over one conspicuous price—the price of government. Local property taxes were the initial target in what quickly turned into a general tax revolt. As housing prices rose, homeowners in many areas of the country confronted steep property tax increases. The problem became acute in California in the 1970s as a result of a good-government reform that required impartial assessments of property at full market value, instead of fractional assessments at the discretion of local assessors. In June 1978, after years of defeating other tax limitation measures, California voters triggered a political earthquake when, by a two-to-one margin, they passed Proposition 13, an amendment to the state constitution that not only cut property taxes by more than half for current owners but limited the ability of both the state and local governments to raise taxes in the future.[78]

The cascade of tax and expenditure limitations that followed— by 1980, thirty-eight states had adopted measures reducing or limiting taxes—had lasting consequences for two reasons.[79] First, the limits were often constitutionally entrenched, permanently restraining taxes and budgets and requiring supermajorities to override those limits. Proposition 13 entrenched rules for assessing future taxes that greatly advantaged current property owners over new buyers, who would owe taxes based on a property's acquisition price. After a purchase, new owners would also lock in a tax privilege that increased in value the longer they held on to the property; the privilege would be especially large for commercial-property owners and affluent homeowners, since tax breaks were bigger the more valuable the real estate.[80] More than forty years later, despite a sea change in California politics, Proposition 13 is still in effect, an entrenched legacy of the late 1970s tax revolt, benefiting insiders over outsiders—longtime property owners over those locked out of the housing market.

The state tax limitations also had lasting consequences because of their impact on national politics. The Republican Party became an antitax party. Before Proposition 13, Republicans had generally maintained that in the interest of a balanced budget, spending would have to be cut first before cutting taxes. The tax revolt led Reagan and other party leaders to reverse that sequence. Federal taxes could now be cut, even without corresponding spending cuts, on the premise that the tax cuts would pay for themselves through faster economic growth. This was the "supply-side" rationale for Reagan's 1981 tax cuts, which reduced income tax rates across the board, slashing the top marginal rate from 70 percent to 50 percent. Although the tax cuts never did pay for themselves, they had political value for Republicans in foreclosing strategies Democrats had followed in expanding welfare-state policies. The ensuing deficits precluded new social initiatives, justified cuts in existing programs, and led many Democrats to become more concerned with deficit reduction than with offering voters a positive alternative.

A second tax cut under Reagan in 1986—bringing the top income tax rate down to 28 percent and reducing the corporate rate from 46 percent to 34 percent—came with a broadening of the tax base on the premise, subsequently not borne out, that the net effect would be revenue-neutral. Corporate tax policy had previously combined high nominal tax rates with investment credits and a variety of deductions that reduced the burden for most companies. The 1986 law cut the selective investment incentives as well as the rates, but while Congress would later enact new credits and deductions, the rate reduction would remain. The net result of all these changes was a redistribution of income in favor of the wealthy. Even with these changes, the federal government continued to depend on a progressive income tax regime, albeit a substantially less progressive one than in the past.[81]

The decline in personal income tax rates and changes in corporate taxation were not limited to the United States. From the early 1970s to 2000, governments in the advanced economies cut the top marginal income tax rate on average from 60 percent to 38 percent, a change that reflected the waning of the special conditions of the Great Conjuncture and the breakdown of the political coalitions that had sustained highly progressive rates.[82] The changes in U.S. corporate taxation in 1986 had a direct effect on policy elsewhere. Governments in the other advanced economies reduced corporate tax rates for fear of losing capital investment and jeopardizing growth; even the Swedish Social Democrats accepted the need to pursue equality on the spending rather than the tax side of fiscal policy. Countries that experienced slower economic growth cut corporate rates more aggressively; those with systems of proportional representation and more veto players moved more slowly.[83] But the downward trend was unrelenting, as conservatives won the battle about what growth required in tax policy and were able to bring about a rollback that favored business and people with high incomes.

Despite these reductions in personal and corporate income taxes, the overall ratio of taxes to GDP in the advanced economies did not fall. Governments compensated for the lost revenue largely by raising regressive consumption and payroll taxes. Social spending, particularly for pensions and health care, continued rising because of demographic, technological, and other changes—and because even the most determined conservative governments could not undo the central institutions of the welfare state. The durability of the NHS in Great Britain and Social Security in the United States shows just how deeply entrenched those institutions had become.

Neoliberal policies may have had a greater impact in Britain than in any other major advanced economy. Thatcher's government not only reduced taxes on the wealthy, weakened unions, and repudiated the commitment to full employment in favor of financial orthodoxy; it also privatized state industries and public housing and sought to introduce market principles into spheres such as education. The biggest privatization measures had a high probability of entrenchment, as it would be very difficult, if not impossible, to return privatized enterprises and housing to state ownership.[84] In a majoritarian system like Britain's, the governing party typically has ample power to carry out its agenda, and the Conservative government under Thatcher and her successor, John Major, held power for an exceptionally long time, from 1979 to 1997. Nonetheless, at the end of those eighteen years, government spending stood at 42 percent of GDP, hardly changed from what it had been when Thatcher was first elected.[85]

The NHS, Labour's most formidable achievement, was a nationalized institution of just the kind that Thatcher sought to privatize. But she pledged, "The NHS is safe with us," and it was only after nearly a decade in office that she undertook a substantial review of its structure.[86] Like two other constitutive moments in the development of Britain's health system—the adoption of Lloyd George's national insurance system in 1911 and the establishment of the NHS in 1948—Thatcher's 1989 review raised fundamental questions of organization and power, as distinct from the ordinary distributive politics of budgets and pay.[87] But her reforms, while imposing internal changes aimed at controlling costs, fell considerably short of the earlier two upheavals in transforming Britain's health care. The NHS remained a universal, tax-financed system. Public support no doubt helps to account for that outcome—polls regularly showed the NHS to be Britain's most popular institution next to the monarchy—but there was another reason as well. The structure of a centrally budgeted national health service enabled

Britain to spend less on health care than any other major democracy. Converting to an insurance system would have raised national health costs and thereby undermined Thatcher's larger aims.

In the United States, Social Security faced challenges during two Republican administrations and also emerged with its basic structure intact. The first stress test came under President Reagan in 1982, when the Social Security Trust Fund confronted a looming shortfall in revenue due to slow wage growth. Conservatives wanted sharp cuts in the program or possibly even privatization, but rather than attempt any radical change, Reagan convened a bipartisan commission, and the crisis was resolved mainly through phased-in increases in both payroll taxes and the standard retirement age. The second stress test came in 2005, when a newly reelected President George W. Bush was soundly rebuffed in his effort to turn Social Security into a system of private accounts.

Like the NHS, Social Security is a popular program with the backing of well-organized beneficiaries, but that support is itself a consequence of the program's structure. The designers of Social Security framed it as providing benefits that are earned through work, paid for through earmarked taxes, and therefore an obligation for the government to provide. President Roosevelt saw the earmarked payroll "contributions" as a barrier to repeal. In response to an aide's criticism that the taxes were regressive, Roosevelt said: "With those taxes in there, no damn politician can ever scrap my social security program. Those taxes aren't a matter of economics, they're straight politics."[88] Though the program grew slowly at the beginning, it became self-reinforcing. Together with Medicare, Social Security drew seniors into engagement with government and helped turn them into a political powerhouse.[89] Even the programs' limitations became a source of strength; they created a market for supplementary insurance and financial services for retirees, a primary source of revenue for what became America's most powerful beneficiary group, the American Association of Retired Persons, now known just by its acronym, AARP.

Social Security, moreover, became entrenched in social structure. Americans counted on it not only for themselves but also to avoid having to support their aging parents. A government that sought to end Social Security would be seen as violating an implicit contract that people relied on in planning their lives. Yet amid reports suggesting Social Security would eventually go bankrupt, many Americans were dubious about its future, so Bush might have made some headway on private accounts if not for one additional consideration known as the "double payment" problem. In 1939, chiefly as a result of criticism by conservatives, amendments to Social Security had put the program on a pay-as-you-go basis, reversing the earlier plan to accumulate a large trust fund to pay future benefits (conservatives worried that the trust fund would lead to program expansion).[90] A pay-as-you-go system, however, is inherently difficult to privatize: If current workers put their Social Security payments into their own individual accounts, where would the money come from to pay current beneficiaries? The double payment problem might have been manageable at a time of federal budget surplus, but in 2005 projected deficits were high because of Bush's earlier tax cuts. To finance new individual accounts, the federal government would have had to undertake some combination of three unpleasant measures—raising taxes, increasing borrowing, or cutting benefits for current retirees. Under these circumstances, Bush's proposal collapsed in the face of overwhelming opposition.

Internationally, large unfunded commitments in mature, pay-as-you-go public pension systems have generally stymied full-scale privatization. Instead, governments have responded to fiscal pressures by incrementally raising contributions and reducing benefits, usually through multiparty agreements to diffuse the blame for retrenchment. Only when pension programs have been recent and their unfunded obligations have therefore been more manageable has privatization been feasible, and in those cases the outcome has depended on the relative strength of left and right parties.[91] One such instance of privatization came in Britain, where Thatcher was able to put a recently established supplementary pension program on a path to extinction by offering incentives for enrollment in "personal pensions"—though at the cost of a huge scandal when financial-services companies were shown to have misrepresented their products.[92]

The limits of neoliberal efforts to roll back core welfare state programs highlight the importance of the costs of change—the costs, in these cases, of switching from state-oriented to market-oriented policies. Some of the obstacles to neoliberal measures did reflect strategic choices in the original design of public programs. As an analysis of the formation of the NHS points out, Labour Party leaders in the 1940s "acted strategically to lock in egalitarian aspects of their choices, creating structures that reduced opportunities for subsequent Conservative governments to undermine the redistributive character of the system."[93] Roosevelt revealed the same kind of political calculation when he defended the earmarked payroll tax as preventing any "damn politician" from scrapping Social Security in the future. But emergent costs, like the double payment problem, may have created even stronger obstacles to privatization than strategic design choices at the inception of welfare-state institutions. Different forms of privatization have different fiscal implications. Privatizing state assets (for example, selling state enterprises) provides a one-time boost to state budgets; contracting out of public services may also achieve budgetary savings. But in cases like the NHS and Social Security, where privatization would create new budgetary and social costs, the existing institutions have been far more likely to survive.

Rolling back any public program is likely to threaten its beneficiaries and therefore have political costs. The sheer size of the constituencies created by the welfare state raises those political costs to an exceptionally high level. This was one reason why the "new politics" of the welfare state, as Paul Pierson argued in 1994, did not mirror the earlier period of welfare-state expansion, when labor unions had often played a crucial role. Instead of depending for their support wholly on the original forces that produced their enactment, the programs generated self-reinforcing feedback, including the growth of client groups like AARP.[94] But in the new economic and political environment, not all beneficiaries were equally capable of defending their interests; AARP was an exceptional case, not the rule. Groups that were poorly organized and less closely tied to a major party were not able to exert that kind of influence.[95]

Insiders and Outsiders

The postwar welfare state would have come under pressure in the late twentieth century even without the economic shocks of the 1970s and the ensuing partisan and ideological shifts. As a result of structural change in the economy, employment was shifting from manufacturing to services, and slower productivity growth in services was bound to impede growth rates overall. Increased global trade was accelerating the loss of manufacturing jobs, particularly for low-skill work that could be bought more cheaply in low-wage countries. But with or without globalization, post-industrial societies were deindustrializing societies, and deindustrialization posed an enormous challenge to unions and therefore to the political foundations of parties on the left that supported progressive tax and spending policies. Some social insurance programs, notably old-age pensions and health insurance, had been introduced with relatively low costs, but those costs were destined to rise as the systems matured, populations aged, and medical care became more specialized and complex. At a time of growing opposition to higher taxes, the rising costs of pensions and health care squeezed other social expenditures.

These changed conditions made it difficult not only to sustain redistributive policies in full but also to respond to new demands for protection against risk. While some long-protected groups would have their benefits locked in, some new or less politically connected groups of claimants would find themselves locked out. A politics of insiders and outsiders, a dual structure of rights, developed. The dualities were defined in relation to the labor market, systems of social protection, and moral ideas of social worth. Employees who continued to have jobs in the primary labor market were more likely to receive the full benefits of the postwar settlement, while those who worked in the more precarious, secondary labor market had little or no protection. The division was partly by gender, partly by race and citizenship, and partly by generation. When women entered the labor force in large numbers, many of them found part-time jobs or other forms of contingent work, without the full benefits that came with standard employment. The same was true of ethnic minorities and immigrants. Young adults just entering their working years were also far more likely to be unemployed or to get jobs without the protections the older generation received.

The extent of these economic disparities varied with a country's institutions and policies. This was also a period when women and minorities were fighting for equal rights and equal pay and seeking changes in both employment practices and public policies. Many of their claims received recognition in laws and policies prohibiting discrimination and requiring new procedures for affirmative action and other means of redress or compensation. Other demands—for example, for parental leave and child care—sought, if not an entirely new welfare state, at least a substantial updating of the old one. It was just in these years, however, that governments were hit by the rising costs of existing pension and health-care programs amid pressure from voters not to raise taxes.

Deindustrialization and higher unemployment rates intensified the pressures on governments created by the fiscal squeeze. Full employment had been an integral part of the postwar welfare state in Europe. Between 1955 and 1973, the unemployment rate had averaged 2.1 percent in the six core countries of the European Economic Community (France, Germany, Britain, the Netherlands, Denmark, and Belgium). From 1982 to 2000, however, the average jobless rate in the same countries climbed to 8.2 percent, with much of the increase coming in long-term unemployment.[96] In the fifteen core Organisation for Economic Co-operation and Development (OECD) countries as of 1975, only 15 percent of the unemployed suffered jobless spells longer than twelve months, but that proportion rose to 40 percent or higher in the years after 1982.[97] The old recipe for full employment, a competitive export sector, was no longer sufficient. To meet global competition, European industrial firms modernized and downsized, leaving workers to find jobs in other sectors.

The loss of industrial jobs was only one factor in the decline of unions that began in the 1980s. After more than three decades of growth in most of the advanced economies, unions lost ground even within manufacturing. The old Fordist systems of mass production had tended to concentrate workers in large plants and separate them from management; the demands of global competition and advent of new technology encouraged a shift to more flexible systems of production in smaller and flatter organizations that were less conducive to unionization. In Great Britain, legislation passed under Thatcher led to an exceptionally sharp fall in union density (the ratio of union members to all wage and salary

earners) from 51 percent in 1979 to 33 percent in 1995. In the
United States, Reagan's policies reinforced a decline in unionization that had been under way since the mid-1950s; after falling
from a peak of 35 percent in 1954 to 21 percent in 1979, union
density dropped to 16 percent in 1989. Even in Europe's coordinated market economies, employers in the 1980s sought to gain
concessions from labor and decentralize negotiations on the
grounds that rising global competition made it imperative to lower
costs and increase flexibility. The more unions were entrenched
nationally, the better able they were to resist the global market
forces and national pressures tending to weaken them. Where they
were relatively weak to begin with, they fell even further in membership and power. According to an analysis at the end of the
1990s, unions were unable to maintain membership at the levels
they had reached two decades earlier if they did not run an unemployment insurance system (as they did in the Scandinavian countries and Belgium) or did not combine workplace unionism with
corporatist bargaining at higher levels.[98]

With manufacturing employment in decline, the advanced
economies had to create more jobs in services, but most of those
jobs were traditionally low in pay and stagnant in productivity.
Here the different systems of political economy and social protection in the advanced economies diverged.[99] During the 1980s and
1990s, the United States generated robust growth in private-sector
service jobs, many of them, however, low-paying, insecure, and
without benefits. Unemployment was kept in check, but inequality
increased. The Nordic countries also created jobs in services, but
they did so primarily in the public sector and with full social protections, at the cost of increased pressure on government budgets
and taxes. In continental Europe, however, the creation of new ser-
vice-sector employment lagged because of the high fixed costs of
labor due to mandatory social insurance benefits, relatively egalitarian wages, and strict job protections that made it difficult to fire
workers.

The linkage between employment and social insurance, the
distinguishing feature of the Bismarckian welfare state, was also
a primary source of its problems in adapting to post-industrial
change. The costs of social insurance fell entirely on labor and

impeded the development of private employment at the low end of
the labor market. Bismarckian social insurance was also premised
on male breadwinners, with women and children deriving protection mainly from their husbands and fathers. Although coverage
varied by occupation, governments had extended social insurance
to nearly their entire population, a change made possible in the
postwar era by full employment. The system worked as long as the
structure of the economy and families remained the same. But with
slow growth, deindustrialization, rising unemployment, women's
increased entry into the labor force, higher rates of family breakup,
and aging populations, the system's underlying premises broke
down. Financing existing benefits became more difficult, and new
social risks developed with the rise of single-parent families and
increased needs for child care and care of the aged.

In the 1980s, continental European governments initially
sought to preserve traditional arrangements by raising social insurance taxes and encouraging "labor-shedding" policies such as early
retirement. But these measures left fewer workers to support the
social insurance system. As this approach became unsustainable,
governments turned to policies that distinguished between labor-
market insiders and outsiders, a process called "dualization." The
protections for insiders were largely preserved, while firms and
governments institutionalized a lower status and less protection for
outsiders. This process went along with a retreat from standard
employment as governments adopted deregulatory policies to
increase labor-market flexibility and allow for part-time jobs, temporary employment contracts, and self-employment. Instead of
encouraging firms to shed employees, governments were spurring
more people to work and, in an important shift, beginning to
address the new social risks by expanding parental leave and
child care.[100]

But the earlier postwar expansion of social insurance now went
into reverse as governments in continental Europe made it more
difficult to qualify for earnings-related pensions and unemployment insurance, and instead provided a lower tier of tax-financed,
means-tested benefits. These policies effectively subsidized low-
wage employment by reducing social insurance taxes. Dualization
was not the same as economic liberalization in the Thatcherite

sense; it arose from coalitions of the "social partners," the organized workers and employers in the core economy. These groups,
as Bruno Palier and Kathleen Thelen write in regard to France
and Germany, defended the traditional standards of protection for
themselves but were "no longer able to serve the leadership functions they once did of providing crucial collective goods for all."[101]

The Nordic countries were more successful in maintaining
collective goods, though social protections eroded there too. As a
result of social democratic influence, Sweden and its neighbors had
developed distinctly comprehensive and egalitarian institutions:
universal social insurance, public provision of social services, a
strong labor movement committed to equal pay for equal work
across firms and industries, and support for gender equality and
female employment. These countries also stood out for their generous spending on public education and their workers' high levels
of skill and information-age literacy. After an economic crisis
and budgetary retrenchment in the early 1990s limited the use of
the public sector to increase service employment, the Nordic
countries expanded service jobs in two other ways. They developed
knowledge-intensive industries at the high end of the labor market,
while also deregulating temporary work and making other changes
that put the burden of retrenchment on labor-market outsiders,
just as continental European countries did. But the Nordic countries remained more egalitarian, especially on issues affecting
women, and they had faster economic growth than continental Europe from the early 1990s until the global financial crisis in 2008.[102]

Despite the many differences between the United States and
European countries, American developments in labor markets and
social policy moved along a parallel path from the 1980s through
the early 2000s. In the labor market, standard employment in full-
time jobs declined as firms made increasing use of independent
contractors, subcontractors, and temp agencies. Dualization took
the form of an increase in precarious work. With weaker unions
and fewer legal protections, however, labor-market insiders in the
United States were less able to defend their benefits than their
counterparts in Europe were. Social protection within the firm—
the private welfare state—eroded as companies cut back pension
and health-care obligations and shifted risks to employees.[103]

American social policy—the public welfare state—also saw changes that in some respects paralleled European developments, though the parallels are not widely appreciated because the systems are so different. The great dividing line in American antipoverty policy is the distinction between the deserving and undeserving poor. Under means-tested welfare programs, aid traditionally went only to the deserving—to the blind, disabled, and aged poor and to low-income single mothers with children—but not to able-bodied working-age adults. Even government financing of health care developed according to who was considered deserving. The uninsured became concentrated not among the poorest of the poor, many of whom qualified for Medicaid, but among the poor holding low-wage jobs, an apparent contradiction of the idea that Americans valued and rewarded work. Congress might have eliminated the dualism in social protection with European-style universal policies such as family allowances and national health insurance, except that these were politically blocked. Instead, the lines between the deserving and undeserving were redrawn in the 1990s. Mothers and children on welfare were reassigned to the undeserving category and given less public support, while the working poor were reconceived as deserving and given more support.

The end of the cash assistance program Aid to Families with Dependent Children represents one of the few times in recent history that a long-established welfare policy was overturned. The program was vulnerable not only because of the usual political weaknesses of targeted aid to the poor, but also because of the racially inflected animus against its beneficiaries and the symbolic status it had acquired in the conservative backlash against the liberalism of the 1960s. By the 1990s, moreover, with most mothers joining the workforce, it became harder for liberals to defend a program that enabled low-income mothers to stay home with their children; as an alternative, liberals looked to policies rewarding work that could win wider support. Elected president in 1992 after pledging to end "welfare as we know it," Bill Clinton was responsible for two big changes in antipoverty policy. With Democrats still in control of Congress in 1993, he greatly enlarged the Earned Income Tax Credit, which served as a wage supplement for the working poor. Then, in 1995, with Republicans in control of Congress and over the protests of his liberal aides, Clinton signed legislation replacing the traditional cash assistance program with a more restrictive policy, pointedly called Temporary Assistance for Needy Families to emphasize the limited duration of aid (leaving the federal food stamp program as the equivalent of a national minimum guaranteed income). In the tight labor market of the late 1990s, the emphasis on work initially looked like a success. The long-run effect of Clinton's policies, though, was to increase inequality *among* the poor, boosting the position of low-wage workers but eliminating the safety net for others who fell into deep poverty.[104]

The expanded Earned Income Tax Credit and food stamps were not the only ways the federal government supplemented low wages. From the 1980s through the enactment of the Affordable Care Act in 2010, Congress extended eligibility for Medicaid to the working poor. In different ways, both European and American policies were trying to move "from welfare to workfare." As globalization and technological change were battering the low end of labor markets, governments were using public benefits not financed with payroll taxes to bolster incomes and employment.

When the Great Recession struck in 2008–9, it brought out the welfare state's continuing importance as well as its limits. Social insurance systems and other programs continued to offer protection against destitution and serve as automatic stabilizers. In the United States, the poverty rate would have increased by 4.5 percentage points without government transfers, but it actually rose only by half a point, thanks to measures taken under Barack Obama to extend unemployment insurance and other forms of aid, including tax cuts aimed at the poor and middle class. The tax system became markedly more progressive under Obama, with what was effectively a negative income tax for people below the poverty line and, in his second term, sharp increases in taxes on capital gains and top incomes.[105] Expansionary fiscal and monetary policies helped make the U.S. recovery more rapid than that of most other countries. Despite the general limits imposed by the European Union on deficit spending, European institutions also adopted more expansionary policies in 2008–9 than they had in response to the recessions in 1974–76 and 1980–82.[106] In a sense, Keynesianism was back, if only for the emergency.

The Great Recession showed that the capitalist democracies still had the institutional capacities to address an economic crisis and mitigate the damage. But while governments prevented a repeat of the catastrophe of the 1930s, they had not prevented the Great Recession from happening. Millions of their citizens lost their jobs and homes, only to see governments bail out financial institutions that bore responsibility for the disaster. The stark inequities of state intervention ruined any possibility of a renewal of confidence in progressive government, even where it brought about a recovery.

In 2002, the sociologist Harold Wilensky wrote, "The welfare state persists through thick and thin, through prosperity and recession, through changes in party coalitions, even through shifts of regimes."[107] That assessment is still accurate if the measure is aggregate social spending or the survival of social insurance and other central welfare-state institutions. The net effect of taxes and spending continues to be progressive. Yet that effect, especially in the Anglophone world, has not been large enough to offset rising inequalities in the market given the decline of unions, liberalization of trade, and other changes that have weakened labor's leverage in relation to both employers and public policy. The changed political and fiscal environment has also severely constrained governments' responses to the new post-industrial social risks. Yet some important steps have been taken to supplement the incomes of low-wage workers, promote employment, and provide for parental leave and child care. Social protections for workers in non-standard jobs will be at the center of conflict in coming years.

Since the mid-1970s, the political economy of capitalism has simultaneously evolved in new ways and regressed toward old patterns. Post-industrialism and new technology have brought much of the novelty; neoliberal policy has brought much of the regression. Together, they have contributed to globalization and the emergence of a new online world that has had some of the characteristics of the old laissez-faire. These forces have shaped the era since the end of what I have called the Great Conjuncture, the sequence of world wars and economic crises in the mid-twentieth century that created exceptional conditions for the expansion of the state and reduction

of inequality. Even without globalization, the shift to a post-industrial economy was going to displace workers from industrial jobs
and deprive others of the path to the middle class that those jobs
once provided. As advances in robotics, artificial intelligence, and
other technologies continue, the pressures on labor will be unrelenting and challenge even the governments that are the most sup-
portive of labor's interests. But unsupportive policies make things
tougher. By weakening unions and social protections and accelerating the pace of change, neoliberal policies have made post-industrial
adjustment more difficult.

Many native-born workers see those difficulties as arising from
increased immigration. They remember a time, in the early postwar
decades, when their incomes were rising and their societies were
more homogenous, and they associate the former condition with the
latter. In both Europe and the United States, nativist resentment of
immigrants now figures centrally in political conflict, including conflict over social protection and the welfare state. Anger against immigrants has sometimes been associated with opposition to high
levels of public spending, but it has also led to another response.
Many of the native born who are concerned about immigration do
not necessarily oppose social spending, at least the spending from
which they benefit; indeed, they may oppose immigration partly in
the belief that it threatens their own interests in social protection
and economic security. As right-wing parties have turned toward
populist appeals, it should be no surprise, therefore, to see them
abandoning neoliberalism and embracing "welfare chauvinism"—a
welfare state "for us, not for them"—as right-wing populist parties
in Europe have already done. The radical right in Europe began
winning elections when it dropped right-wing economics.[108]

The idea of an exclusive welfare state has historical precedents.[109] If the right-wing populist parties of the twenty-first century do get their way, they may prove, once again, that the welfare
state "persists through thick and thin . . . even through shifts of regimes." But it would be a very different welfare state from the one
that the Western democracies built by fusing social protection with
liberal principles of universalism and nondiscrimination. Whether
that progressive vision will survive is now a central question in the
unexpected crisis that liberal democracy now faces.

CHAPTER SIX

Democracy and the Politics
of Entrenchment

THREE DECADES AFTER THE fall of Soviet communism, the liberal democratic world finds itself haunted not by one specter but by two—oligarchy and populist nationalism. At a time of rising economic inequality, neither the resurgence of oligarchic power nor the spread of popular discontent should be surprising. But in Europe and the United States, contrary to what one might have expected, the antisystem movements that have mobilized popular discontent have not emerged chiefly on the left, as they did in in the age of industrial capitalism. Instead, the threat to liberal democratic institutions arises from the forces on the right that are beset by fears of demographic and national decline and receptive to authoritarian appeals. As it has done before, a nationalist and populist right offers a politics of resentment against ethnic minorities and a narrative of national betrayal by cosmopolitan elites. In that narrative, new leaders need to take stern measures on behalf of the people to protect them against immigrants and terrorists, unfair rules imposed from abroad, and malign influences in the media and other elite institutions. The niceties of the law cannot be allowed to stand in the way.

Democracies, as I have been arguing in this book, operate at two levels. In ordinary politics, the contending parties take the rules of the system as given and fight over what they understand to be reversible policies and power arrangements. But in the politics of entrenchment, they fight over choices that have foundational implications and that they anticipate will be hard to undo. Unlike ordinary politics, struggles over entrenchment offer a distinctive prize—irreversibility, or as close to it as the institutions of a society can come. Constitutional design is a familiar example, but the politics of entrenchment is not limited to constitutions. Other means, both domestic and international, can also be used to make policies hard to reverse and to achieve and reinforce long-term dominance.

Two conditions heighten interests in strategic entrenchment: political polarization and uncertainty about the future. If a group or party shares considerable common ground with its main rivals and potential successors, it has less reason to try to entrench itself, with all the opposition that will arouse. But when the ideological distance is great, so is the incentive to adopt measures that will be hard for the other side to reverse. That interest will be greater when a party or group is insecure about the future and believes it faces the risk of decline. The key moment for entrenchment may be when a group or party still holds power, or is capable of being mobilized to achieve it, before the dreaded long-term shifts become unstoppable. It may then pursue strategies of entrenchment as a form of political insurance, aiming to prevent its adversaries from subsequently changing policies or from ever gaining power at all.

These conditions—high levels of polarization and fear of demographic and political decline among white majorities—now exist in the United States and many European countries. The supporters of right-wing populist leaders and parties see themselves as facing a threat of irreversible change in society and are therefore looking to bring about irreversible change in law and public institutions. While the rise of populist nationalism today poses many dangers, these are the most troubling: changes in constitutional law and other policies that will be self-reinforcing and threaten to entrench illiberal and antidemocratic power for the long term.

The idea that democracies would self-destruct is an old one, but in recent decades, internal collapse did not seem a serious possibility in the well-established democracies. From the ancient to the early modern world, most republics were short-lived, a pattern that classical political thought attributed to an inevitable cycle of birth, decay, and death in human affairs. Even after modern representative democracies developed on a stable basis, a version of the classic cyclical pattern persisted on a global scale. In Europe, authoritarian reversals followed both the French Revolution and the revolutions of 1848. The same kind of regression wiped out the democratic gains made in the aftermath of World War I. A reverse wave from the late 1940s to the 1960s eliminated some of the new democracies established around the world after World War II and the retreat of European colonialism.[1]

In the late twentieth century, however, representative government and related liberal institutions made such extensive advances internationally that they took on an aura of irreversibility. After the collapse of the Soviet Union, the United States stood alone as a global power, and liberal democracy appeared to have no ideological rival. Political analysts in the 1990s and early 2000s usually interpreted the breakdown of communist and authoritarian regimes as the start of democratic transitions, as though that was their only possible destination. Many of these new regimes, however, adopted only the formalities of constitutions and elections, not the protections of rights that democracy requires, and soon they were authoritarian in all but name. Some working democracies also broke down, "backsliding" in a process that was slower and, at least initially, more ambiguous than in past reverse waves. Instead of generals seizing power in a coup, self-aggrandizing elected leaders have typically entrenched themselves through steps that formally comply with the law.[2]

Still, as recently as 2015, authoritarian reversals were relatively few, and there was at least a plausible case that talk of a global "democratic recession" was exaggerated.[3] But the reverse wave has continued as antisystem parties and leaders have gained support and entered governments even in European countries regarded as successfully consolidated democracies. A variety of measures of public opinion show diminished support for democracy and increased receptivity to alternatives.[4] What has come especially as a shock is that the reverse wave has hit the United States, with the election in 2016 of a president who disdains democratic norms, embraces authoritarian leaders, and undermines the international institutions supporting liberal democracy.

With the rise of populist nationalism, the liberal world now faces two different stress tests. One is to the national political institutions that embody the principles of liberal democracy. The other is to the international institutions where political liberalism has become entangled with neoliberal economics, and democratic influences are at best weak and indirect. As I write, it is impossible to know how the present crisis will turn out. It may be a brief historical parenthesis or the prologue to a full-scale authoritarian reversal and nationalist revival. The two current threats to liberal democracy are not entirely separate. The return of oligarchical power and the rise of populist nationalism overlap and have even come together, nowhere more clearly than in the presidency of Donald Trump.

OLIGARCHY AS POPULISM

Though seemingly opposed, oligarchy and populism are often linked. In some countries they feed off each other, with populists winning support in reaction to oligarchic governments and vice versa. This has been the pattern in relatively new and unsettled democracies in Latin America and Southeast Asia that oscillate between oligarchic and populist control. The defining feature of such political systems is neither their oligarchic nor populist phases but their repeated swerving back and forth.[5]

Oligarchy and populism may also be linked more directly, when opportunistic wealthy elites join with majority ethnic or religious groups in an alliance against other elites and minorities. Oligarchy here coalesces with populism, not the egalitarian populism of the left directed against the rich but the exclusionary populism of the right directed against ethnically and culturally defined others, who are portrayed as alien to a people's historic identity and true interests. An alliance in which oligarchs provide the resources, while right-wing populists provide the political framing and the following, makes sense for both. Oligarchs have the money and often the media that populists need, and populism provides as good a mask for oligarchy as the political imagination can devise.

The term "oligarchy" need not refer only to regimes where a wealthy few directly control the state. According to a more general conception, oligarchy exists wherever wealth is concentrated and those who control it also have exceptional power over the government policies that affect them. If we think of oligarchy that way, as Jeffrey Winters suggests, it can coexist with democracy as long as officials do not encroach on the prerogatives of the wealthy. On many issues—think of abortion or gay rights—the superrich may come down on different sides, but they are less likely to cancel each other out on matters, such as taxes, that bear directly on their shared economic interests. As Winters points out, an entire "wealth defense industry," consisting of lawyers, accountants, and lobbyists, has arisen in the United States to protect wealth through the manipulation of the tax code, regulatory system, and inheritance laws. "The degree of oligarchy in a society," he argues, "depends on how concentrated wealth is in a few hands, and how easily wealth power can be converted into political power."[6]

Oligarchical power has been a recurrent pattern in European and American history. Landed aristocracies dominated European societies well into the modern era. The slaveholding oligarchy of the South shaped American political development through the antebellum period. Financial and industrial capital did the same in both Europe and America in the late nineteenth and early twentieth centuries. All of these forms of oligarchic dominance became so deeply entrenched that they long seemed impossible to overturn. It took the revolutions of the eighteenth century to overthrow the systems of patrimonial inheritance and the power of landed oligarchy in the United States and France. It took the Civil War and Reconstruction to end slavery's sway over the early American republic. It took the rise of labor movements and parties of the left in Europe to put labor on a position of relative equality with capital, and in the United States it took the reform movements of the Populist and Progressive eras and the New Deal to rein in the plutocracy. Each of these counter-oligarchic movements transformed politics and society in a more democratic direction, but none achieved a permanent victory. Economic and political development has brought with it not only new forms and concentrations of wealth but also new ways of converting wealth into political power.

As I argued in Chapters 2 and 3, wealth may be converted into political power through at least four channels: the control of a specific type of domain (such as a plantation or corporation), concentrations and combinations of ownership (such as concentrated wealth or monopoly), privileged political and legal representation and access (such as differential voting rights and financing of candidates and parties), and the structural indispensability of capital for investment and growth. Soaring wealth at the top is only part of the reason for the recent return of oligarchical power. Changes in law and political economy have also facilitated the conversion of wealth into political power through each of the four channels.

1. Owners' and managers' control of a domain such as a corporation depends on the power of other parties in that domain. The decline of unions throughout the advanced economies has given employers more unilateral domain control and therefore a foundation for greater political power. Labor has effectively lost many of its old weapons, such as the strike, as business has made more use of contingent labor and outsourcing.

2. Concentrations and combinations of ownership depend on tax and competition policies. The sharp reduction in progressive income and estate taxes has facilitated the concentration of wealth. Monopoly power has also grown as antitrust enforcement has waned and firms in many industries have consolidated, while new forms of monopoly power have emerged in the central platforms of the online economy.

3. Privileged political access has increased as a result of two different sets of developments affecting the elected and non-elected branches of government. In the United States, political campaigns have required ever-increasing funds at a time when the Supreme Court has effectively eliminated limits on contributions, giving enormous influence to big donors (only partially offset by online capacities to raise money from smaller contributors). On both sides of the Atlantic, the removal of policy decisions

from the elected branches of government to counter-majoritarian institutions such as central banks has provided another channel for money's increased influence on policy.

4. Structural dependence on capital for economic growth has increased as governments have deregulated finance, enabling the owners of wealth and those who invest it on their behalf to move it anywhere in the global economy with a few keystrokes.

Some of these developments, notably the decline in labor's power, have been more pronounced in the Anglophone countries than in continental Europe. The rise in economic inequality since 1980 has also been greater in the Anglophone world.[7] But as I noted in the previous chapter, labor has lost power in Europe too. As employment has shifted from manufacturing to services, it has shifted away from the most heavily unionized industries. Although the trends vary from one country to another, membership in unions and the share of the workforce covered by collective bargaining agreements have fallen throughout most of western Europe.[8] At the same time, the growth of global trade and free-trade agreements have weakened labor's bargaining position. After going into effect in 1993, the Treaty on European Union guaranteed the free movement of capital, goods, and people among the member states. Between 2004 and 2007, the EU expanded that free-trade area with the admission of twelve states, chiefly eastern European countries with low wages and low levels of social protection. As a result, employers could more easily relocate operations to the east, and the citizens of those countries could migrate freely to the west. In addition, the EU and other international institutions made other policy decisions weakening labor rights and unions' bargaining power.[9]

The economic policy failures of both national governments and transnational institutions in the 1990s and early 2000s contributed to growing support for populist nationalism, particularly among working-class constituencies. In much of eastern Europe, including the former East Germany, post-communist economic performance did not match expectations, and even where economic growth was strong, as in Poland, many people were left out of the gains. In western Europe, governments were asking their native-born populations to accept increasing numbers of immigrants, many from outside Europe, in an era of slow growth and persistently high unemployment. Non-Europeans had begun arriving after World War II, when some former colonial subjects migrated to Europe and guest workers were recruited from Turkey, the Middle East, and North Africa to meet labor shortages. A politically significant backlash developed only later, when the postwar boom ended but many of those foreign workers stayed and raised families. The western European countries also began admitting large numbers of refugees from Africa and the Middle East during the 1980s and 1990s.[10]

For countries that had been relatively homogeneous in the early postwar years, the changes were dramatic. The ethnic minority population in Great Britain, for example, went from under 100,000 in the 1950s to more than eight million today; Germany went from one million guest workers in 1964 to a population of about 17 million immigrants and their descendants.[11] By the early 2000s, surveys were registering rising hostility to immigration, with respondents saying that immigrants made crime worse, took away jobs, and received more in welfare benefits than they paid in taxes.[12] Religious differences heightened the social tensions; the growth of Islamic communities aroused opposition not only from conservative Christians but also from secular liberals, and Islamist terrorism in the early 2000s inflamed those tensions further. A poll in 2017 found an average of 50 percent of respondents in EU countries agreeing with the statement "There are so many foreigners in our country, sometimes I feel like a stranger."[13]

The United States has seen a major demographic shift, too. As a result of restrictive immigration laws adopted in the 1920s, the United States had also been relatively homogeneous in the early postwar decades, but by the early 2000s the foreign-born population reached its highest level in a century. Although the United States has a longer and deeper tradition than European countries of receiving and assimilating immigrants, anti-immigrant feeling increased in America as well.[14]

Economic disappointments and rising anger about immigration provided a political opening for new right-wing populist parties and for the leaders of existing parties to reorient their rhetoric and policies. In some western European countries, such as Denmark, populist parties had originated in the antitax movements of the 1970s, while other right-wing parties, such as France's National Front, had connections to earlier fascist and Nazi groups. In search of wider support, these parties ditched their old antigovernment posture and distanced themselves from unsavory historical associations. Now they focused on immigration restrictions, became advocates of welfare-state protections for the native born, and refashioned themselves as defenders of popular rule against the elitist impositions of the EU. The great prize was the support of workers who in both Europe and the United States felt they had been abandoned by the parties of the left that they had supported in the past. Once central to politics as well as the economy, white workers have increasingly come to believe they have been demoted and marginalized while others have pushed in front of them. The fear of a way of life slipping away has been especially acute in declining industrial and rural communities, the areas that have provided the most votes for antisystem parties.[15]

Besides being anti-elitist, the new populists are antipluralist. Claiming that they alone represent the people, they practice what Jan-Werner Müller calls "an exclusionary form of identity politics" that denies legitimacy to the claims of outgroups and to other political views. "Put simply," Müller writes, "populists do not claim 'We are the 99 percent.' What they imply instead is 'We are the 100 percent.' " This antipluralism affects how populists govern. Since they see themselves as the nation's only true representatives, they openly convert the state bureaucracy into their own partisan instrument by removing independent professionals and civil servants who put obstacles in their path. They shower benefits on favored constituencies and use the powers of the state against their enemies in a pattern of "discriminatory legalism" ("for my friends, everything; for my enemies, the law").[16]

Populist parties in power have also directed the fruits of state power to allies in the private sector through government contracts, licenses, and regulatory policies.[17] Mutually advantageous relations between populists in power and business allies have been especially important in the control of the media. The regimes don't need to shut down opposition media or bring them under direct state ownership. Instead, they pressure the owners of troublesome newspapers and broadcast stations to sell them to business allies who enjoy the government's largesse and are dependent on it. The result is media capture, the subordination of the media to oligarchic interests close to the regime.[18] In the world of crony capitalism, enrichment and entrenchment go happily together.

Donald Trump embodies this fusion of oligarchy and populism and the simultaneous pursuit of enrichment and entrenchment. Long before the 2016 election, observers were talking about America entering a "second gilded age," an understanding of our time that has found its purest expression in Trump's politics, enterprises, and aesthetic. After his connections to Russian oligarchs drew attention during the 2016 campaign, the *Washington Post* columnist Anne Appelbaum wrote, "The real problem with Trump isn't that he is sympathetic to Russian oligarchs, it's that he *is* a Russian oligarch"—or as she went on to explain, he is "an oligarch in the Russian style—a rich man who aspires to combine business with politics and has an entirely cynical and instrumental attitude toward both."[19] Both as a candidate and in office, Trump has proven himself a master of the exclusionary identity politics that define right-wing populism. The key to that politics is the fingering of elites and minorities as involved in a joint conspiracy against the people. The story Trump tells is of a great national betrayal by leaders whose immigration, trade, and national security policies allowed in Muslim terrorists, Mexican criminals, and cheap imports from China that have stolen American jobs. At the same time, he flaunts his personal wealth and ability to avoid paying taxes and signs tax legislation that offers little to the working-class voters who put him in office but a great deal to the Republican donor class and Trump himself. The contradictions are so open and flagrant that "exposing" them may seem only to belabor the obvious.

It is a mistake to try to fit into a coherent political philosophy all of the practices and policies of the Trump presidency or other right-wing governments claiming to be populist. Whatever they say, most of what they do is best understood from the standpoint of political entrenchment. An exclusionary conception of the people serves them not only when they start out on the road to power, but in keeping power once they achieve it. Limiting immigration, denying immigrants a path to citizenship, and obstructing the electoral participation of minority citizens are all means of entrenchment. Populists do not just polarize the public with extreme proposals and incendiary language when they campaign for office; polarization becomes a continuing practice of governing, a means of reaffirming and deepening the divides that populists count on to retain support. Similarly, populists have a continuing need to identify "enemies of the people," whether those are in the media, the universities, transnational institutions, or the "deep state" inside their own state bureaucracy. The presence of those enemies explains why criticism from those quarters or the facts they report can be dismissed as "fake news," and why the government is justified in whatever measures it takes. As Steven Levitsky and Daniel Ziblatt argue, capturing the "referees"—the law enforcement, tax, and regulatory authorities that are supposed to be independent and nonpartisan—is a critical step for authoritarians.[20] Capturing those institutions not only shields political leaders from investigation but gives them the power to destroy their opponents. This is all about entrenchment. And as long as populist regimes care about maintaining a semblance of legality, one form of entrenchment is of special long-term value, and that is capture of the constitution itself.

CONSTITUTIONAL CAPTURE

Constitutional democracy rests on the premise that when ordinary politics fails, constitutional protections will limit the damage. If elected leaders and their appointees fail to uphold their responsibilities, threaten to violate individual rights, and try to perpetuate themselves in office, constitutions and courts are there as a backstop to ensure that officials stay within the law, rights are safeguarded, and the voters have an opportunity to throw out the incumbents. That is the theory. But if democracy can go wrong in ordinary politics, why can't the politics of entrenchment go wrong too? When constitutions are drafted or amended, they are not immune from the influence of powerful interests. Why should constitutional change be any more reliably democratic than ordinary political change?

This is the problem of constitutional capture—the capture of an ostensibly liberal democratic constitution for purposes that are neither liberal nor democratic. Regulatory agencies may be captured by the industries they are supposed to regulate. So, too, constitutions and supreme courts may be captured by parties and powerful interests that the constitution is supposed to regulate. But while regulatory capture distorts one sector of the economy, constitutional capture distorts the entire political system. The greatest danger is what Kim Lane Scheppele calls a "constitutional coup." A constitutional coup is constitutional because it satisfies formal legal requirements, but it is a coup because it achieves "a substantively anti-constitutional result, including, in the extreme case, transforming a state in plain sight from a constitutional democracy to an autocracy."[21] The prime historical example is what happened in Germany in 1933. Shortly after the Nazis won a plurality of legislative seats, the new chancellor, Adolf Hitler, persuaded President Paul von Hindenberg to declare a state of emergency, suspending an array of rights. The rationale for the state of emergency was a fire in the Reichstag (parliament) allegedly set by a Communist; the arrest of Communist representatives then turned the Nazi plurality of seats into a majority. Subsequent legislation authorized Hitler's cabinet to govern by decree, the suspended rights were never restored, and what had been a democracy was transformed into a dictatorship through formally legal means.

Scheppele's contemporary example of a constitutional coup is what happened in Hungary after the Fidesz Party under Viktor Orban won a free election in 2010 with 53 percent of the vote. Under Hungary's electoral rules, that 53 percent of the vote gave Fidesz two-thirds of the legislative seats, and under Hungary's "lightly entrenched" constitution, a two-thirds vote of the legislature was sufficient for constitutional revisions. (Actually, the constitution at the time required a four-fifths vote to decide on constitution-drafting procedures, but Fidesz reduced that requirement to two-thirds with a two-thirds vote.) Orban's government then proceeded to rewrite the constitution, pack the constitutional court, and change election rules and procedures to ensure that opposition to its policies would be ineffectual.

In both the Nazi and Hungarian cases, a single election opened the way to constitutional capture. Many other constitutions create several hurdles for constitutional revision, which can at least force the leaders of a government intent on entrenching new rules to go back to the voters for a confirming election, or to seek the approval of other branches in the national government or other levels of government. Separate procedures for initiating and ratifying amendments help to create a series of tests of public sentiment. Article 5 of the U.S. Constitution sets out two ways of initiating amendments and two ways of ratifying them. They can be initiated by a two-thirds vote of both houses of Congress or by two-thirds of the state legislatures calling for a "convention for proposing amendments" (the latter method has so far never been used). Amendments then have to be ratified by three-fourths of the states, either by their legislatures or by specially elected conventions, as Congress may decide. So arduous are the requirements that relatively few amendments have been approved. But as a result, many of the most important constitutional changes have taken place in other ways, especially through changes in the membership and doctrines of the Supreme Court.

Nonetheless, the political difficulty of making and sustaining major constitutional changes in the United States may still be a safeguard of democracy. In his three-volume constitutional history *We the People*, Bruce Ackerman argues that the great "constitutional moments"—the adoption of the Constitution, Reconstruction, the New Deal, and the civil rights revolution—have been affirmations of popular sovereignty. Developing a theory of what he calls "dualist democracy," Ackerman distinguishes transformations of "higher lawmaking" from ordinary politics and argues that the key democratic basis of higher lawmaking is not Article 5 but the separation of powers. Constitutional transformations typically pit a reforming institution (often but not always the presidency) against a resisting institution. The resulting clashes among presidents, Congress, and the Supreme Court force the advocates of constitutional reform to run an institutional gauntlet—including multiple public confrontations and a series of elections—before they can consolidate the

changes. A dualist democracy, Ackerman argues, is appropriate because popular involvement in politics varies from decade to decade.
"During periods of constitutional politics," he writes, "the higher
lawmaking system encourages an engaged citizenry to focus on
fundamental issues and determine whether any proposed solution
deserves its considered support. During periods of normal politics,
the system prevents the political·elite from undermining the hard-
won achievements of the People 'behind the citizenry's back.' "[22]

The ultimate democratic safeguard, according to Ackerman, is
the need for sustained popular mobilization to bring about constitutional change. Democratic political participation, however, partly
depends on whether those in power solicit or suppress it. Elections
also do not necessarily turn on constitutional questions; economic
conditions or other unrelated political conflicts may be more decisive. The constitutional transformations that figure centrally in
Ackerman's analysis did enlarge the scope of both the national government and democratic citizenship. But just as there have been
reverse waves of democratization around the world, so there have
been reverse waves in American history. The Reconstruction
amendments were supposed to protect the rights of African Americans but were used to sanctify the rights of corporations. The
achievements of both the New Deal and civil rights revolutions
have been partly reversed, and more reversals may be on the way.
Despite its democratic moments, America has had long periods
when concentrated wealth has dominated both politics and the
courts. Economic inequality is a structural source of political inequality that the law has not rectified. Building on those structural
advantages, a conservative political party can use a combination of
means—some complying with legal norms, others not—to entrench constitutional changes that narrow the scope of government
and citizenship, as long as that party continues to win several elections in a row and secures enough seats on the Supreme Court to
consolidate its hold.

The United States was already in the midst of a reverse wave
before the 2016 election, and it is not hard to envision scenarios
that would put the nation's democratic achievements even more
gravely at risk than they are now. One involves the untraveled road
of a new constitutional convention. Another involves exploiting

the structural weaknesses of progressive politics and consolidating constitutional change through the Supreme Court.

The provision in Article 5 for a constitutional convention is a potentially explosive but not impossible option. Conservative groups backed by wealthy donors have been promoting the idea; some advocates claim twenty-eight states have open applications for a convention, just six short of the thirty-four required, though that calculation ignores mutually contradictory stipulations in the resolutions passed by state legislatures.[23] If Hillary Clinton had won the 2016 presidential election, conservatives might have responded to the prospective liberal shift in the Supreme Court by mobilizing to pass consistent calls for a convention. In that sense, Trump's election may have averted a constitutional crisis, at least of the sort that a convention might produce.

The Constitution is silent on how a new constitutional convention would work. It prescribes no limits on a convention's authority and no rules for such basic decisions as how states are to be represented (the original Convention in 1787 gave each state delegation one vote). Even though some states have called for a convention to propose a balanced-budget amendment, a convention could set its own agenda.[24] Despite being called only to amend the Articles of Confederation, the 1787 Convention wrote a new constitution, and instead of following the requirement under the Articles for unanimous approval of amendments, it set a requirement of only three-fourths of the states for ratification. A new convention could also set new ratification criteria. If disputes arose about its procedures or outcome, the Supreme Court would have no jurisdiction to resolve them; disputes over the ratification of amendments, the Court has said, are "political questions" outside its purview.[25] A convention would be a desperate move by a party that had greater power in the states than at the national level and decided to use that power to try to transform the constitutional order.

The more likely path to constitutional capture by the right is through the gradual democratic backsliding that is already taking place. That path involves strategically weakening progressive constituencies, maximally using executive powers, and consolidating partisan control of the Supreme Court.

Republicans have opportunities to entrench themselves in power partly because of structural disadvantages that progressives face. The U.S. Senate underrepresents the most populous states, where, it now happens, Democrats are concentrated. Democratic senators on average represent more constituents and have received more votes than Republican senators, but they are nevertheless, as of 2019, in the minority. By 2040, according to demographic projections, 30 percent of the population, spread over the less urbanized states, will choose 70 percent of the Senate, making it even less nationally representative.[26] That 30 percent will be not only disproportionately rural but also disproportionately white. (If the 30 percent of Americans projected to control 70 percent of the Senate consisted primarily of racial minorities, the odds of reforming the structure of the Senate would miraculously improve, notwithstanding the constitutional obstacles.) In addition, thanks to the high spatial concentration of Democrats in metropolitan areas, many more Democratic votes for the House of Representatives and state legislatures are "wasted" in districts where Democrats have overwhelming majorities. Perhaps most important, Democratic support comes disproportionately from groups that tend to vote at lower rates, including low-income minorities, immigrants, and the young.

The last two of these structural disadvantages can then be magnified by strategically chosen electoral rules. The spatial concentration of Democratic voters makes them highly susceptible to extreme partisan and racial gerrymanders. The Democratic vote can also be reduced through a variety of facially neutral election rules that disproportionately affect lower-income groups, such as requirements for specific forms of government-issued identification, disenfranchisement of ex-felons, and purges of less frequent voters from the rolls. Limited voting hours, fewer polling places in cities, and other measures that make voting more difficult or time-consuming can also produce the same results. Historically, the techniques of voter suppression have changed, but the intent remains what it was in the past—reducing the votes and thereby the voice of minorities and the poor for purposes of political entrenchment.[27]

Although unions have declined, they remain an important base of the Democratic Party and a prime target for conservatives.

Republicans have used their power at the state level to enact right-to-work laws that deny unions the ability to require workers to pay "fair share" fees for representing them in collective bargaining. The loss of that financing then throws unions on the defensive, forcing them to devote resources to holding on to members. Right-to-work laws have substantial political effects. They decrease contributions to Democratic campaigns, make it less likely that Democratic voters will be contacted to vote, and reduce the votes Democratic candidates receive.[28]

The measures disadvantaging Democrats do not make it impossible for them to win national elections. They raise the hurdle Democrats have to overcome, requiring them to have the support not just of a majority of the people but of a supermajority. When they enjoy especially wide support and win a wave election, they can interrupt entrenchment and possibly stop it—but the structural handicaps owing to the nature of the Senate, spatially concentrated supporters, and reliance on low-turnout constituencies appear to be long-term.

With Trump in power, Republicans face fewer obstacles to targeted voter suppression. Instead of enforcing voting rights, the Trump administration has focused on the phantom menace of illegal voting by immigrants. During the 2016 election, Trump repeatedly said he might not accept the results because of election fraud, and since then he has falsely claimed that millions of illegal votes were cast against him. It is easy to dismiss such comments, but they have laid down the predicate for a refusal by Trump and other Republicans to give up power in a close election.

Executive aggrandizement has been the path to democratic breakdown in other countries, and the United States may not be nearly as well protected against that risk as Americans have traditionally assumed. The modern presidency is an awesomely powerful institution, with broad authority over law enforcement, economic and social regulation, tax collection, trade agreements, intelligence, and national security. Democracy has worked as well as it has, which is far from perfectly, only because of unwritten norms that have demanded forbearance in the partisan and personal use of those powers.[29] A president determined to test the limits of presidential powers could make a mockery of the idea of a system of checks and balances.

Republicans' resort to voter suppression and their silence in the face of Trump's violations of democratic norms have raised serious questions about how committed they are to democratic institutions. "If conservatives become convinced that they cannot win democratically, they will not abandon conservatism. They will reject democracy," writes David Frum, former speechwriter for George W. Bush. "The stability of American society depends on conservatives' ability to find a way forward from the Trump dead end, toward a conservatism that cannot only win elections but also govern responsibly, a conservatism that is culturally modern, economically inclusive, and environmentally responsible, that upholds markets at home and U.S. leadership internationally."[30] It is indeed the lesson of much past history that for democracy to work, conservatives must see a practical "way forward" for themselves within it. But their leaders may not choose that path, and many of their supporters may not want it.

The nightmare scenario on the model of the Reichstag fire is that President Trump or a like-minded successor would use an episode such as a terrorist incident as a pretext for entrenching his own power and suspending civil liberties. Under the separation of powers, Congress and the judiciary are supposed to prevent the president from aggrandizing his powers, but in an era of polarized political parties, there is no counting on a divided and irresolute Congress to stop a single-minded and resolute president. And the Supreme Court has a long history of according "near-total deference to the executive" when the government claims that national security is at stake.[31]

But it is unnecessary to speculate about what the Court might do in a crisis, when it has already done so much without a crisis to facilitate political entrenchment. The conservative movement has become more sophisticated about entrenching its power and the constitutional tenets that support it. When Richard Nixon had four Supreme Court nominations in his first term, conservatives were not prepared with candidates they had vetted or with a clear conception of their objectives. But in the following decades, with the financial support of wealthy right-wing donors, the conservative movement built a formidable legal network to develop the ideas, strategies, and people to ensure that when the opportunities arose for judicial appointments and legal breakthroughs, they could take full advantage of them.[32] The judges and justices whom Republicans have named to the courts in recent decades reflect that strategic awareness.

Supreme Court appointments are to some extent a lottery because of the unpredictable relationship between presidential terms and judicial retirements and deaths—but not entirely so. Justices often retire at a time when a president with their views can replace them. The five-to-four decision in *Bush v. Gore* in 2000 to suspend the recount of votes in Florida on the basis of a rule the Court said could never be applied again not only put the presidency in Republican hands; it also ensured that the Republican majority on the Court would stay the majority with new Republican appointees. After the death of Justice Antonin Scalia in February 2016, the Republican majority in the Senate also invented a previously unknown rule—this time, that a president could not fill a court vacancy in the final year of his term—to block any consideration of Barack Obama's nominee, Merrick Garland, for the seat filled the next year when Trump nominated Neil Gorsuch.

Even with bare five-to-four majorities, the Court has rewarded Republicans with a series of decisions about voting rights, campaign finance reform, and gerrymandering that have helped give the party an edge in elections. The Court's decisions about the rights of corporations and unions have been especially important not only for partisan but for oligarchic entrenchment. The "rights revolution" is usually thought of as the advance of the rights of racial minorities, women, gays and lesbians, and other historically disadvantaged groups. But no rights movement has had more success than the movement for corporate rights, though, unlike the others, it did not involve popular protest aimed at changing public opinion. On the contrary, it has proceeded without popular support but succeeded nonetheless. Leveraging rights established for other groups has been one basis of that success; corporations now enjoy nearly all the rights of individuals, except the right to vote.[33] But thanks to the Court, corporations now have expanded rights to influence votes. In *Citizens United* in 2010, the Court overturned a century-old ban on the ability of corporations to use money from their general treasuries to influence elections, on the grounds that the law infringed on free speech (previously, corporations could set up "political action committees" to collect contributions from employees). Unions have long been prohibited from using union dues for political purposes, and in right-to-work states, they cannot require workers they represent even to pay a share of the costs of representation. But in the *Janus* case in 2018, the Court took a further step when it decided, also on the basis of free speech, that public-employee unions cannot negotiate agreements that require workers to pay "fair share" fees. The decision effectively applied the right-to-work laws to the public sector throughout the country. In short, the Supreme Court interprets the First Amendment as allowing corporations to use all the resources at their disposal to influence elections and as denying unions the resources they require to exert countervailing influence.

In the now dominant legal understanding, as Joseph Fishkin and William Forbath point out, the Constitution is blind to oligarchical power and serves only to limit what legislators can do in response to it. But an alternative tradition of constitutional thought that Fishkin and Forbath call the "Anti-Oligarchy Constitution" looks upon the choices differently. It holds that "we cannot keep our constitutional democracy—our 'republican form of government'—without constitutional restraints against oligarchy and a political economy that maintains a broad middle class, accessible to everyone." From Andrew Jackson through the Populists and Progressives to Franklin Roosevelt and the New Deal, this was a central idea in the American political and legal tradition.[34]

The disappearance of that tradition from the Supreme Court does not mean it need be lost forever; on the contrary, its deep roots and long persistence should give grounds for confidence that it can be recovered again. But for there to be any chance of a revival of limits on oligarchic and monopoly power, democracy itself will have to survive the stress tests it faces now.

DEMOCRACY'S STRESS TESTS

Entrenched institutions, as I have emphasized throughout this book, are hard but not impossible to undo, and they consequently may have one additional effect that goes unnoticed until they are in trouble. They may create a false sense of security and lead those who control them to overreach. This is a classic source of the decline of empires and the defeat of dictatorships that overstretch their resources in war, but it has not been their problem alone.

When the liberal democracies and capitalism stood in triumph after the collapse of Soviet communism, their leaders also overreached. It was not just foolish to believe the whole world would follow the West's example; overconfidence also led to reckless decisions at home. In the making of policies about finance, trade, and labor, all of the lessons from the 1930s about the dangers of unfettered markets were forgotten. The post-industrial transition was going to be hard enough; the insecurities created by the weakening of social protections and financial regulation made it even tougher. As the digital revolution advanced, the people with the relevant skills and resources, who could expect to be on the creative, disrupting side of "creative destruction," gave little thought to what the disrupted and despairing might do as their world crumbled. In their enthusiasm for diversity, the winners also underestimated the backlash against immigration. The evidence is strong for long-term net social gains from trade, technological change, and immigration, but lecturing the losers about the need to be adaptable and tolerant was never going to be as persuasive as a promise to put their interests first.

Now both the international and domestic institutions that have supported liberal democracies are at risk. Internationally, the advocates of constitutionalism and democracy underestimated the potential for a resurgence of surviving authoritarian regimes. Just as important, they underestimated the risks of institutional capture from within the long-established democracies. Least of all did they imagine the emergence of an illiberal international alliance linking the world's authoritarian and populist leaders, including the president of the United States.

Democracy is always a gamble, but in ordinary politics the stakes are only short-term wins and losses. The stakes escalate when the prospects rise for entrenchment. The legitimate reason for an entrenched constitution is to prevent the wrong turns of a moment from wrecking institutions with durable advantages. Constitutionalism provides opportunities for recovery, and to the extent it holds now, there is hope that the setbacks to democracy can be reversed. But maintaining constitutional norms is not enough. The defenders of liberal democracy also need to disentangle it from the errors of recent decades, reverse its tendencies toward oligarchy, and reconstruct the popular basis on which its historical achievements have rested.

Sooner or later, even the richest and most fortunate countries face systemic crises, including crises of their own making. Those are the times when their people, not just their institutions, are tested. Some elections in a democracy are not only about who will hold office for the next term, but about the principles that will govern in the long run. It is an error of the most serious kind to think you are fighting a normal election when you are actually fighting over the constitutional system itself. Let us hope that when those moments of decision come, enough people appreciate what is at stake.

Notes

Introduction

1. John Stuart Mill, *Considerations on Representative Government* (London: Parker, Son and Bourn, 1861), 127–128.

Chapter One. Understanding Entrenchment

1. John R. Searle, *Mind, Language and Society: Philosophy in the Real World* (New York: Basic Books, 1998), 123–124. The application of this distinction to society departs from the original Kantian meaning in that social institutions are not objects of pure intuition. When applied to social rules, the constitutive/regulative distinction defines a range rather than a binary.
2. Giuseppe Tomasi di Lampedusa, *The Leopard*, tr. Archibald Colquhoun (New York: Pantheon, 1960), 40.
3. This conception implies a rejection of other conceptions of institutions as self-enforcing conventions or as shared scripts for action. For a relevant discussion (although a still more circumscribed definition of institutions), see Wolfgang Streeck and Kathleen Thelen, "Introduction: Institutional Change in Advanced Political Economies," pp. 1–39 in Wolfgang Streeck and Kathleen Thelen, eds., *Beyond Continuity: Institutional Change in Advanced Political Economies* (Cary, NC: Oxford University Press, 2005).
4. Jon Elster, *Ulysses and the Sirens: Studies in Rationality and Irrationality* (Cambridge: Cambridge University Press, 1979), 77, 113.
5. Peter Hedström and Peter Bearman, "What Is Analytical Sociology About? An Introductory Essay," in Peter Hedström and Peter Bearman, eds., *The Oxford Handbook of Analytical Sociology* (New York: Oxford University Press, 2009), 3–24.

6. James C. Scott, *Domination and the Arts of Resistance: Hidden Transcripts* (New Haven: Yale University Press, 1990), vi.

7. H. L. A. Hart, *The Concept of Law* (New York: Oxford University Press, 1963), 78–95 (quotation: 92).

8. Terry M. Moe and Michael Caldwell, "The Institutional Foundations of Democratic Government: A Comparison of Presidential and Parliamentary Systems," *Journal of Institutional and Theoretical Economics* (1994), 150: 171–195; Martin Gilens, *Affluence and Influence: Economic Inequality and Political Power in America* (Princeton, NJ: Princeton University Press, 2012), 74, 99, 134; Alfred Stepan and Juan J. Linz, "Comparative Perspectives on Inequality and the Quality of Democracy in the United States," *Perspectives on Politics* (2011), 9: 841–853.

9. Barry D. Baysinger and Henry N. Butler, "Antitakeover Amendments, Managerial Entrenchment, and the Contractual Theory of the Corporation," *Virginia Law Review* (1985), 71: 1257–1303; Gerald F. Davis, "Agents Without Principles: The Spread of the Poison Pill Through the Intercorporate Network," *Administrative Science Quarterly* (1991), 36: 583–513; Marcel Kahan and Michael Klausner, "Lockups and the Market for Corporate Control," *Stanford Law Review* (1996), 48: 1539–1571.

10. On the forms of cumulative advantage, see Thomas A. DiPrete and Gregory M. Eirich, "Cumulative Advantage as a Mechanism for Inequality: A Review of Theoretical and Empirical Developments," *Annual Review of Sociology* (2006), 32: 271–297.

11. W. Brian Arthur, "Competing Technologies, Increasing Returns, and Lock-In by Historical Events," *Economic Journal* (1989), 99: 116–131; W. Brian Arthur, *Increasing Returns and Path Dependence in the Economy* (Ann Arbor: University of Michigan Press, 1994). Paul Krugman disputes Arthur's claims of originality. See "The Legend of Arthur: A Tale of Gullibility at *The New Yorker*," *Slate* (January 15, 1998), at https://slate.com/business/1998/01/the-legend-of-arthur.html.

12. Paul A. David, "Clio and the Economics of QWERTY," *American Economic Review* 75 (1985), 332–337. More recent research has called into question various aspects of the "QWERTY legend," including whether the original design was intended to slow down typists. See Koichi Yasuoka and Motoko Yasuoka, "On the Prehistory of QWERTY," *Zinbun* (2009/2010), no. 42, 161–174.

13. Robin Cowan, "Nuclear Power Reactors: A Study in Technological Lock-In," *Journal of Economic History* (1990), 50: 541–567 (quotations: 552, 567).

14. Paul A. David and Julie Ann Bunn, "The Economics of Gateway Technologies and Network Evolution: Lessons from Electricity Supply History," *Information Economics and Policy* (1988), 3: 165–202.

15. On information cascades, see Sushil Bikhchandani, David Hirchleifer, and Ivo Welch, "A Theory of Fads, Fashion, Custom, and Cultural

Change as Informational Cascades," *Journal of Political Economy* (1992), 992–1026; Abhijit V. Banerjee, "A Simple Model of Herd Behavior," *Quarterly Journal of Economics* (1992), 107: 797–817; Sushil Bikhchandani, David Hirshleifer, and Ivo Welch, "Learning from the Behavior of Others: Conformity, Fads, and Information Cascades," *Journal of Economic Perspectives* (1998), 12: 151–170; and David Easley and Jon Kleinberg, *Networks, Crowds, and Markets: Reasoning About a Highly Connected World* (New York: Cambridge University Press, 2010).

16. Brian Arthur et al., "Path Dependence Processes and the Emergence of Macro-Structure," *European Journal of Operational Research* (1987), 30: 294–230.

17. For the original experiment, see Lisa R. Anderson and Charles A. Holt, "Information Cascades in the Laboratory," *American Economic Review* (1997), 87: 847–862.

18. Matthew J. Salganik, Peter Sheridan Dodds, and Duncan J. Watts, "Experimental Study of Inequality and Unpredictability in an Artificial Cultural Market," *Science* (2006), 311: 854–856.

19. In other words, cascades may have long-term consequences, but it is not the cascade itself that locks in those consequences. For an example of the application of the model to a political revolution, see Susanne Lohmann, "The Dynamics of Information Cascades: The Monday Demonstrations in Leipzig, East Germany, 1989–91," *World Politics* (1994), 47: 42–101. For a model showing how unpopular norms may be socially enforced (that is, through interpersonal pressure rather than top-down authority) as a result of a cascade, see Damon Centola, Robb Willer, and Michael Macy, "The Emperor's Dilemma: A Computational Model of Self-Enforcing Norms," *American Journal of Sociology* (2005), 110: 1009–1040. This is a model of "pluralistic ignorance," a condition in which a majority privately disbelieves in a norm but thinks others uphold it. In the model, the "false believers" become aggressive enforcers out of personal insecurity that they will be outed—and they drive what may appear to be lock-in of the norm. But because the root of the phenomenon is interpersonal ignorance, it takes only the willingness of people to disclose their true beliefs to break lock-in ("look, the emperor has no clothes"). So, like other information cascades, this is a case where the outcome is fragile—unless top-down authority reinforces the outcome of the cascade.

20. For some influential, formative works in the migration of path dependence into historical institutionalism, see Douglass C. North, *Institutions, Institutional Change, and Economic Performance* (New York: Cambridge University Press, 1990); Ruth Berins Collier and David Collier, *Shaping the Political Arena: Critical Junctures, the Labor Movement, and Regime Dynamics in Latin America*, 2nd ed. (Notre Dame, IN: University of Notre Dame Press, 2002 [1991]), 27–39; and Paul Pierson, *Politics in Time: History, Institutions, and Social Analysis* (Princeton, NJ: Princeton

University Press, 2004). Others adding to, modifying, and criticizing the theory of path-dependent development include Jack A. Goldstone, "Initial Conditions, General Laws, Path Dependence, and Explanations in Historical Sociology," *American Journal of Sociology* (1998), 104: 829–845; James Mahoney, "Path Dependence in Historical Sociology," *Theory and Society* (2000), 29: 507–548; B. Guy Peters, Jon Pierre, and Desmond S. King, "The Politics of Path Dependency: Political Conflict in Historical Institutionalism," *Journal of Politics* (2005), 67: 1275–1300; and Scott E. Page, "Path Dependence," *Quarterly Journal of Political Science* (2006), 1: 87–115.

21. North, *Institutions, Institutional Change, and Economic Performance*, 95.
22. Carl J. Friedrich, *Man and His Government* (New York: McGraw-Hill, 1963), 203.
23. For the biological theory, see Stephan Jay Gould and Niles Eldredge, "Punctuated Equilibrium Comes of Age," *Nature* (1993), 366: 223–227. For examples of the borrowings by social scientists, see Stephen D. Krasner, "Approaches to the State: Alternative Conceptions and Historical Dynamics," *Comparative Politics* (1984), 16: 223–246; Frank Baumgartner and Bryan Jones, *Agendas and Instability in American Politics* (Chicago: University of Chicago Press, 1993).
24. For example, James Mahoney writes that in historical sequences characterized by path dependence, "contingent events set into motion institutional patterns or event chains that have deterministic properties." Mahoney, "Path Dependence in Historical Sociology," 507.
25. Giovanni Capoccia and Daniel Keleman, "The Study of Critical Junctures: Theory, Narrative, and Counterfactuals in Historical Institutionalism," *World Politics* (2007), 59: 341–369 (quotation: 343).
26. Jacob S. Hacker, "Privatizing Risk Without Privatizing the Welfare State: The Hidden Politics of Social Policy Retrenchment in the United States," *American Political Science Review* (2004), 98: 243–260; see also Kathleen Thelen, "How Institutions Evolve: Insights from Comparative-Historical Analysis," in James Mahoney and Dietrich Rueschemeyer, eds., *Comparative Historical Analysis in the Social Sciences* (New York: Cambridge University Press, 2003), 208–240; Eric Patashnik, *Reforms at Risk: What Happens After Major Policy Changes Are Enacted* (Princeton NJ: Princeton University Press). Patashnik uses the term "entrenchment" for one of four scenarios for post-enactment politics, along with erosion, reversal, and reconfiguration.
27. This is prime territory for "constructivist" or "constitutive" analyses of institutional change. The importance of "constitutive moments" is a central theme in my book *The Creation of the Media: Political Origins of Modern Communications* (New York: Basic Books, 2004). For discussions of constructivist and constitutive analysis, see Colin Hay, "Constructivist Institutionalism," in Sarah A. Binder, R. A. W. Rhodes, and Bert A. Rockman,

eds., *The Oxford Handbook of Political Institutions* (New York: Oxford University Press, 2009).

28. John F. Padgett and Walter W. Powell, eds., *The Emergence of Organizations and Markets* (Princeton, NJ: Princeton University Press, 2012). For a typology of "gradual but nevertheless transformative change," see Streeck and Thelen, "Introduction: Institutional Change in Advanced Political Economies."

29. Peter Gardenfors, *Knowledge in Flux* (Cambridge, MA: MIT Press, 1988), 87.

30. For the key work in this area, see Mark Granovetter, "Threshold Models of Collective Behavior," *American Journal of Sociology* (1978), 83: 1420–1433. Here I am particularly indebted to Damon Centola, "The Social Origins of Networks and Diffusion," *American Journal of Sociology* (2015), 120: 1295–1338.

31. Clifford Geertz, *The Interpretation of Cultures* (New York: Basic Books, 1973), 259. Geertz calls these ties "primordial," taking the term from Edward Shils, "Primordial, Personal, Sacred and Civil Ties: Some Particular Observations on the Relationships of Sociological Research and Theory," *British Journal of Sociology* (1957), 8: 130–145.

32. Mark Granovetter, "The Strength of Weak Ties," *American Journal of Sociology* (1973), 78: 1360–1380; Duncan J. Watts and Steven H. Strogatz, "Collective Dynamics of 'Small-World' Networks," *Nature* (1998), 393: 440–442.

33. Damon Centola and Michael Macy, "Complex Contagions and the Weakness of Long Ties," *American Journal of Sociology* (2007), 113: 702–734.

34. Florian Znaniecki, *Modern Nationalities* (Urbana: University of Illinois Press, 1952), 82; quoted in Philip E. Converse, "The Nature of Belief Systems in Mass Publics," in David E. Apter, ed., *Ideology and Discontent* (New York: Free Press, 1964), 237.

35. Eugen Weber, *Peasants into Frenchmen: The Modernization of Rural France, 1870–1914* (Stanford, CA: Stanford University Press, 1976), 67.

36. Larry Diamond, *Developing Democracy: Toward Consolidation* (Baltimore: Johns Hopkins University Press, 1999), 18.

37. Norbert Elias, *The Civilizing Process*, rev. ed. (London: Blackwell, 1994 [1939]).

38. What I call "institutional deepening" has some overlap with Phillip Selznick's concept of "thick institutionalization." See *The Moral Commonwealth: Social Theory and the Promise of Community* (Berkeley: University of California Press, 1992), 235.

39. This paragraph draws on the first article I wrote on entrenchment: "Social Categories and Claims in the Liberal State," in Mary Douglas and David Hull, eds., *How Classification Works: Nelson Goodman Among the Social Sciences* (Edinburgh: Edinburgh University Press, 1992). A slightly expanded version appears in *Social Research* 59 (1992), 263–295.

40. Andreas Wimmer, "The Making and Unmaking of Ethnic Boundaries: A Multilevel Process Theory," *American Journal of Sociology* (2008), 113: 970–1022.

41. Steven Teles, *The Rise of the Conservative Legal Movement: The Battle for the Control of Law* (Princeton, NJ: Princeton University Press, 2008), 270.

42. For systematic discussions, see Jon Elster, *Ulysses Unbound: Studies in Rationality, Precommitment, and Constraints* (New York: Cambridge University Press, 2000), and Stephen Holmes, "Precommitment and the Paradox of Democracy," in Holmes, *Passions and Constraint: On the Theory of Liberal Democracy* (Chicago: University of Chicago Press, 1995).

43. Daron Acemoglu and James A. Robinson, *Why Nations Fail: The Origins of Power, Prosperity, and Poverty* (New York: Crown Business, 2012).

44. The term "opportunity hoarding" comes from Charles Tilly, *Durable Inequality* (Berkeley: University of California Press, 1998).

45. Daron Acemoglu et al., "The Environment and Directed Technical Change," *American Economic Review* (2012), 102: 131–166.

46. See my discussion of the "American health policy trap" in *Remedy and Reaction: The Peculiar American Struggle over Health Care Reform*, rev. ed. (New Haven: Yale University Press, 2013).

Chapter Two. Aristocracy and Inherited Wealth

1. Roy Porter, *English Society in the Eighteenth Century* (Harmondsworth: Penguin, 1984), 71.

2. Alexis de Tocqueville, *Democracy in America*, tr. Henry Reeve (New York: Schocken, 1961), 1: 39.

3. John G. Fleming, "Changing Functions of Succession Laws," *American Journal of Comparative Law* (1978), 26: 233–238 (quoting an unpublished paper by Friedman); for Friedman's later work on the subject, see Lawrence M. Friedman, *Dead Hands: A Social History of Wills, Trusts, and Inheritance Law* (Stanford, CA: Stanford Law Books, 2009).

4. Thomas Piketty, *Capital in the Twenty-First Century* (Cambridge, MA: Harvard University Press, 2014), 377–409; Robert J. Gordon, *The Rise and Fall of American Growth* (Princeton, NJ: Princeton University Press, 2016).

5. Jack Goody, Joan Thirsk, and E. P. Thompson, eds., *Family and Inheritance: Rural Society in Western Europe, 1200–1800* (New York: Cambridge University Press, 1976); Jack Goody, "Strategies of Heirship," *Comparative Studies in Society and History* (1973), 15: 3–20.

6. Henry Maine, *Ancient Law* (New York: Dutton, 1917 [1861]); Henry Cabot Lodge, "The Anglo-Saxon Land Law," in Charles Francis Adams, ed., *Essays in Anglo-Saxon Law* (Boston: Little, Brown, 1876), 55–120; David M. Rabban, "From Maine to Maitland via America," *Cambridge Law Journal* (2009), 68: 410–435.

7. Carole Shammas, "English Inheritance Law and Its Transfer to the Colonies," *American Journal of Legal History* 31 (1987), 31: 145–163.

8. A. W. B. Simpson, *A History of the Land Law*, 2nd ed. (New York: Oxford University Press, 1986), 208–241; Zouheir Jamoussi, *Primogeniture and Entail in England: A Survey of Their History and Representation in Literature* ([Tunis]: Centre de publication Universitaire, 1999).

9. Marc Bloch, *Feudal Society* (London: Routledge and Kegan Paul, 1961), 160–175 (quotation: 167).

10. Bloch, *Feudal Society*, 190–208.

11. Richard Huscroft, *The Norman Conquest: A New Introduction* (Harlow, UK: Pearson, 2009); Simpson, *History of the Land Law*, 81–85.

12. George Duby, *The Early Growth of the European Economy* (Ithaca, NY: Cornell University Press, 1974), 168–174.

13. Adam Smith, *The Wealth of Nations* (New York: The Modern Library, 1937), 361–362.

14. Smith, *Wealth of Nations*, 362.

15. In a variant of Smith's account, Maine offered a "political" explanation of primogeniture: "When Patriarchal power is not only *domestic* but *political*, it is not distributed among all the issue at the parent's death, but is the birthright of the eldest son." The decline of state-imposed public order in feudal Europe demanded that the fief serve political purposes: "So long as the land was kept together on which the entire organization rested, it was powerful for defence and attack; to divide the land was to divide the little society, and voluntarily to invite aggression in an era of universal violence. ... Everybody would have suffered by the division of the fief. Everybody was a gainer by its consolidation. The Family grew stronger by the concentration of power in the same hands." Maine, *Ancient Law*, 137–138, 139.

16. Bloch, *Feudal Society*, 329.

17. Max Weber, *Economy and Society*, ed. Guenther Roth and Claus Wittich (New York: Bedminster Press, 1968), 1: 43–46; 3: 1077–1081.

18. Bas Van Bavel and Richard Hoyle, "Introduction: Social Relations, Property and Power in the North Sea Area, 500–2000," in Bas Van Bavel and Richard Hoyle, eds., *Rural Economy and Society in North-western Europe, 500–2000*, vol. 1: *Social Relations: Property and Power* (Turnhout, Belgium: Prepols, 2010), 1–24.

19. J. P. Cooper, "Patterns of Inheritance and Settlement by Great Landowners from the Fifteenth to the Eighteenth Centuries," in Goody, Thirsk, and Thompson, *Family and Inheritance*, 192–327.

20. Lloyd Bonfield, "Strict Settlement and the Family: A Differing View," *Economic History Review*, New Series (1988), 41: 461–466; Douglas Hay and Nicholas Rogers, *Eighteenth Century English Society: Shuttles and Swords* (New York: Oxford University Press, 1997).

21. Peter Laslett, *The World We Have Lost* (London: Methuen & Co., 1965), 200.

22. Lawrence Stone and Jeanne C. Fawtier Stone, *An Open Elite? England, 1540–1880* (New York: Oxford, 1984), 403.

23. Peter H. Lindert, "Who Owned Victorian England? The Debate over Landed Wealth and Inequality," *Agricultural History* (1987), 61: 37.

24. Judith J. Hurwich, "Inheritance Practices in Early Modern Germany," *Journal of Interdisciplinary History* (1991), 23: 699–718; see also Cooper, "Patterns of Inheritance and Settlement by Great Landowners from the Fifteenth to the Eighteenth Centuries," and Evelyn Cecil, *Primogeniture: A Short History of Its Development in Various Countries and Its Practical Effects* (London: John Murray, 1895).

25. Gordon S. Wood, *The Radicalism of the American Revolution* (New York: Random House, 1991), 45.

26. Shammas, "English Inheritance Law and Its Transfer to the Colonies," 161.

27. Joan Thirsk, "The European Debate on Customs of Inheritance, 1500–1700," in Goody, Thirsk, and Thompson, *Family and Inheritance*, 177–191.

28. Alan Ryan, *Property* (Minneapolis: University of Minnesota Press, 1987), 23–31; Niccolò Machiavelli, *Seven Books on the Art of War*, tr. Henry Neville (1675), First Book, at http://oll.libertyfund.org/titles/984.

29. James Harrington, *The Commonwealth of Oceana; and, A System of Politics* (New York: Cambridge University Press, 1992 [1656]), 11, 57.

30. J. G. A. Pocock, *The Ancient Constitution and the Feudal Law: A Study of English Historical Thought in the Seventeenth Century* (New York: Cambridge University Press, 1987 [1957]), 128–144.

31. Harrington, *Commonwealth of Oceana*, 109.

32. John Adams to James Sullivan, May 26, 1776, in Charles Francis Adams, ed., *The Works of John Adams, Second President of the United States* (Boston, 1858), IX, 176–177; cited in James L. Huston, *Securing the Fruits of Labor: The American Concept of Wealth Distribution, 1765–1900* (Baton Rouge: Louisiana State University Press, 1998), 21.

33. Smith, *Wealth of Nations*, 364.

34. Bavel and Hoyle, "Introduction: Social Relations, Property and Power in the North Sea Area, 500–2000," 10 (spelling Americanized).

35. Thomas Paine, *The Rights of Man*, in Ian Shapiro and Jane E. Calvert, eds., *Selected Writings of Thomas Paine* (New Haven: Yale University Press, 2014), 210, 211.

36. Edmund Burke, *An Appeal from the New to the Old Whigs* (1791), reprinted in *The Works of the Right Honourable Edmund Burke* (London: John C. Nimmo, 1887), vol. 4, at http://www.gutenberg.org/files/15700/15700-h/15700-h.htm#APPEAL.

37. Thomas Jefferson, "Autobiography, 1743–1790," in *Thomas Jefferson: Writings*, ed. Merrill D. Peterson (New York: Library of America, 1984), 32.

38. Jefferson, "Autobiography, 1743–1790," 44.

39. Stanley Katz, "Republicanism and the Law of Inheritance in the American Revolutionary Era," *Michigan Law Review* (1977), 76: 1–29.
40. Bernard Bailyn, "Political Experience and Enlightenment Ideas in Eighteenth-Century America," *American Historical Review* (1962), 67: 345.
41. Holly Brewer, "Entailing Aristocracy in Colonial Virginia: 'Ancient Feudal Restraints' and Revolutionary Reform," *William and Mary Quarterly* (1997), 54: 307–346.
42. Jens Beckert, *Inherited Wealth* (Princeton, NJ: Princeton University Press, 2008), 119–130.
43. Beckert, *Inherited Wealth*, 23–49.
44. Beckert, *Inherited Wealth*, 131–156 (quotation: 146).
45. David Cannadine, *The Decline and Fall of the British Aristocracy* (New Haven, CT: Yale University Press, 1990), 89.
46. Christopher Dyer and Richard Hoyle, "Britain, 1000–1750," in Bavel and Richard Hoyle, *Rural Economy and Society in North-western Europe*, 51–78.
47. Paul Brassley, Richard Hoyle, and Michael Turner, "Britain, 1750–2000," in Bavel and Hoyle, *Rural Economy and Society in North-western Europe*, 81; Lindert, "Who Owned Victorian England?"
48. Pierre Rosanvallon, *A Society of Equals* (Cambridge, MA: Harvard University Press, 2013), 10.
49. Alexander Gerschenkron, *Bread and Democracy in Germany* (Ithaca, NY: Cornell University Press, 1946); Barrington Moore, *Social Origins of Dictatorship and Democracy* (Boston: Beacon Press, 1966); Daniel Ziblatt, "Does Landholding Inequality Block Democratization? A Test of the 'Bread and Democracy' Thesis and the Case of Prussia," *World Politics* (2008), 60: 610–641.
50. Carles Boix, *Democracy and Redistribution* (New York: Cambridge University Press, 2003), 40, 88–92.
51. Ben Ansell and David Samuels, "Inequality and Democratization: A Contractarian Approach," *Comparative Political Studies* (2010), 43: 1543–1574; Christian Houle, "Inequality and Democracy: Why Inequality Harms Consolidation but Does Not Affect Democratization," *World Politics* (2009), 61: 589–622.
52. Rosanvallon, *Society of Equals*, 31.

Chapter Three. Racial Slavery as an Entrenched Contradiction

1. On the flourishing condition of the South's economy, see Robert William Fogel, *Without Consent or Contract: The Rise and Fall of American Slavery* (New York: W. W. Norton, 1989), and Sven Beckert, *Empire of Cotton: A Global History* (New York: Alfred A. Knopf, 2014). The view I take here is that the southern and northern economies were varieties of capitalism, not that the South was precapitalist, much less anticapitalist.

2. Beckert, *Empire of Cotton*, 243; Lee Soltow, *Men and Wealth in the United States, 1850–1870* (New Haven: Yale University Press, 1971), 101.

3. David Eltis, "Slavery and Freedom in the Early Modern World," pp. 25–49 in Stanley Engerman, ed., *Terms of Labor: Slavery, Serfdom, and Free Labor* (Stanford, CA: Stanford University Press, 1999); David Eltis, *The Rise of African Slavery in the Americas* (New York: Cambridge University Press, 2000), 1–28; David Brion Davis, *The Problem of Slavery in the Age of Revolution, 1770–1823* (Ithaca, NY: Cornell University Press, 1975); Beckert, *Empire of Cotton*, 38.

4. I am indebted to a memo from Jason Windawi on this point.

5. Winthrop Jordan, *White over Black: American Attitudes Toward the Negro, 1550–1812* (Chapel Hill: University of North Carolina Press, 1968), 48–52; Thomas D. Morris, " 'Villeinage . . . As It Existed in England, Reflects But Little Light on Our Subject': The Problem of the Sources of Southern Slave Law," *American Journal of Legal History* (1988), 32: 95–137.

6. Robin Blackburn, *The Making of New World Slavery: From the Baroque to Modern* (London: Verso, 1997), 97–123; David Brion Davis, *Challenging the Boundaries of Slavery* (Cambridge, MA: Harvard University Press, 2009), 14–27.

7. Jordan, *White over Black*, 61–63; Eltis, "Slavery and Freedom in the Early Modern World"; Edmund S. Morgan, *American Slavery, American Freedom: The Ordeal of Colonial Virginia* (New York: Norton, 1975), 126.

8. Morgan, *American Slavery, American Freedom*, 154–55; Gordon S. Wood, *The Radicalism of the American Revolution* (New York: Knopf, 1992), 53–54.

9. Evsey D. Domar, "Causes of Slavery or Serfdom," *Journal of Economic History* (1970), 30: 1832; see also Barbara Solow, "Slavery and Colonization," pp. 21–42 in Barbara L. Solow, ed., *Slavery and the Rise of the Atlantic System* (New York: Cambridge University Press, 1991).

10. The following account of slavery in colonial Virginia relies heavily on Morgan, *American Slavery, American Freedom*.

11. Morgan, *American Slavery, American Freedom*, 296–307; David W. Galenson, "Economic Aspects of the Growth of Slavery in the Seventeenth-Century Chesapeake," pp. 265–92 in Solow, *Slavery and the Rise of the Atlantic System*.

12. Jordan, *White over Black*, 78–82; Morgan, *American Slavery, American Freedom*, 306–337; Rosemary Brana-Shute and Randy J. Sparks, eds., *Paths to Freedom: Manumission in the Atlantic World* (Columbia: University of South Carolina Press, 2009).

13. Jordan, *White over Black*, 66–71 (Body of Liberties quoted, 67); Wendy Warren, *New England Bound: Slavery and Colonization in Early America* (New York: Liveright, 2016).

14. Ira Berlin, *Many Thousands Gone: The First Two Centuries of Slavery in North America* (Cambridge, MA: Belknap Press of Harvard University

Press, 1998), 8–10, 97–98. For the original distinction, see Moses I. Finley, *Ancient Slavery and Modern Ideology*, ed. Brent D. Shaw (Princeton, NJ: Markus Wiener, 1998 [1980]), 147–150, 274.

15. Morgan, *American Slavery, American Freedom*, 296.
16. Berlin, *Many Thousands Gone*, 177–182.
17. Berlin, *Many Thousands Gone*, Table 1, 369–371.
18. Robin L. Einhorn, *American Taxation, American Slavery* (Chicago: University of Chicago Press, 2014), 7.
19. Thomas Jefferson to John Holmes, Monticello, April 22, 1820, in Andrew A. Lipscomb and Albert Ellery Bergh, eds., *The Writings of Thomas Jefferson* (Washington, DC, 1903), 15: 248–250.
20. Davis, *The Problem of Slavery in the Age of Revolution*, 470–501; David Waldstreicher, *Slavery's Constitution: From Revolution to Ratification* (New York: Hill and Wang, 2009), 39.
21. Jordan, *White over Black*, 291; Gary B. Nash, *Race and Revolution* (New York: Rowman & Littlefield, 1990), 8–12.
22. Arthur Zilversmit, *The First Emancipation: The Abolition of Slavery in the North* (Chicago: University of Chicago Press, 1967); Gary B. Nash and Jean R. Soderlund, *Freedom by Degrees: Emancipation in Pennsylvania and Its Aftermath* (New York: Oxford University Press, 1991); Joanne Pope Melish, *Disowning Slavery: Gradual Emancipation and "Race" in New England, 1780–1860* (Ithaca, NY: Cornell University Press, 1998).
23. Eva Sheppard Wolf, "Manumission and the Two-Race System in Early National Virginia," pp. 309–337 in Brana-Shute and Sparks, *Paths to Freedom*; Nash, *Race and Revolution*, 18.
24. Michael D. Chan, "Alexander Hamilton on Slavery," *Review of Politics* (2004), 66: 207–231 (Hamilton quoted, 217).
25. Benjamin Quarles, *The Negro in the American Revolution* (Chapel Hill: University of North Carolina Press, 2012 [1961]); Cassandra Pybus, "Jefferson's Faulty Math: The Question of Slave Defections in the American Revolution," *William and Mary Quarterly*, 3rd ser. (2005), 62: 243–264.
26. Adam Smith, *The Wealth of Nations* (New York: Random House, 1937), 366.
27. Robert Fogel and Stanley Engerman, "Philanthropy at Bargain Prices: Notes on the Economics of Gradual Emancipation," *Journal of Legal Studies* (1974), 3: 377–401.
28. Alejandro de la Fuente and Ariela Gross, "Comparative Studies of Law, Slavery and Race in the Americas," *Annual Review of Law and Social Science* (2010), 6: 475.
29. Fogel, *Without Consent or Contract*, 228–229. Taking into account the additional cost of sugar between 1835 and 1842, Fogel estimates the British outlay for emancipation to be more than £40 million.
30. Don E. Fehrenbacher, *The Slaveholding Republic: An Account of the United States Government's Relations to Slavery* (New York: Oxford University Press, 2001), 27–28, 253–258 (Jefferson quoted, 27).

31. Max M. Edling, *A Revolution in Favor of Government: Origins of the U.S. Constitution and the Making of the American State* (New York: Oxford University Press, 2003); Gordon S. Wood, *The Creation of the American Republic* (Chapel Hill: University of North Carolina Press, 1998 [1969]).

32. Fehrenbacher, *The Slaveholding Republic*, 28–35; Waldstreicher, *Slavery's Constitution*, 71–105; Sean Wilentz, *No Property in Man: Slavery and Antislavery at the Nation's Founding* (Cambridge, MA: Harvard University Press, 2018).

33. For the skeptical view that the three-fifths clause was a penalty, see Fehrenbacher, *The Slaveholding Republic*, 29–33, 40–41; for the opposed view, see Akhil Reed Amar, *America's Constitution: A Biography* (New York: Random House, 2005), 88–98, and Leonard L. Richards, *The Slave Power: The Free North and Southern Domination, 1780–1860* (Baton Rouge: Louisiana State Press, 2000), 32–37.

34. Fehrenbacher, *The Slaveholding Republic*, 33–35, 135–137. On the origins of the provision regarding slave imports and the exclusion of any explicit reference therein to slaves as property, see Wilentz, *No Property in Man*, 72–100.

35. Amar, *America's Constitution*, 21–39 (Madison quoted, 38).

36. See Madison's notes for July 12, 1787: http://consource.org/document/james-madisonsnotes-of-the-constitutional-convention-1787-7-12/.

37. Stanley L. Engerman, "Slavery and Emancipation in Comparative Perspective: A Look at Some Recent Debates," *Journal of Economic History* (1986), 46: 320.

38. Garry Wills, *Lincoln at Gettysburg: The Words That Remade America* (New York: Simon & Schuster, 1992).

39. Fehrenbacher, *The Slaveholding Republic*, 37–38 (Madison quoted, 37); Waldstreicher, *Slavery's Constitution*, 114 (Pinckney quoted).

40. Fehrenbacher, *The Slaveholding Republic*, 47.

41. James L. Huston, *Calculating the Value of the Union: Slavery, Property Rights, and the Economic Origins of the Civil War* (Chapel Hill: University of North Carolina Press, 2003), 16, 27–28.

42. Fehrenbacher, *The Slaveholding Republic*, 10–11.

43. Beckert, *Empire of Cotton*, 105.

44. Paul Frymer, *Building an American Empire: The Era of Territorial and Political Expansion* (Princeton, NJ: Princeton University Press, 2017), 21 (quoting Tocqueville).

45. Adam Rothman, *Slave Country: American Expansion and the Origins of the Deep South* (Cambridge, MA: Harvard University Press, 2005); Beckert, *Empire of Cotton*, 105.

46. Fogel, *Without Consent or Contract*, 34; for a review of contrary or at least complicating evidence, see Gavin Wright, *Slavery and American Economic Development* (Baton Rouge: Louisiana State University Press, 2006).

47. *State v. Mann*, 13 N.C. 263 (N.C. 1830), For background on the case, see Mark V. Tushnet, *Slave Law in the American South: State v. Mann in History and Literature* (Lawrence: University Press of Kansas, 2003).

48. Walter Johnson, *River of Dark Dreams: Slavery and Empire in Cotton Kingdom* (Cambridge, MA: Belknap Press of Harvard University Press, 2013), 12–13.

49. Robin Blackburn, "Introduction," pp. 1–13 in Brana-Shute and Sparks, *Paths to Freedom*; Wolf, "Manumission and the Two-Race System in Early National Virginia"; Manisha Sinha, *The Counterrevolution of Slavery: Politics and Ideology in Antebellum South Carolina* (Chapel Hill: University of North Carolina Press, 2000), 14–15. On the various possible explanations for the restriction of manumission in the American South, see Orlando Patterson, *Slavery and Social Death: A Comparative Study* (Cambridge, MA: Harvard University Press, 1982), 259–261.

50. Robert William Fogel and Stanley L. Engerman, *Time on the Cross: The Economics of American Negro Slavery* (Boston: Little, Brown, 1974); Fogel, *Without Consent or Contract*.

51. Carl F. Kaestle, *Pillars of the Republic: Common Schools and American Society, 1780–1860* (New York: Hill and Wang, 1983), 206–210; Eugene D. Genovese, *The Political Economy of Slavery* (New York: Pantheon, 1967), 157–179.

52. James Henry Hammond, "Letter to an English Abolitionist" (1845), in Drew Gilpin Faust, ed., *The Ideology of Slavery: Proslavery Thought in the Antebellum South* (Baton Rouge: Louisiana University Press, 1981), 190. On Hammond, see Carol Bleser, ed., *Secret and Sacred: The Diaries of James Henry Hammond, a Southern Slaveholder* (New York: Oxford University Press, 1988).

53. James Oakes, *The Ruling Race: A History of American Slaveholders* (New York: W. W. Norton, 1998 [1982]), 38–40; Albert W. Niemi, "Inequality in the Distribution of Slave Wealth: The Cotton South and Other Southern Agricultural Regions," *Journal of Economic History* (1977), 37: 747–754.

54. Henry L. Watson, "Conflict and Collaboration: Yeomen, Slaveholders, and Politics in the Antebellum South," *Journal of Social History* (1985), 10: 273–298; Adam Rothman, "The 'Slave Power' in the United States, 1783–1865," pp. 78–79 in Steve Fraser and Gary Gerstle, eds., *Ruling America: A History of Wealth and Power in a Democracy* (Cambridge, MA: Harvard University Press, 2005).

55. Einhorn, *American Taxation, American Slavery*, 7.

56. William Freehling, *Prelude to Civil War: The Nullification Controversy in South Carolina, 1816–1836* (New York: Harper, 1966), 89–90; Sinha, *The Counterrevolution of Slavery*, 12–14.

57. Richards, *The Slave Power*, 56–62, 69, 94, 112–120.

58. On the Missouri Compromise, see Sean Wilentz, *The Rise of American Democracy: Jefferson to Lincoln* (New York: W. W. Norton, 2006), 218–240;

Nolan McCarty, Keith T. Poole, and Howard Rosenthal, "Congress and the Territorial Expansion of the United States," in David W. Brady and Mathew D. McCubbins, eds., *Party, Process, and Political Change in Congress: New Perspectives on the History of Congress* (Stanford, CA: Stanford University Press, 2002), 1: 392–451.

59. On the emergence of political antislavery, see Eric Foner, *Free Soil, Free Labor, Free Men: The Ideology of the Republican Party Before the Civil War* (New York: Oxford University Press, 1970); on homesteaders versus slave-owners, see Frymer, *Building an American Empire*, 140–150.

60. Larry E. May, *Manifest Destiny's Underworld: Filibustering in Antebellum America* (Chapel Hill: University of North Carolina Press, 2002), 45–52, 52–79; Amar, *America's Constitution*, 266–67 (Brown quoted, 267).

61. Matthew Karp, *This Vast Southern Empire: Slaveholders at the Helm of American Foreign Policy* (Cambridge, MA: Harvard University Press, 2016), 5–7 (Adams quoted, 5).

62. Fehrenbacher, *The Slaveholding Republic*, 11–12; Foner, *Free Soil, Free Labor, Free Men*, 73–102 (Chase quoted, 76, 83).

63. *Dred Scott v. Sandford*, 60 U.S. 393. On the contradictions and incoherence of Taney's opinion, see Don E. Fehrenbacher, *The Dred Scott Case: Its Significance in American Law and Politics* (New York: Oxford University Press, 1978), esp. 335–364.

64. Foner, *Free Soil, Free Labor, Free Men*, 97–98; Eric Foner, *The Fiery Trial: Abraham Lincoln and American Slavery* (New York: W. W. Norton, 2010), 99–100.

65. Charles A. Beard and Mary R. Beard, *The Rise of American Civilization* (New York: Macmillan, 1927), 2: 55–56 (Hammond quoted, 55).

66. Foner, *The Fiery Trial*, 145–153 (Lincoln quoted, 153); "Message of Jefferson Davis to the Provisional Congress of the Confederate States of America," April 29, 1861, at http://avalon.law.yale.edu/19th_century/csa_m042961.asp.

67. William H. Seward, "On the Irrepressible Conflict," Rochester, New York, October 25, 1858, at http://www.nyhistory.com/central/conflict.html.

68. Fehrenbacher, *The Slaveholding Republic*, 307.

69. Michael Vorenberg, *Final Freedom: The Civil War, the Abolition of Slavery, and the Thirteenth Amendment* (New York: Cambridge University Press, 2001), 1–7.

70. May, *Manifest Destiny's Underworld*, 278–279 (Lincoln quoted, 279).

71. Vorenberg, *Final Freedom*, 18–22. The two ratifying states were Maryland and Ohio. Although Illinois also ratified the Corwin amendment, its ratification was invalid because it did so by a state convention instead of by the state legislature, as Congress had specified.

72. Foner, *The Fiery Trial*, 167–216.

73. Foner, *The Fiery Trial*, 240–247.

74. Gary W. Gallegher, *The Union War* (Cambridge, MA: Harvard University Press, 2011), 75–82 (Lincoln to Wisconsin representatives, 75); Foner, *The Fiery Trial*, 249–256.

75. For a superb review of the issues, see Seymour Drescher and Pieter C. Emmer, eds., *Who Abolished Slavery? Slave Revolts and Abolitionism, A Debate with João Pedro Marques* (New York: Berghahn Books, 2010).

76. W. E. B. Du Bois, *Black Reconstruction: An Essay toward a History of the Part which Black Folk Played in the Attempt to Reconstruct Democracy in America, 1860–1880* (New York: Harcourt, Brace, 1935), 63–68.

77. Vorenberg, *Final Freedom*, 36–40, 222–233; Bruce Ackerman, *We the People*, vol. 2: *Transformations* (Cambridge, MA: Harvard University Press, 1998), 136–159.

78. Vorenberg, *Final Freedom*, 176–210.

79. B. R. Mitchell, ed., *Abstract of British Historical Statistics* (Cambridge: Cambridge University Press, 1962), 396.

80. Total outlays in 1860 were $63 million. U.S. Department of Commerce, *Historical Statistics of the United States, Colonial Times to 1970* (Washington, DC: Government Printing Office, 1975), 2: 1114.

81. Beard and Beard, *The Rise of American Civilization*, 2: 100, 52–121. They were not the first to characterize the Civil War as revolutionary. For an analysis of the history of that idea, see James M. McPherson, *Abraham Lincoln and the Second American Revolution* (New York: Oxford University Press, 1991), 3–42.

82. Vorenberg, *Final Freedom*, 190–191; Eric Foner, *Reconstruction: America's Unfinished Revolution, 1863–1877* (New York: HarperCollins, 2014 [1988]), 198–216, 253–261; Ackerman, *We the People*, vol. 2, 186–206.

83. Eric Foner, *Nothing but Freedom: Emancipation and Its Legacy* (Baton Rouge: Louisiana State University Press, 1983), 39–40.

84. Daron Acemoglu and James A. Robinson, "De Facto Political Power and Institutional Persistence," *American Economic Review* 96 (2006), 325–330.

85. Jay R. Mandle, "Black Economic Entrapment After Emancipation in the United States," in Frank McGlynn and Seymour Drescher, eds., *The Meaning of Freedom: Economics, Politics, and Culture After Slavery* (Pittsburgh: University of Pittsburgh Press, 1992), 69–84; Foner, *Reconstruction: America's Unfinished Revolution*, 69–70, 158–163; Roger L. Ransom and Richard Sutch, *One Kind of Freedom: The Economic Consequences of Emancipation* (Cambridge, MA: Harvard University Press, 1977).

86. Patterson, *Slavery and Social Death*, 13.

87. McPherson, *Abraham Lincoln and the Second American Revolution*, 16–22.

88. For the original study, see Charles Wallace Collins, *The Fourteenth Amendment and the States* (Boston: Little, Brown, 1912), 129–138; for a recent historical account of how the amendment was diverted from its original purpose, see Adam Winkler, *We the Corporations: How American Businesses Won Their Civil Rights* (New York: Liveright, 2018), 113–160.

Chapter Four. The Conservative Design of Liberal Democracy

1. Thomas Jefferson to James Madison, September 6, 1789, at http://www.let.rug.nl/usa/presidents/thomas-jefferson/letters-of-thomas-jefferson/jefl81.php; letter to Samuel Kercheval, July 12, 1816, quoted in Zachary Elkins, Tom Ginsburg, and James Melton, *The Endurance of National Constitutions* (New York: Cambridge University Press, 2009), 1.

2. Daniel Ziblatt, *Conservative Parties and the Birth of Democracy* (New York: Cambridge University Press, 2017).

3. For overviews of the subject, see Josep M. Colomer, ed., *Handbook of Electoral System Choice* (New York: Palgrave Macmillan, 2004); Shaun Bowler, "Electoral Systems," in Sarah Binder et al., eds., *Oxford Handbook of Political Institutions* (New York: Oxford University Press, 2008), 578–594; and Bernard Grofman, "The Impact of Electoral Laws on Political Parties," in Donald A. Wittman and Barry R. Weingast, eds., *Oxford Handbook of Political Economy* (New York: Oxford University Press, 2008), 103–115.

4. Arend Lijphart, *Patterns of Democracy: Government Forms and Performance in Thirty-Six Countries* (New Haven: Yale University Press, 2012), 2; G. Bingham Powell, Jr., *Elections as Instruments of Democracy: Majoritarian and Proportional Visions* (New Haven: Yale University Press, 2000).

5. Alberto Alesina and Edward L. Glaeser, *Fighting Poverty in the U.S. and Europe: A World of Difference* (New York: Oxford University Press, 2004), 97–107. On PR and redistribution, see Markus Crepaz, "Inclusion Versus Exclusion: Political Institutions and the Welfare State," *Comparative Politics* (1998), 31: 61–80; Torstein Persson and Guido Tabellini, *Political Economics: Explaining Economic Policy* (Cambridge, MA: MIT Press, 2000); Torben Iversen and David Soskice, "Electoral Institutions and the Politics of Coalitions: Why Some Democracies Redistribute More Than Others," *American Political Science Review* (2006), 100: 165–181.

6. Alberto Penadés, "Choosing Rules for Government: The Institutional Preferences of Early Socialist Parties," in J. M. Maravell and Ignacio Sanchez-Cuenca, eds., *Controlling Governments* (New York: Cambridge University Press, 2008), 202–246. Although the following differ in their analyses, they share an emphasis on the strategic choices of elites in electoral system change: Carles Boix, "Setting the Rules of the Game: The Choice of Electoral Systems in Advanced Democracies," *American Political Science Review* (1999), 93: 609–624; Carles Boix, "Electoral Markets, Party Strategies, and Proportional Representation," *American Political Science Review* (2010), 104: 404–413; Josep M. Colomer, "The Strategy and History of Electoral System Choice," pp. 3–78 in Colomer, *Handbook of Electoral System Choice*; Amel Ahmed, *Democracy and the Politics of Electoral System Choice* (New York: Cambridge University Press, 2013). For an earlier formulation, see Stein Rokkan, *Citizens, Elections, Parties: Approaches to*

the *Comparative Study of the Process of Development* (New York: McKay, 1970), 157–158. See also Daniel Ziblatt, "How Did Europe Democratize?," *World Politics* (2006), 58: 311–338.

7. Josep M. Colomer, "On the Origins of Electoral Systems and Political Parties: The Role of Elections in Multi-member Districts," *Electoral Studies* (2007), 26: 262–273; Ahmed, *Democracy and the Politics of Electoral System Choice*, 15–17, 65–66.

8. In the effort to promote minority representation from urban areas (the "minorities" in this case being the more affluent voters), some governments also experimented with other electoral rules. Under the "limited ballot," for example, a voter in a district with three seats might be able to cast only two votes; under the "cumulative ballot," voters in that same district might each be given three votes, which they could cast entirely for one candidate. The rationale for these alternatives was to give minorities in multi-member districts a better chance to elect a representative. Both alternatives, however, could be gamed by parties that coordinated their supporters' balloting, and neither caught on. Colomer, "The Strategy and History of Electoral System Choice," 35–36; Ahmed, *Democracy and the Politics of Electoral System Choice*, 67, 123–125.

9. Ahmed, *Democracy and the Politics of Electoral System Choice*, 166–182. For the two other of the earliest adopters of PR, see Bo Särlik, "Party and Electoral System in Sweden," in Bernard Grofman and Arend Lijphart, eds., *The Evolution of Electoral and Party Systems in the Nordic Countries* (New York: Agathon, 2002), 225–269; Leif Lewin, "Sweden: Introducing Proportional Representation from Above," pp. 265–278 in Colomer, *Handbook of Electoral System Choice*; and Jan Sundberg, "The Electoral System of Finland: Old, and Working Well," pp. 67–100 in Grofman and Lijphart, *The Evolution of Electoral and Party Systems in the Nordic Countries*.

10. André Blais, Agnieszka Dobrzynska, and Indridi H. Indridason, "To Adopt or Not to Adopt Proportional Representation: The Politics of Institutional Choice," *British Journal of Political Science* (2005), 35: 182–190. See also Jonathan Rodden, "Back to the Future: Endogenous Institutions and Comparative Politics," in Mark Lichbach and Alan Zuckerman, eds., *Comparative Politics: Rationality, Culture, and Structure*, 2nd ed. (New York: Cambridge University Press, 2009), 333–357.

11. Colomer, "The Strategy and History of Electoral System Choice," 47.

12. Georg Lutz, "Switzerland: Introducing Proportional Representation from Below," in Colomer, *Handbook of Electoral System Choice*, 279–293.

13. Thomas Cusack, Torben Iversen, and David Soskice, "Economic Interests and the Origins of Electoral Systems," *American Political Science Review* (2007), 101: 373–391; for critiques and evaluations of this argument, see Marcus Kreuzer, "Historical Knowledge and Quantitative Analysis: The Case of the Origins of Proportional Representation," *American Political*

Science Review (2010), 104: 369–392; Ahmed, *Democracy and the Politics of Electoral System Choice*, 12–13.

14. Erik J. Engstrom, *Partisan Gerrymandering and the Construction of American Democracy* (Ann Arbor: University of Michigan Press, 2013), 43–55.

15. Ahmed, *Democracy and the Politics of Electoral System Choice*, 117–135; Peter Catterall, "The British Electoral System, 1885–1970," *Historical Research* (2000), 73: 156–174.

16. D. E. Butler, *The Electoral System in Britain Since 1918*, 2nd ed. (Oxford: Clarendon Press, 1963), 40–47; Ahmed, *Democracy and the Politics of Electoral System Choice*, 135–138.

17. The recent British experience can also be read as further evidence of the entrenchment of majoritarianism. From 1979 to 1992, the Conservatives triumphed in four straight elections, though they never received more than 44 percent of the vote and won large majorities of seats only because of a divided opposition. The Thatcherite revolution would probably not have been possible with proportional representation. Consequently, support for electoral-system change grew among Labour as well as the Liberals (later Liberal Democrats). Yet, as in the 1920s, Labour reversed itself when it had the opportunity to change the system. After winning power in 1997 (with 43 percent of the votes but 63 percent of seats), Labour reneged on an earlier promise to put a form of proportional representation to a vote in a national referendum. National electoral reform again became a possibility after the 2010 elections, when the Conservatives fell short of a majority of seats, turned to the Liberal Democrats to form a coalition government, and agreed to hold a national referendum on the "alternative vote" (AV) or "instant runoff" system. The referendum resulted in a resounding defeat. AV, however, belongs to the majoritarian family; voters choose representatives in single-member districts. But they rank candidates, and if none receives a majority of first-preference votes, the votes for the candidate finishing last are reallocated according to the voters' second preferences—a process that is repeated until a candidate passes 50 percent. Thus the system is majoritarian, but it bolsters the position of third parties. Under the name "ranked-choice voting," the system has been adopted in some U.S. cities as well as the state of Maine.

18. See Colomer, "The Strategy and History of Electoral System Choice"; Bowler, "Electoral Systems."

19. Colomer, "The Strategy and History of Electoral System Choice," 58; on mixed-member systems, see Matthew Sobarg Shugart and Martin P. Wattenberg, eds., *Mixed-Member Electoral Systems: The Best of Both Worlds?* (New York: Oxford University Press, 2001).

20. For the argument that risk aversion leads political actors to choose rules that reduce their probability of being "absolute losers," see Colomer, "The Strategy and History of Electoral System Choice," 7.

21. David Denemark, "Choosing MMP in New Zealand: Explaining the 1993 Electoral Reform," in Shugart and Wattenberg, *Mixed-Member Electoral Systems*, 70–95.

22. See in this connection Samuel Issacharoff and Richard H. Pildes, "Politics as Markets: Partisan Lockups of the Democratic Process," *Stanford Law Review* (1998), 50: 643–717, and Michael J. Klarman, "Majoritarian Judicial Review: The Entrenchment Problem," *Georgetown Law Journal* (1997), 85: 491–553.

23. Lijphart, *Patterns of Democracy*, 206–211.

24. Martin Shapiro, "The Success of Judicial Review and Democracy," in Martin Shapiro and Alec Stone Sweet, *On Law, Politics, and Judicialization* (New York: Oxford University Press, 2002); C. Neal Tate and Torbjorn Vallinder, eds., *The Global Expansion of Judicial Power* (New York: New York University Press, 1995).

25. Simone Polillo and Mauro F. Guillén, "Globalization Pressures and the State: The Worldwide Spread of Central Bank Independence," *American Journal of Sociology* (2005), 110: 1764–1802.

26. Christopher Crowe and Ellen E. Meade, "The Evolution of Central Bank Governance Around the World," *Journal of Economic Perspectives* (2007), 21: 72.

27. Tom Ginsburg, *Judicial Review in New Democracies: Constitutional Courts in Asian Cases* (New York: Cambridge University Press, 2003), 18, 25.

28. Ran Hirschl, *Towards Juristocracy: The Origins and Consequences of the New Constitutionalism* (Cambridge, MA: Harvard University Press, 2004).

29. John B. Goodman, "The Politics of Central Bank Independence," *Comparative Politics* (1991), 23: 329–349 (quotation: 334).

30. Delia M. Boylan, *Defusing Democracy: Central Bank Autonomy and the Transition from Authoritarian Rule* (Ann Arbor: University of Michigan Press, 2001), 108.

31. Douglas C. North and Barry R. Weingast, "Constitutions and Commitment: The Evolution of Institutional Governing Public Choice in Seventeenth-Century England," *Journal of Economic History* (1989), 49: 803–832. The key in determining whether commitments were credible was not just the number of institutional veto players, but what party controlled them. See David Stasavage, "Credible Commitment in Early Modern Europe: North and Weingast Revisited," *Journal of Law, Economics, & Organization* (2002), 18: 155–186.

32. For other accounts of the sources of England's "financial revolution," see John Brewer, *The Sinews of Power: War, Money, and the English State, 1688–1783* (New York: Knopf, 1989); Henry Roseveare, *The Financial Revolution, 1660–1760* (New York: Longman, 1991); P. G. M. Dickson, *The Financial Revolution in England: A Study in the Development of Public Credit, 1688–1756* (New York: St. Martin's Press, 1967); Mark Kishlansky, *A Monarchy Transformed: Britain, 1603–1714* (New York: Penguin, 1996).

33. Ginsburg, *Judicial Review in New Democracies*, 60–64.
34. Thomas C. Schelling, *Micromotives and Macrobehavior* (New York: Norton, 1978); Stephen Holmes, "Gag Rules or the Politics of Omission," in Jon Elster and Rune Slagstad, eds., *Constitutionalism and Democracy* (New York: Cambridge University Press, 1988), 19–58.
35. For a review, see Frank Dobbin, Beth Simmons, and Geoffrey Garrett, "The Global Diffusion of Public Policies: Social Construction, Coercion, Competition, or Learning?," *Annual Review of Sociology* (2007), 33: 449–472.
36. Ginsburg, *Judicial Review in New Democracies*, 6.
37. See, for example, Alberto Alesina and Lawrence H. Summers, "Central Bank Independence and Macroeconomic Performance: Some Comparative Evidence," *Journal of Money, Credit and Banking* (1993), 25: 151–162.
38. Sylvia Maxfield, *Gatekeepers of Growth: The International Political Economy of Central Banking in Developing Countries* (Princeton, NJ: Princeton University Press, 1997). In a study of changes in central banking laws during the 1990s, Simone Polillo and Mauro Guillén find that bank independence increased with a nation's exposure to foreign trade, investment, and multilateral lending and that the more a given country traded with other countries that had an independent central bank (or competed with such countries), the more independent its own central bank became. Polillo and Guillén, "Globalization Pressures and the State."
39. Alex Cukierman, "Central Bank Independence and Monetary Policy-Making Institutions: Past, Present and Future," *European Journal of Political Economy* (2008), 24: 722–736.
40. Guillermo O'Donnell and Philippe Schmitter, "Tentative Conclusions About Uncertain Democracies," Part 4 of Guillermo O'Donnell, Philippe Schmitter, and Laurence Whitehead, eds., *Transitions from Authoritarian Rule* (Baltimore: Johns Hopkins University Press, 1986), 5.
41. Mark Blyth, *Great Transformations: Economic Ideas and Institutional Change in the Twentieth Century* (New York: Cambridge University Press, 2002), 7, 8–11.
42. Alasdair Roberts, *The Logic of Discipline: Global Capitalism and the Architecture of Government* (New York: Oxford University Press, 2010).
43. Robert O. Keohane, *After Hegemony: Cooperation and Discord in the World Political Economy* (Princeton, NJ: Princeton University Press, 1984), 116–125 (quotation: 117).
44. Alec Stone Sweet, *The Judicial Construction of Europe* (New York: Oxford University Press, 2004); Maurice Adams, Federico Fabbrini, and Pierre Larouche, *The Constitutionalization of European Budgetary Constraints* (Portland, OR: Hart, 2014).
45. Andrew Moravcsik, "The Origins of Human Rights Regimes: Democratic Delegation in Postwar Europe," *International Organization* (2000), 54: 217–252; see also Beth A. Simmons, *Mobilizing for Human Rights: In-*

ternational Law in Domestic Politics (New York: Cambridge University Press, 2009). Simmons finds mixed evidence: long-established democracies were quickest to ratify two human rights treaties, while "newly transitioned" democracies were quickest to ratify three others (82, 86). Emphasizing the role of civil society in compliance, Simmons identifies polities with "fluid" institutions as those where the treaties are most likely to have their biggest effect (16). In both the Moravcsik and Simmons accounts, actors use entrenchment devices to overcome risk.

46. Stephen Haggard, "The Institutional Foundations of Hegemony: Explaining the Reciprocal Trade Agreements Act of 1934," *International Organization* (1988), 42: 91–119; Michael A. Bailey, Judith Goldstein, and Barry R. Weingast, "The Institutional Roots of American Trade Policy: Politics, Coalitions, and International Trade," *World Politics* (1997), 49: 309–338.

47. Keohane, *After Hegemony*, 118.

48. Dani Rodrik, *The Globalization Paradox* (New York: W. W. Norton, 2011), 67–88; Rodrik credits the distinction between shallow and deep integration to Robert Lawrence.

49. Emilie M. Hafner-Burton and Kiyoteru Tsutsui, "Human Rights in a Globalizing World: The Paradox of Empty Promises," *American Journal of Sociology* (2005), 110: 1373–1411; Simmons, *Mobilizing for Human Rights*.

50. Kim Lane Scheppele, "The Global Patriot Act," *American Prospect* (September 2011), 49–50.

51. Steven Levitsky and Lucan Way, "The Durability of Revolutionary Regimes," *Journal of Democracy* (2013), 24: 5–17.

52. Ziblatt, *Conservative Parties and the Birth of Democracy*; Gerard Alexander, *The Sources of Democratic Consolidation* (Ithaca, NY: Cornell University Press, 2002).

53. O'Donnell and Schmitter, "Tentative Conclusions About Uncertain Democracies."

54. Daron Acemoglu and James A. Robinson, *Economic Origins of Dictatorship and Democracy* (New York: Cambridge University Press, 2006), 34.

55. Susan Alberts, Chris Warshaw, and Barry R. Weingast, "Democratization and Countermajoritarian Institutions: Power and Constitutional Design in Self-Enforcing Democracy," in Tom Ginsburg, ed., *Comparative Constitutional Design* (New York: Cambridge University Press, 2012), 69–100.

56. Alfred Stepan, Juan J. Linz, and Yogendra Yadav, *Crafting State-Nations: India and Other Multinational Democracies* (Baltimore: Johns Hopkins University Press, 2011).

Chapter Five. Entrenching Progressive Change

1. Lucy Barnes and Peter A. Hall, "Neoliberalism and Social Resilience in the Developed Democracies," in Peter A. Hall and Michèle Lamont, eds.,

Social Resilience in the Neoliberal Era (New York: Cambridge University Press, 2013), 209–238.

2. Peter H. Lindert, "The Rise and Future of Progressive Redistribution," October 2017, Commitment to Equity (CEQ) Institute, Tulane University, Working Paper 73.

3. Tali Kristal, "Good Times, Bad Times: Postwar Labor's Share of National Income in Capitalist Democracies," *American Sociological Review* (2010), 75: 729–763.

4. Richard Rose, "Maximizing Tax Revenue While Minimizing Political Costs," *Journal of Public Policy* (1985), 5: 289–320. On the analysis of fiscal regimes, see Andrew Monson and Walter Scheidel, "Studying Fiscal Regimes," in Monson and Scheidel, eds., *Fiscal Regimes and the Political Economy of Premodern States* (New York: Cambridge University Press, 2015), 3–28.

5. M. E. Robinson, *Public Finance*, introd. by J. M. Keynes (New York: Harcourt Brace, 1922), 92.

6. Paul Pierson, *Dismantling the Welfare State? Reagan, Thatcher, and the Politics of Retrenchment* (New York: Cambridge University Press, 1994), 39–50.

7. Clem Brooks and Jeff Manza, *Why Welfare States Persist: The Importance of Public Opinion in Democracies* (Chicago: University of Chicago Press, 2007). For an important qualification, see Charlotte Cavaillé and Kris-Stella Trump, "Two Facets of Social Policy Preferences," *Journal of Politics* (2015), 77: 146–160.

8. Jacob S. Hacker, "Privatizing Risk Without Privatizing the Welfare State: The Hidden Politics of Social Policy Retrenchment in the United States," *American Political Science Review* (2004), 98: 243–260; Kathleen Thelen, "How Institutions Evolve: Insights from Comparative-Historical Analysis," in James Mahoney and Dietrich Rueschemeyer, eds., *Comparative Historical Analysis in the Social Sciences* (New York: Cambridge University Press, 2003), 208–240.

9. Lindert, "The Rise and Future of Progressive Redistribution."

10. Business did not always or even usually support the development of social protection, but at least elements of business did so under certain political conditions. On the German case, see Thomas Paster, "Business and Welfare State Development: Why Did Employers Accept Social Reforms?," *World Politics* (2013), 65: 416–451; on the variable influence of business in the United States, see Jacob S. Hacker and Paul Pierson, "Business Power and Social Policy: Employers and the Formation of the American Welfare State," *Politics and Society* (2002), 30: 277–325.

11. This schema is adapted from Walter Korpi and Joakim Palme, "The Paradox of Redistribution and the Strategy of Equality: Welfare State Institutions, Inequality and Poverty in the Western Countries," *American Sociological Review* (1998), 63: 661–687.

12. Gøsta Esping-Andersen, *The Three Worlds of Welfare Capitalism* (Princeton, NJ: Princeton University Press, 1990).

13. Gaston V. Rimlinger, *Welfare Policy and Industrialization in Europe, America, and Russia* (New York: John Wiley & Sons, 1971), 89–90; Peter Baldwin, *The Politics of Social Solidarity: Class Bases of the European Welfare State, 1875–1975* (New York: Cambridge University Press, 1990), 59–60; E. P. Hennock, *British Social Reform and German Precedents: The Case of Social Insurance, 1880–1914* (Oxford: Clarendon Press, 1987), 185–186; Esping-Andersen, *Three Worlds of Welfare Capitalism*, 60.

14. Baldwin, *The Politics of Social Solidarity*, 60–65, 85–94.

15. L. T. Hobhouse, *Liberalism* (New York: H. Holt, 1911); Michael Freeden, *The New Liberalism: An Ideology of Social Reform* (Oxford: Clarendon Press, 1978); Hennock, *British Social Reform and German Precedents*, Part 2 (Churchill quotation: 169).

16. Policy outcomes before the New Deal, Hacker and Pierson write, "conform to a simple rule of thumb: reforms that threatened to raise costs significantly for a large number of firms engaged in interstate competition were very unlikely to pass." Hacker and Pierson, "Business Power and Social Policy," 293. For the alternative view emphasizing limited state capacity as a barrier to social insurance, see Theda Skocpol, *Protecting Soldiers and Mothers: The Political Origins of Social Policy in the United States* (Cambridge, MA: Harvard University Press, 1992), 248–310. On the battle over health insurance, see Paul Starr, *Remedy and Reaction: The Peculiar American Struggle over Health Care Reform*, rev. ed. (New Haven: Yale University Press, 2013), 27–34.

17. Carl F. Kaestle, *Pillars of the Republic: Common Schools and American Society, 1780–1860* (New York: Hill and Wang, 1983); Albert Fishlow, "The American Common School Revival: Fact or Fancy?," in Henry Rosovsky, ed., *Industrialization in Two Systems: Essays in Honor of Alexander Gerschenkron* (New York: Wiley, 1966), 40–67; Emily Zackin, *Looking for Rights in All the Wrong Places: Why State Constitutions Contain America's Positive Rights* (Princeton, NJ: Princeton University Press, 2013), 67–105; Claudia Goldin, "America's Graduation from High School: The Evolution and Spread of Secondary Schooling in the Twentieth Century," *Journal of Economic History* (1998), 58: 345–374.

18. Simon Kuznets, "Economic Growth and Income Inequality," *American Economic Review* (1955), 45(1): 1–28; Harold Wilensky, *The Welfare State and Equality* (Berkeley: University of California Press, 1975), 15–28.

19. James O'Connor, *The Fiscal Crisis of the State* (New York: St. Martin's Press, 1973).

20. Karl Polanyi, *The Great Transformation* (Boston: Beacon Press, 1957 [1944]); Mark Blyth, *Great Transformations: Economic Ideas and Institutional Change in the Twentieth Century* (New York: Cambridge University Press, 2002), 4.

21. See Christopher H. Achen and Larry M. Bartels, *Democracy for Realists: Why Elections Do Not Produce Responsive Government* (Princeton, NJ: Princeton University Press, 2017), Ch. 7.

22. Thomas Piketty, *Capital in the Twenty-First Century* (Cambridge, MA: Harvard University Press, 2014), 272, 275, 291–294; Claudia Goldin and Robert A. Margo, "The Great Compression: The Wage Structure in the United States at Mid-Century," *Quarterly Journal of Economics* (1992), 107: 1–34.

23. Richard M. Titmuss, "War and Social Policy," in his *Essays on "The Welfare State"* (Boston: Beacon Press, 1969 [1958]), 75–87 (quotation: 82).

24. William Beveridge, *Social Insurance and Allied Services* (London: His Majesty's Stationery Office, 1942); Brian Abel-Smith, "The Beveridge Report: Its Origins and Outcomes," *International Social Security Review* (1992), 45: 5–16.

25. Alan T. Peacock and Jack Wiseman, *The Growth of Public Expenditure in the United Kingdom* (Princeton, NJ: Princeton University Press, 1961); Karen A. Rasler and William R. Thompson, "War Making and State Making: Government Expenditures, Tax Revenues, and Global Wars," *American Political Science Review* (1985), 79: 491–507.

26. This is the general approach of the "power resources" tradition: Walter Korpi, *The Democratic Class Struggle* (Boston: Routledge and Kegan Paul, 1983); Esping-Andersen, *Three World of Welfare Capitalism*.

27. Margaret Weir, "Ideas and Politics: The Acceptance of Keynesianism in Britain and the United States," in Peter A. Hall, ed., *The Political Power of Economic Ideas: Keynesianism Across Nations* (Princeton, NJ: Princeton University Press, 1989), 53–86.

28. Peter A. Hall, "Conclusion: The Politics of Keynesian Ideas," in Hall, ed., *The Political Power of Economic Ideas*, 376–377.

29. Detlev Zollner, "Germany," in Peter Kohler and Hans F. Zacher, eds., *The Evolution of Social Insurance, 1881–1981* (New York: St. Martin's Press, 1982), 81. For the contrast with Keynesianism, see Christopher S. Allen, "The Underdevelopment of Keynesianism in the Federal Republic of Germany," in Hall, *The Political Power of Economic Ideas*, 263–289.

30. Gøsta Esping-Andersen, *Politics Against Markets: The Social Democratic Road to Power* (Princeton, NJ: Princeton University Press, 1985), Ch. 3.

31. For a survey, see José Harris, "Society and the State in Twentieth-Century Britain," in F. M. L. Thomson, ed., *Cambridge Social History of Britain, 1750–1950* (New York: Cambridge University Press, 2008), 3: 63–117.

32. Caricature of the "liberal" model is characteristic of much of the tradition in comparative research based on Esping-Andersen's typology of the "three worlds" of welfare capitalism, although Esping-Andersen himself writes that "liberalism's accommodation of social protection is in practice much more elastic than is normally thought." *Three Worlds of Welfare Capitalism*, 44.

33. Ira Katznelson, *Fear Itself: The New Deal and the Origins of Our Time* (New York: Liveright, 2013); Alan Brinkley, *The End of Reform: New Deal Liberalism in Recession and War* (New York: Alfred A. Knopf, 1995).

34. William E. Leuchtenburg, *The Supreme Court Reborn: The Constitutional Revolution in the Age of Roosevelt* (New York: Oxford University Press, 1995), 82–162.

35. Bruce Western, *Between Class and Market: Postwar Unionization in the Capitalist Democracies* (Princeton, NJ: Princeton University Press, 1997), 29–49; Peter A. Hall and David Soskice, eds., *Varieties of Capitalism: The Institutional Foundations of Comparative Advantage* (New York: Oxford University Press, 2001).

36. Nelson Lichtenstein, *State of the Union: A Century of American Labor*, rev. ed. (Princeton, NJ: Princeton University Press, 2013), 114–118.

37. Alberto Alesina and Edward Glaeser, *Fighting Poverty in the U.S. and Europe* (New York: Oxford University Press, 2004), 133–182. Alesina and Glaeser suggest that the relationship between race and redistribution is also contingent on "entrepreneurial politicians" stirring up racial animosity as a way of fighting redistribution (136). Other writers call attention to cases where political parties and leaders have created national or subnational identities that bind together groups and support spending on public goods. See Prerna Singh, *How Solidarity Works for Welfare: Subnationalism and Social Development in India* (New York: Cambridge University Press, 2015).

38. *The New York Times*, January 4, 1971. Nixon never did say, "We are all Keynesians now," although that line is often attributed to him.

39. Piketty, *Capital in the Twenty-First Century*, 505, 507.

40. Kenneth Scheve and David Stasavage, *Taxing the Rich: A History of Fiscal Fairness in the United States and Europe* (Princeton, NJ: Princeton University Press, 2016), 55–56.

41. Thomas Piketty and Emmanuel Saez, "How Progressive Is the U.S. Federal Tax System? A Historical and International Perspective," *Journal of Economic Perspectives* (2007), 21: 3–24.

42. For the classic accounts, see Louis Hartz, *The Liberal Tradition in America* (New York: Harcourt Brace, 1955), and Seymour Martin Lipset, *American Exceptionalism: A Double-Edged Sword* (New York: W. W. Norton, 1996).

43. It is theoretically possible to turn the income tax into a progressive consumption tax by raising marginal rates while excluding savings from taxable income. But the constituencies that prefer a consumption tax generally have no interest in making it progressive.

44. The direct taxation of wealth also has the potential to produce substantial revenue on a progressive basis, but at higher levels of economic development, the mobility of capital constrains the ability to tax it directly. The structural dependence of states on capital—their need for investment—has

prevented even the countries that have adopted comprehensive taxes on wealth from taxing it heavily. The most common wealth taxes are property and inheritance taxes. But since property taxes are mainly limited to real property and exclude financial wealth, they hit the home-owning middle class harder than top wealth holders. As one-time levies, taxes on estates and inheritances produce only a limited flow of revenue, though they may significantly reduce the concentration of wealth and dynastic entrenchment.

45. Paul Smith, ed., *Lord Salisbury on Politics: A Selection from His Articles in the Quarterly Review, 1860–1883* (New York: Cambridge University Press, 1972), 155, as cited by Daniel Ziblatt, *Conservative Parties and the Birth of Democracy* (New York: Cambridge University Press, 2017), 28.

46. Isabela Mares and Didac Queralt, "The Non-Democratic Origins of Income Taxation," *Comparative Political Studies* (2015), 48(14): 1974–2009.

47. Mares and Queralt, "The Non-Democratic Origins of Income Taxation"; Margaret Levi, *Of Rule and Revenue* (Berkeley: University of California Press, 1988), 122–144; Piketty, *Capital in the Twenty-First Century*, 498–499.

48. These two phases can be further subdivided: W. Elliot Brownlee distinguishes five tax regimes in U.S. history. See his *Federal Taxation in America: A Short History*, rev. ed. (New York: Cambridge University Press, 2004).

49. Max M. Edling and Mark D. Kaplanoff, "Alexander Hamilton's Fiscal Reform: Transforming the Structure of Taxation in the Early Republic," *William and Mary Quarterly*, 3rd ser. (2004), 61: 713–744; Alvin Rabushka, *Taxation in Colonial America* (Princeton, NJ: Princeton University Press, 2008).

50. Richard Bensel, *The Political Economy of American Industrialization* (New York: Cambridge University Press, 2000), 457–509. For the classic account of tariff politics, see F. W. Taussig, *The Tariff History of the United States*, 8th ed. (New York: G. P. Putnam's Sons, 1931).

51. *Pollock v. Farmers' Loan & Trust Co.*, 157 U.S. 429 (1895). In a 1796 case, *Hylton v. United States*, concerning a tax on carriages, the Court had agreed with the government's counsel, none other than Alexander Hamilton, who said that the term "direct tax" in the Constitution referred to land and capitation taxes and a general tax on property. See Sidney Ratner, *Taxation and Democracy* (New York: John Wiley & Sons, 1967 [1942]), 193–214.

52. On the movement for the progressive income tax, see Ratner, *Taxation and Democracy*, 298–320; John D. Buenker, *The Income Tax and the Progressive Era* (New York: Garland, 1985); Bennett D. Baack and Edward John Ray, "Special Interests and the Adoption of the Income Tax in the United States," *Journal of Economic History* (1985), 45: 607–625; and Ajay Mehrotra, " 'More Mighty Than the Waves of the Sea': Toilers, Tariffs, and the Income Tax Movement, 1880–1913," *Labor History* 45 (2004), 165–198.

53. Brownlee, *Federal Taxation in America*, 55.

54. Scheve and Stasavage, *Taxing the Rich*, 76–86.

55. Rosella Cappella Zielinski, *How States Pay for Wars* (Ithaca, NY: Cornell University Press, 2016), 110–111.

56. Scheve and Stasavage, *Taxing the Rich*, 5–7, 135–159 (quotation: 157).

57. Thomas Piketty, *Les hauts revenus en France au XXème siècle* (Paris: Grasset, 2001), 255, 263.

58. Carl Shoup, "Sales Taxes as Phenomena of Economic Crises," *Proceedings of the Annual Conference on Taxation under the Auspices of the National Tax Association* (October 1–5, 1934), 27: 90–101.

59. On tax policy in World War I, see Brownlee, *Federal Taxation in America*, 59–72.

60. Brownlee, *Federal Taxation in America*, 73–83.

61. Brownlee, *Federal Taxation in America*, 81–133.

62. Peacock and Wiseman, *The Growth of Public Expenditure in the United Kingdom*, xxiv.

63. Carolyn Jones, "Mass-Based Income Taxation: Creating a Taxpaying Culture, 1940–1952," in W. Elliot Brownlee, ed., *Funding the Modern American State, 1941–1995: The Rise and Fall of the Era of Easy Finance* (Cambridge: Cambridge University Press, 1996), 107–147; James T. Sparrow, " 'Buying Our Boys Back': The Mass Foundations of Fiscal Citizenship, 1942–1954," *Journal of Policy History* (2008), 20: 263–826.

64. Gustavo A. Flores-Macías and Sarah E. Kreps, "Political Parties at War: A Study of American War Finance, 1789–2010," *American Political Science Review* (2013), 107: 833–848.

65. Ajay K. Mehrotra, *Making the Modern American Fiscal State: Law, Politics, and the Rise of Progressive Taxation, 1877–1929* (New York: Cambridge University Press, 2013), 376–383; Monica Prasad, *The Land of Too Much: American Abundance and the Paradox of Poverty* (Cambridge, MA: Harvard University Press, 2012), 104–109.

66. Vito Tanzi, *Taxation in an Integrating World* (Washington, DC: Brookings Institution, 1995), 17–31.

67. Sven Steinmo, *Taxation and Democracy: Swedish, British, and American Approaches to Financing the Modern State* (New Haven: Yale University Press, 1993), 85–91, 121–135, 196; Jude C. Hays, "Globalization and Capital Taxation in Consensus and Majoritarian Democracies," *World Politics* (2003), 56: 79–113; Thomas R. Cusack and Pablo Beramendi, "Taxing Work," *European Journal of Political Research* (2006), 45: 43–73; Pablo Beramendi and David Rueda, "Social Democracy Constrained: Indirect Taxation in Industrialized Democracies," *British Journal of Political Science* 37 (2007), 619–641.

68. Junko Kato, *Regressive Taxation and the Welfare State* (Cambridge: Cambridge University Press, 2003), 27.

69. On the development of value-added taxation, see Richard Eccleston, *Taxing Reforms: The Politics of the Consumption Tax in Japan, the United States, Canada and Australia* (Northampton, MA: Edward Elgar, 2007); Michael

Keen and Ben Lockwood, "The Value Added Tax: Its Causes and Consequences," *Journal of Development Economics* (2009), 92: 138–151; and Kathryn James, *The Rise of the Value-Added Tax* (New York: Cambridge University Press, 2015).

70. Eccleston, *Taxing Reforms*, 43–44.

71. Harold L. Wilensky, *Rich Democracies: Political Economy, Public Policy, and Performance* (Berkeley: University of California Press, 2002), 379–383; Monica Prasad and Yingying Deng, "Taxation and the Worlds of Welfare," *Socio-Economic Review* (2009), 7(3): 431–457.

72. Jacob S. Hacker, *The Divided Welfare State: The Battle over Public and Private Social Benefits in the United States* (New York: Cambridge University Press, 2002), 239–241. On the politics of tax expenditures, see also Suzanne Mettler, *The Submerged State: How Invisible Government Policies Undermine American Democracy* (Chicago: University of Chicago Press, 2011).

73. For the full argument, see Starr, *Remedy and Reaction*.

74. Here, as in the preceding chapter, I emphasize the constitutive role of ideas in neoliberal change in the late twentieth century, in line with constructivist or discursive branches of institutionalism (see, for example, Blyth, *Great Transformations*). The contrast is with purely structural explanations of neoliberalism, as in this claim: "The structure called forth the necessary ideology." Monica Prasad, *The Politics of Free Markets: The Rise of Neoliberal Economic Policies in Britain, France, Germany, and the United States* (Chicago: University of Chicago Press, 2006), 50.

75. On the intellectual and political origins of the neoliberal movement, see Jan-Werner Müller, *Contesting Democracy: Political Ideas in Twentieth-Century Europe* (New Haven: Yale University Press, 2011), 150–154, 221–222; Angus Burgin, *The Great Persuasion: Reinventing Free Markets Since the Depression* (Cambridge, MA: Harvard University Press, 2012), and Daniel Stedman Jones, *Masters of the Universe: Hayek, Friedman, and the Birth of Neoliberal Politics* (Princeton, NJ: Princeton University Press, 2012).

76. Martha Derthick and Paul J. Quirk, *The Politics of Deregulation* (Washington, DC: Brookings Institution, 1985), 40–45, 105–108.

77. This is the history of economic inequality that Piketty gives in *Capital in the Twenty-First Century*. Piketty acknowledges the primacy of changing political forces but says little about them.

78. Robert Kuttner, *The Revolt of the Haves: Tax Rebellions and Hard Times* (New York: Simon and Schuster, 1980); David O. Sears and Jack Citrin, *Tax Revolt: Something for Nothing in California* (Cambridge, MA: Harvard University Press, 1985).

79. For the number of states, see David Lowery and Lee Sigelman, "Understanding the Tax Revolt: Eight Explanations," *American Political Science Review* (1981), 75: 963–974. I use the term "cascade" here in the sense discussed in Chapter 1. Such processes ordinarily are fragile—the tax revolt itself was short-lived—but the results may be entrenched through political

and institutional change, as they were in this case because the policies enacted often took the form of amendments to state constitutions.

80. Isaac William Martin, *The Permanent Tax Revolt: How the Property Tax Transformed American Politics* (Stanford, CA: Stanford University Press, 2008), 5–14.

81. Cathie J. Martin, *Shifting the Burden: The Struggle over Growth and Corporate Taxation* (Chicago: University of Chicago Press, 1991), 159–189; Piketty, *Capital in the Twenty-First Century*, 508–512.

82. Scheve and Stasavage, *Taxing the Rich*, 55–56.

83. Mark Hallerberg and Scott Basinger, "Internationalization and Changes in Tax Policy in OECD Countries: The Importance of Domestic Veto Players," *Comparative Political Studies* (1998), 31: 321–352; Duane Swank, "Taxing Choices: International Competition, Domestic Institutions and the Transformation of Corporate Tax Policy," *Journal of European Public Policy* (2016), 23: 571–603.

84. James Cronin, "Embracing Markets, Bonding with America, Trying to Do Good: The Ironies of New Labor," in James Cronin, George W. Ross, and James Shoch, eds., *What's Left of the Left: Democrats and Social Democrats in Challenging Times* (Durham, NC: Duke University Press, 2011), 116–140.

85. Wilensky, *Rich Democracies*, 232.

86. For this discussion, I rely on Rudolf Klein, *The New Politics of the NHS*, 5th ed. (Oxford: Radcliffe, 2006), Chs. 5–6 (quotation: 112).

87. See Patricia Day and Rudolf Klein, "Constitutional and Distributional Conflict in British Medical Politics: The Case of General Practice, 1911–1991," *Political Studies* (1992), 40: 462–478.

88. Luther Gulick, "Memorandum on Conference with FDR Concerning Social Security Taxation, Summer, 1941," http://www.ssa.gov/history/Gulick.html. On the strategic entrenchment of Social Security, see also Martha Derthick, *Policymaking for Social Security* (Washington, DC: Brookings Institution, 1979), 417.

89. Andrea Louise Campbell, *How Policies Make Citizens: Senior Political Activism and the American Welfare State* (Princeton, NJ: Princeton University Press, 2003).

90. Derthick, *Policymaking for Social Security*, 142–144.

91. John Myles and Paul Pierson, "The Comparative Political Economy of Pension Reform," in Paul Pierson, ed., *The New Politics of the Welfare State* (Oxford: Oxford University Press, 2001), 305–333.

92. The Thatcher reforms did not just seek to divert enrollment from the State Earnings-Related Pension System (SERPS), which had been established in the mid-1970s to supplement the low, flat-benefit public pension for those without occupational pensions. The reforms also offered incentives to opt out of occupational pensions into personal accounts. Ironically, however, the ensuing scandal led to more stringent regulation of financial

services than had previously existed. Nonetheless, Thatcher's reforms were a turning point: Britain today no longer offers a public, earnings-related, defined-benefit pension. See Alan M. Jacobs and Steven Teles, "The Perils of Market Making: The Case of British Pension Reform," in Mark K. Landy, Martin A. Levin, and Martin Shapiro, eds., *Creating Competitive Markets: The Politics of Regulatory Reform* (Washington, DC: Brookings Institution Press, 2007), 157–183; and, for later developments, Marek Naczyk, "Unemployment and Pensions Protection in Europe: The Changing Role of Social Partners. PROWELFARE Country Report: United Kingdom," OSE Paper Series, Research Paper No. 22 (Brussels: European Social Observatory, 2016), 21–40.

93. Timothy Hicks, "Partisan Strategy and Path Dependence: The Post-War Emergence of Health Systems in the UK and Sweden," *Comparative Politics* (2013), 207–226.

94. Pierson, *Dismantling the Welfare State?*, 1–9, 164–165. For recent assessments of Pierson's arguments, see "Pierson's *Dismantling the Welfare State?*: A Twentieth Anniversary Reassessment," *PS: Political Science & Politics* (2015), 48(2).

95. Kay Lehman Schlozman, Sidney Verba, and Henry E. Brady, *The Unheavenly Chorus: Unequal Political Voice and the Broken Promise of Democracy* (Princeton, NJ: Princeton University Press, 2012), Ch. 11.

96. Walter Korpi, "Welfare-State Regress in Western Europe: Politics, Institutions, Globalization, and Europeanization," *Annual Review of Sociology* (2003), 29: 589–609.

97. Patrick Emmenegger, Silja Häusermann, Bruno Palier, and Martin Seeleib-Kaiser, "How We Grow Unequal," in Patrick Emmenegger, Silja Häusermann, Bruno Palier, and Martin Seeleib-Kaiser, eds., *The Age of Dualization: The Changing Face of Inequality in Deindustrializing Societies* (New York: Oxford University Press, 2012), 3–26.

98. Bernhard Ebbinghaus and Jelle Visser, "When Institutions Matter: Union Growth and Decline in Western Europe, 1950–1995," *European Sociological Review* (1999), 15: 135–158. See also Western, *Between Class and Market*, 145, 156–192; Larry J. Griffin, Holly J. McCammon, and Christopher Botsko, "The 'Unmaking' of a Movement? The Crisis of U.S. Trade Unions in Comparative Perspective," in Maureen Hallinan, David Klein, and Jennifer Glass, eds., *Change in Societal Institutions* (New York: Plenum, 1990), 169–194; Bruce Western and Jake Rosenfeld, "Workers of the World Divide: The Decline of Labor and the Future of the Middle Class," *Foreign Affairs* (2012), 91: 88–99.

99. My analysis here follows Torben Iversen and Anne Wren, "Equality, Employment, and Budgetary Restraint: The Trilemma of the Service Economy," *World Politics* (1998), 50: 507–546; for later follow-up, see Anne Wren, ed., *The Political Economy of the Service Transition* (New York: Oxford University Press, 2013).

100. Emmenegger et al., *The Age of Dualization*; Martin Seeleib-Kaiser, "The End of the Conservative German Welfare State Model," *Social Policy and Administration* (2016), 50: 219–240. Seeleib-Kaiser argues that Germany looks more like a liberal regime as a result of social security cuts and more Nordic as a result of new policies for child care.

101. Bruno Palier and Kathleen Thelen, "Dualization and Institutional Complementarities: Industrial Relations, Labor Market and Welfare State Changes in France and Germany," in Emmenegger et al., *The Age of Dualization*, 201–225 (quotation: 201).

102. For contrasting views, see Jonas Pontusson, "Once Again a Model: Nordic Social Democracy in a Globalized World," in Cronin, Ross, and Shoch, *What's Left of the Left*, 89–115; and Johan Bo Davidsson, "Dualising the Swedish Model: Insiders and Outsiders and Labour Market Policy Reform in Sweden: An Overview," in Sotiria Theodoropoulou, ed., *Labour Market Policies in the Era of Pervasive Austerity: A European Perspective* (Bristol: Policy Press at the University of Bristol, 2018).

103. David Weil, *The Fissured Workplace* (Cambridge, MA: Harvard University Press, 2014); Jacob S. Hacker, *The Great Risk Shift* (New York: Oxford University Press, 2008).

104. David T. Ellwood, *Poor Support: Poverty in the American Family* (New York: Basic Books, 1988); David T. Ellwood, "Welfare Reform as I Knew It: When Bad Things Happen to Good Policies," *American Prospect* (1996), 22–29; Jason DeParle, *American Dream: Three Women, Ten Kids, and a Nation's Drive to End Welfare* (New York: Penguin, 2005); Kathryn J. Edin and H. Luke Shaefer, *$2.00 a Day: Living on Almost Nothing in America* (Boston: Houghton Mifflin Harcourt, 2015); Christopher Jencks, "Why the Very Poor Have Become Poorer," *New York Review of Books*, June 9, 2016.

105. On the reasons for Obama's failure to get credit for progress in reducing inequality, see Paul Starr, "Achievement Without Credit: The Obama Presidency and Inequality," in Julian Zelizer, ed., *The Presidency of Barack Obama: A First Historical Assessment* (Princeton, NJ: Princeton University Press, 2018), 45–61.

106. Nancy Bermeo and Jonas Pontusson, "Coping with Crisis: An Introduction," in Nancy Bermeo and Jonas Pontusson, eds., *Coping with Crisis: Government Reactions to the Great Recession* (New York: Russell Sage Foundation Press, 2012), 1–32.

107. Wilensky, *Rich Democracies*, 232.

108. Maureen A. Eger and Sarah Valdez, "Neo-Nationalism in Western Europe," *European Sociological Review* (2015), 31: 115–130; Sasha Polakow-Suransky, *Go Back Where You Came From: The Backlash Against Immigration and the Fate of Western Democracy* (New York: Nation Books, 2017), 50–52; Tom Edsall, "The Rise of 'Welfare Chauvinism,'" *New York Times*, December 16, 2014.

109. Racism played a part not just in the Nazi adaptation of the German welfare state but in the early history of Swedish social democracy and even in the New Deal. See Carly Elizabeth Schall, *The Rise and Fall of the Miraculous Welfare Machine: Immigration and Social Democracy in Twentieth-Century Sweden* (Ithaca, NY: Cornell University Press, 2016), 45–46; Ira Katznelson, *When Affirmative Action Was White* (New York: W. W. Norton, 1985).

Chapter Six. Democracy and the Politics of Entrenchment

1. Samuel P. Huntington, *The Third Wave: Democratization in the Late Twentieth Century* (Norman: University of Oklahoma Press, 1991).

2. Nancy Bermeo, "On Democratic Backsliding," *Journal of Democracy* (2016), 27: 5–19; Steven Levitsky and Daniel Ziblatt, *How Democracies Die* (New York: Crown, 2018).

3. Larry Diamond, "Democracy's Deepening Recession," Atlantic.com, May 2, 2014, https://www.theatlantic.com/international/archive/2014/05/the-deepening-recession-ofdemocracy/361591/; Steven Levitsky and Lucan Way, "The Myth of Democratic Recession," in Larry Diamond and Marc F. Plattner, eds., *Democracy in Decline? A* Journal of Democracy Book (Baltimore: Johns Hopkins University Press, 2015), 58–76.

4. Yascha Mounk, *The People Versus Democracy* (Cambridge, MA: Harvard University Press, 2018), 99–131.

5. Dan Slater, "Democratic Careening," *World Politics* (2013), 65: 729–763.

6. Jeffrey A. Winters, *Oligarchy* (New York: Cambridge University Press, 2011), 10–11; Jeffrey A. Winters, "Oligarchy and Democracy," Huffington Post, April 24, 2014, http://www.huffingtonpost.com/jeffrey-winters/oligarchy-and-democracy-i_b_5206368.html.

7. Anthony B. Atkinson and Thomas Piketty, *Top Incomes over the Twentieth Century: A Contrast Between Continental European and English-Speaking Countries* (New York: Oxford University Press, 2007).

8. For data on changes in union density from 1980 to 2011 in seventeen European countries, see Claus Schnabel, "Trade Unions in Europe: Dinosaurs on the Verge of Extinction?," Centre for Economic Policy Research, November 18, 2013, https://voxeu.org/article/trade-unions-europe; on bargaining coverage, see Jelle Visser et al., "Trends in Collective Bargaining Coverage: Stability, Erosion, or Decline?," International Labor Organization, November 1, 2017, http://www.ilo.org/global/topics/collective-bargaining-labourrelations/publications/WCMS_409422/lang—en/index.htm.

9. Robert Kuttner, *Can Democracy Survive Global Capitalism?* (New York: W. W. Norton, 2018), 124–136.

10. John Judis, *The Populist Explosion: How the Great Recession Transformed American and European Politics* (New York: Columbia Global Reports, 2016).

11. Mounk, *The People Versus Democracy*, 165.

12. John Sides and Jack Citrin, "European Opinion About Immigration: The Role of Identities, Interest, and Information," *British Journal of Political Science* (2007), 37: 477–504, Table 1.

13. 2017 Bertelsmann Foundation poll, cited in Timothy Garton Ash, "Liberal Europe Isn't Dead Yet. But Its Defenders Face a Long, Hard Struggle," *The Guardian*, July 9, 2018, https://www.theguardian.com/commentisfree/2018/jul/09/liberal-europe-isnt-dead-struggle.

14. Marisa Abrajano and Zoltan L. Hajnal, *White Backlash: Immigration, Race, and American Politics* (Princeton, NJ: Princeton University Press, 2015); Daniel J. Hopkins, "Politicized Places: Explaining Where and When Immigrants Provoke Local Opposition," *American Political Science Review* (2010), 104: 40–60. Some research suggests that as a result of social desirability bias, public opinion polling has underestimated opposition to immigration: Alexander L. Janus, "The Influence of Social Desirability Pressures on Expressed Immigration Attitudes," *Social Science Quarterly* (2010), 91: 928–946; Leonardo Bursztyn, Georgy Egorov, and Stefano Fiorin, "From Extreme to Mainstream: How Social Norms Unravel," NBER Working Paper 23415, May 2017.

15. Justin Gest, *The New Minority: White Working Class Politics in an Ange of Immigration and Inequality* (New York: Oxford University Press, 2016).

16. Jan-Werner Müller, *What Is Populism?* (Philadelphia: University of Pennsylvania Press, 2016), 3, 45.

17. Neil Buckey and Andrew Byrne, "Viktor Orban's Oligarchs: A New Elite Emerges in Hungary," *Financial Times*, December 17, 2017, https://www.ft.com/content/ecf6fb4e-d900–11e7-a039c64b1c09b482.

18. Anya Schiffrin, "Government and Corporations Hinder Journalists with 'Media Capture,' " *Columbia Journalism Review*, August 29, 2017. See also Reporters Without Frontiers, "Media Oligarchs Go Shopping" (2016), https://rsf.org/sites/default/files/2016-rsf-report-media-oligarchs-gpo-shopping.pdf.

19. Anne Appelbaum, "The Secret to Trump: He's Really a Russian Oligarch," *Washington Post*, August 19, 2016.

20. Levitsky and Ziblatt, *How Democracies Die*.

21. Kim Lane Scheppele, "Constitutional Coups and Judicial Review: How Transnational Institutions Can Strengthen Peak Courts at Times of Crisis," *Transnational Law and Contemporary Problems* (2014), 23: 51–117.

22. Bruce Ackerman, *We the People*, vol. 2: *Transformations* (Cambridge, MA: Harvard University Press, 1998), 6. Ackerman himself has become critical of "triumphalist" writing about the Constitution, including his own: "The triumphs of the presidency in the past have prepared the way for a

grim future. The office that has sustained a living tradition of popular sovereignty threatens to become its principal agent of destruction." See *The Decline and Fall of the American Republic* (Cambridge, MA: Harvard University Press, 2010), 4.

23. The groups pushing for a convention include the American Legislative Exchange Council (ALEC) and Citizens for Self-Government, both funded by David and Charles Koch. ALEC offers an Article V handbook for state lawmakers: "Proposing Constitutional Amendments by a Convention of the States," https://www.alec.org/app/uploads/2016/06/2016-Article-V_FINAL_WEB.pdf; Jeffrey A. Kimble, "Acknowledging the Elephant in the Room: The Congressional Obstacle to the Balanced Budget Amendment Task Force's Effort to Achieve a Convention Call," Compact for America, January 25, 2016, http://docs.wixstatic.com/ugd/e48202_f127027 c82734a108bbfbe6520100812.pdf. For background on the campaign, see Josh Keefe, "The Koch Brothers Want a New Constitution—And They're Closer Than You Think," *International Business Times*, July 14, 2017, http://www.ibtimes.com/political-capital/koch-brothers-want-new-constitution-theyre-closeryou-think-2552039.

24. Walter E. Dellinger, "The Recurring Question of the 'Limited' Constitutional Convention," *Yale Law Journal* (1979), 88: 1623–1640; letter from Chief Justice Warren Burger to Phyllis Schlafly, June 22, 1988, http://constitution.i2i.org/files/2013/11/Burger-letter2.pdf.

25. *Coleman et al. v Miller,* 307 U.S. 433 (1939).

26. Daniel Markovits and Ian Ayres, "The U.S. Is in a State of Perpetual Minority Rule," *Washington Post*, November 8, 2018; David Wasserman, "The Congressional Map Has A Record-Setting Bias Against Democrats: And It's Not Just 2018," FiveThirtyEight, August 7, 2017, at https://fivethirtyeight.com/features/the-congressional-map-is-historically-biased-toward-the-gop/; Paul Waldman, "We're Living in an Age of Minority Rule," *Washington Post*, July 10, 2018; the state population projections for 2040 come from the Weldon Cooper Center for Public Service of the University of Virginia: https://demographics.coopercenter.org/national-population-projections.

27. For some recent accounts, see Carol Anderson, *One Person, No Vote: How Voter Suppression Is Destroying Our Democracy* (New York: Bloomsbury, 2018); Ari Berman, *Give Us the Ballot: The Modern Struggle for Voting Rights in America* (New York: Farrar, Straus and Giroux, 2015); and Jim Rutenberg, "A Dream Undone: Inside the 50-year Campaign to Roll Back the Voting Rights Act," *New York Times*, July 29, 2015.

28. James Feigenbaum, Alexander Hertel-Fernandez, and Vanessa Williamson, "From the Bargaining Table to the Ballot Box: Political Effects of Right to Work Laws," NBER Working Paper No. 24259, January 2018; see also Alexander Hertel-Fernandez, "Policy Feedback as Political Weapon: Conservative Advocacy and the Demobilization of the Public Sector Labor Movement," *Perspectives on Politics* (2018), 16: 364–379.

29. Levitsky and Ziblatt, *How Democracies Die*.
30. David Frum, "An Exit from Trumpocracy," *The Atlantic*, January 18, 2018, at https://www.theatlantic.com/politics/archive/2018/01/frum-trumpocracy/550685/.
31. Jed S. Rakoff, "Don't Count on the Courts," *New York Review of Books*, April 5, 2018, 46–47. See also Tom Ginsburg and Aziz Huq, "How We Lost Constitutional Democracy," in Cass Sunstein, ed., *Can It Happen Here?* (Dey Street Books, 2018), 135–156 (quotation: 151).
32. Steven Teles, *The Rise of the Conservative Legal Movement: The Battle for the Control of Law* (Princeton, NJ: Princeton University Press, 2008).
33. Adam Winkler, *We the Corporations: How American Businesses Won Their Civil Rights* (New York: Liveright, 2018), xvi.
34. Joseph Fishkin and William E. Forbath, "The Anti-Oligarchy Constitution," *Boston University Law Review* (2014), 94: 669–696; for a similar view, see Ganesh Sitaraman, *The Crisis of the Middle-Class Constitution* (New York: Alfred A. Knopf, 2017).

Index